D1604984

EASTER □ MICHAELMAS □ CHRISTMAS DAY □ PURIM □ WORLD DAY OF PRAYER □ PASSOVER □ LAMMAS □ RATHA YATRA □ THANKSGIVING □ ASHURA □ YULE □ BAISAKHI □ LANTERN FESTIVAL

Religious Holidays and Calendars

An Encyclopaedic Handbook

RAMADAN □ LENT □ YOM KIPPUR □ MARDI GRAS

WORLD DAY OF PRAYER □ PASSOVER □ LAMMAS □ RATHA YATRA □ THANKSGIVING □ ASHURA □ YULE □ BAISAKHI □ LANTERN FESTIVAL

PURIM □

CHRISTMAS DAY □

MICHAELMAS □

EASTER □

Religious Holidays and Calendars

An Encyclopaedic Handbook

By
Aidan Kelly,
Peter Dresser and
Linda M. Ross

□ RAMADAN □ LENT □ YOM KIPPUR □ MARDI GRAS

Penobscot Building
Detroit, MI 48226

Library of Congress Cataloging-in-Publication Data

Kelly, Aidan A.
    Religious holidays and calendars : an encyclopaedic handbook / by
Aidan Kelly, Peter Dresser, and Linda M. Ross.
       p. cm.
    Includes bibliographical references (p.) and indexes.
    ISBN 1-55888-348-7 (lib. bdg. : acid-free paper)
    1. Calendars—History.   2. Fasts and feasts.   I. Dresser, Peter
D.   II. Ross, Linda M.   III. Title.
CE6.K45   1993
529'.3—dc20
                                                92-41189
                                                   CIP

Omnigraphics, Inc.

* * *

Frank R. Abate, *Vice President, Dictionaries*
Eric F. Berger, *Vice President, Production*
Laurie Lanzen Harris, *Vice President, Editorial Director*
Peter E. Ruffner, *Vice President, Administration*
James A. Sellgren, *Vice President, Operations and Finance*

* * *

Frederick G. Ruffner, Jr., *Publisher*

Copyright © 1993
Omnigraphics, Inc.

ISBN 1-55888-348-7

∞

This book is printed on acid-free paper meeting the ANSI Z39.48 Standard. The
infinity symbol that appears above indicates that the paper in this book meets that
standard.

Printed in the United States of America

Table of Contents

Introduction vii

Part One: The History of Calendars

1. **Basic Questions All Calendars Must Answer** 3

2. **Lunar and Lunisolar Calendars: Western Traditions** 8
    The Babylonian Calendar 8
    The Hebrew Calendar 9
    The Greek Calendar 12
    Evolution of the Christian Feasts 15
    British Traditions 18

3. **Lunar and Lunisolar Calendars: Eastern Traditions** 29
    The Islamic Calendar 29
    The Calendars of India 31
    The Buddhist Calendar 33
    The Chinese Calendar 34

4. **Solar Calendars** 44
    The Egyptian Calendar 44
    The Roman Calendar and Julian Reform 45
    The Gregorian Reform of the Roman Calendar 47

5. **Calendar Reforms Since the Mid-Eighteenth Century** 50

    The French Republican Calendar 50

    Twentieth Century Reform Proposals 51

Part Two: Alphabetical Catalogue of Religious Holidays 55

Bibliography 125

Monthly Index of Holidays 129

Religions Index 137

Master Index 145

Introduction

Scope and Audience

Religion and the calendar have been linked since antiquity. From the time of the ancient Egyptian and Babylonian civilizations, members of the religious community determined how time was to be divided—in days, months, and years—and which days were ordinary, and which were holy, or holidays. Thus an important aspect of the history of the world's religions is revealed in the origin of their holidays as well as the calendars created to chart them.

Religious Holidays and Calendars: An Encyclopedic Handbook offers the researcher—whether student, scholar, or seeker—an overview of the time-keeping and holiday traditions of the world's major religions. Other reference works in the field focus on Christian and Jewish holidays or the traditions of a single religion such as Islam. This *Handbook*, however, while providing extensive information on the familiar holidays of the world's majority faiths, also describes the primary holy days and festivals of America's minority religions as practiced here or in the country of origin. The reader will also find details on holidays of smaller or newer organizations—such as the Theosophical Society, the Church of Scientology, and Neo-paganism. No existing source covers the unique relationship of religious calendars *and* religious holidays as does this *Handbook*.

Although the *Handbook* does list several major saints' days such as St. Patrick's Day, it does not attempt to cover the myriad of saints' days observed in both the Roman Catholic and Orthodox traditions. This is information requiring a volume of its own.

Organization

Part 1—Essays Lay the Foundation

For a complete understanding of the origin of religious holidays, the *Handbook* opens with a unique discussion of religious calendars. Five essays take readers through history revealing the rules that societies have set up to measure time and decide which days are ordinary and which are holy. The dating designation used throughout the text was selected to reflect all the religions discussed, but it may be unfamiliar to some readers. While the year numbers correspond to the B.C./A.D. system, the letters BCE (Before Common Era) replace B.C. and CE (Common Era) replace A.D.

Part 2—An A-Z Catalog Builds an All-Encompassing Source

Each of the nearly 300 entries in this section provides the following information as depicted in the sample entry below: 1) name of religious holiday; 2) date on which the holiday is celebrated on either the Western civil calendar, a religious calendar, or both; 3) a brief discussion of the holiday's history and/or current practice (either in the U.S. or abroad).

Sample Entry

1) **Lailat al Miraj**
2) *27th of Rajab*
3) Muslim commemoration of the ascension or night journey of Muhammad, when he ascended into Heaven and received instructions from God on the number of times daily prayer is required. Celebrated on the 27th of Rajab, the seventh month of the Islamic calendar. A holiday in six countries.

Bibliography and Indexes

A bibliography of all sources used in compiling the *Handbook* will help researchers pursuing further study of religious holidays and calendars.

Three indexes assure users of quick access to desired information. A **Monthly Index of Holidays** helps researchers needing an overview of all the holidays observed within the months of the Western civil calendar. A **Religions Index** guides users looking for all the holidays associated with Bahai, Islam, or other religion. And a **Master Index** lists all persons, holidays, organizations, events, and over 1,000 other significant terms mentioned in Parts 1 and 2 of *Religious Holidays and Calendars*.

Comments Welcome

Users are invited to send information about religious holidays not listed. Comments or suggestions on improving subsequent editions are also welcome. Please contact:

The Editors
Religious Holidays and Calendars
Omnigraphics Inc.
Penobscot Building
Detroit, MI 48226

Phone: 313-961-1340
Toll-Free: 800-234-1340
Fax: 800-875-1340

Part One

The History of Calendars

Chapter 1

Basic Questions
All Calendars Must Answer

Essential Role of Calendars Throughout History

Societies have created calendars to order time in a systematic manner—a need which all human civilizations share. Like many other fundamental commodities in life, the calendar is so ordinary yet so important that one can hardly imagine a time when it did not exist. Its significance is so great that in many cultures the institution and maintenance of dating systems have been given sacred status and have fallen under the jurisdiction of religious authorities.

The history of calendars attests to human ingenuity. As one begins to consider the state of the world before the evolution of the calendar, two questions invariably arise: How did people recognize their need for a calendar, and what did they do to construct one? Answers to these questions are intricately woven into the fabric of history and celebrate the wonder of human resourcefulness and creativity. Many different cultures have their own calendars, and the characteristics of these calendars are as diverse as the societies that developed them. All calendars, however, serve the common purpose of enabling people to work together to accomplish specific goals.

During the twentieth century, the Western civil calendar has become the international standard for business and diplomatic purposes, but many other calendars are also used by various religions, nations, and societies.

Origins of the Calendar

In the broadest sense, a calendar consists of the set of rules that a society uses to determine which days are ordinary and which are holy or holidays.

The earliest calendars were informal. Thousands of years ago, most people lived in small tribal societies which were based on hunting and gathering as a means of survival. The time-keeping methods of these groups would have been fairly uncomplicated because people could easily coordinate activities by word of mouth. Certainly they used days and perhaps even months as indications of time, but their needs probably did not demand anything more complex such as a year, decade, or century. However, over the course of history, more and more people shifted from small hunting and gathering tribes to larger communities based on agriculture; this shift required that people become more interdependent with each other for survival. For example, farmers and city dwellers must come to the marketplace at the same time if they are going to do business. Therefore, the need for a tool to arrange these societal events became apparent.

Ancient Egyptians and Babylonians systematize their calendars. The first people to formally address the need to integrate social activities were the ancient Babylonians and Egyptians. These two societies were similar in their agricultural base and demographics—large populations spread over significant expanses of land. The most common reason for the citizens of these empires to gather together would be the observance of religious festivals which would take place at regular intervals. Both societies recognized the necessity of a central time-reckoning system to facilitate the timely arrival of people to these festivals and placed the responsibility for the formation of this system into the hands of their respective religious communities.

To develop their calendars, both groups followed similar approaches. They divided time into three major divisions—what we now recognize as days, months, and years–and then went about calculating the exact duration of each category. The questions to be answered by the ancient Babylonians and Egyptians are the questions all subsequent calendar makers have had to address:

> How long is a day?
> How long is a month?
> How long is a year?

These values may seem obvious to a modern day observer, but it actually took centuries of ongoing observations, measurements, and calculations to set them.

How Long is a Day?

The basic building block of all calendars is the day. The length of the day is set by the amount of time in which the earth completes one rotation on its axis.

During the fifth century B.C.E. (Before Common Era, which is equivalent to the term B.C.), the Babylonians divided this duration of time into twenty-four segments which we now know as hours. However, because accurate measurement of seconds and even minutes was not possible until the sixteenth century C.E. (Common Era, equivalent to A.D.), the length of those hours has not always been fixed.

Using the sun to measure the day. Originally, the position of the sun was used to record the passing of time during the day. The problem with this was twofold. First, because of the nature of the earth's revolution of the sun, the point at which the sun passes any given point from one day to the next varies slightly. Second, the devices used to mark the movement of the sun, such as sundials, were not precise and could not compensate for the change in the earth's position relative to the sun from season to season. For instance, according to a sundial, an hour in northern latitudes would have been twice as long in the summer as it would have been in the winter.

Early observers must have noted a pattern in the cycle of light and darkness. Even though the length of light and darkness varied, they were always balanced with each other. When light grew shorter, dark grew longer and vice versa. In any case, the custom of counting one period of light and one period of darkness as a unit for the purpose of time-keeping seemed natural.

A starting point is established. A question developed, however, about when to mark the beginning of this time-keeping unit. Two points seemed to make the most sense: sunrise or sunset. Hebrew culture chose to designate sunset as the beginning of a day. As a result, their sabbaths and holy days began at sunset on the evening before the daytime of the festival. This tradition carried over into Christian traditions and gave rise to the celebrations of "eves" such as Christmas Eve, New Year's Eve, and Halloween (All Hallow's Eve). Other groups chose sunrise as the beginning of the day.

Yet, because the balance of light and dark in the day was always shifting, societies still faced inconsistencies when using the sunrise or sunset to indicate the onset of the day. Because of the logistics of governing people over grand expanses of land, large empires were particularly troubled with widely varying starting points for the day. Theoretically, the day could begin several hours later in the western portion of an empire than it did in the eastern part. Therefore, societies began searching for a more constant point of origin for the day.

Astronomers in ancient Rome observed that no matter what time the sun rose or set, the time between the points at which the sun was directly overhead from day to day was always the same. The Romans established the point at which the sun was directly overhead as the beginning of the day. As history progressed, people realized that if there was a fixed time for midday, there would also be a fixed time exactly opposite that in the middle of the night— midnight. Once this was recognized, the advantages of naming midnight as the beginning of the day became clear. Rather than changing a date in the middle of the business day, the change could be made at night when most people were sleeping—or at least most business was not being conducted. Therefore, midnight became the most commonly accepted changing point for the day.

Classical water-clocks increase accuracy. Around 150 B.C.E., the water-clock or clepsydra came into use by the Greeks and Romans. These water-clocks measured time by allowing a steady flow of water to drip through a small opening into a collection chamber which was marked to indicate the passage of hours as the chamber filled. As the technical sophistication of clepsydras increased, a float attached to a rod was added to the collection chamber. As the water level rose, the rod moved, turning a gear with a pointer on one side. This pointer moved around a numbered dial which indicated the passage of hours.

During the middle-ages, an improvement in the design of the clock was made by replacing water with slowly descending weights to turn the gear. This change allowed the clocks to be mounted in the towers of churches which established a central time source for entire towns. However, even with all of these advances, the measurement of time was still not reliable.

Pendulums swing into action. In 1581, Galileo's discovery that a pendulum moved at a constant rate of speed provided a basis for more accurate time-keeping. Building on this notion, the Dutch astronomer Christiaan Huygens invented a clock around 1657 in which a pendulum was kept moving by descending weights; the regular swinging of the pendulum moved the gears of the clock. Huygens's method proved to be quite precise, eventually allowing for the division of the hour into minutes and minutes into seconds.

How Long is a Month?

The division of days into hours was very important, but a method of ordering a succession of days into larger units of time was necessary for long term planning. The development of what we now call a month, which is based on the rotation of the moon around the earth, grew out of such an attempt to organize days together. How people began to ob-serve the phases of the moon to define the month is not known, but evidence from ancient civilizations suggests that it was done very early in the history of mankind.

Watching the phases of the moon. Early observers noted patterns in the changing shape of the moon. Perhaps initially their observations began at the point when the moon appeared as a thin crescent in the eastern sky just after sunset. Then, a few nights later, the crescent would have grown to a half-circle which was rounded on the western side and flat on the eastern side. Several days would pass and the moon would appear to have grown a hump on its previously flattened eastern side. (*Gibbous*, from a Latin word meaning "hump" is the name of this phase of the moon.) About a week later, a full shiny disc would appear in the east almost exactly as the sun disappeared in the west. The full moon would last only one night; the next night the moon would rise in its gibbous phase, this time the western side would be slightly flatter than the eastern side. The western side would grow flatter each night until it became a half moon again about one week after the full moon had appeared. The process would continue for another week until the crescent moon appeared with its curve toward the east. Finally, one week later, no moon would appear. This phase became known as the new moon.

A month is the time that passes between one new moon and the next. The length of this period, called the synodical month, is about twenty-nine and one-half days.

The priest declares a new month. When people were first beginning to use the phases of the moon as a basis for their month, the duty of watching for the new moon was very solemn and was administered by the religious leaders of the community. This tradition lasted long after astronomers had developed methods by which the appearance of the new moon could be predicted. In fact, it is from such an ancient Roman tradition that the word calendar comes. Each month, the high priest would watch for the new moon; when it occurred, he would *calare* (the Latin word for "declare") a new month. The first day of the month was called *calends* from which we derive our word calendar—a chart which records all of the *calends*.

What is the sidereal month? Ancient observers may have believed that the moon actually changed shapes, but astronomers soon discovered that this was not the case. While they were watching the skies, they certainly studied the moon's companions, the stars. As they did, they discovered that the moon changed its place nightly in relation to the other heavenly bodies. By observing the change in position night after night, they determined that it took about 27 days for the moon to come back to the first position in which it had been observed. This cycle was named the sidereal month and is slightly shorter than the synodical month.

Although the modern Western civil calendar is based on the synodical month, other calendars such as the Hindu calendar which is based on the constellations of the zodiac, use the sidereal month. As time measurement has become more precise, the length of the sidereal month has been discovered to be 27 days, 7 hours, 43 minutes, and 11.5 seconds. The precision of this value has become important as astronomers have grappled with nature to divulge the secret of the length of the year.

How Long is a Year?

Ascertaining the length of the year has been the most difficult issue faced by calendar makers. Although measuring the length of a complete cycle of seasons may not seem complicated, it actually creates significant problems for calendar systems.

In hunting and gathering societies, the need for time measurement beyond a month was not of extreme importance. Agrarian cultures, however, depend heavily on the ability to predict optimal planting and harvesting times—a process requiring an understanding of the cycles of weather. The inhabitants of ancient farming communities began to observe the weather in relation to the phases of the moon.

As the early astronomers watched, they observed a pattern of seasons. Each season contained several new moons or months. The seasons were marked by either warm or cold temperatures or a high or low level of precipitation and repeated after the passage of twelve months. These observations originally defined the year.

Babylonians and Egyptians disagree. In the fifth century B.C.E., the Babylonians and Egyptians both arrived at a specific number of days in the year, but their conclusions were different. For some unknown reason, the Babylonians claimed that the year was 360 days long while the Egyptians more accurately estimated the year at 365 days. The discrepancy between the two lengths of the year has always been puzzling.

One possibility for the difference is that the Babylonians simply miscalculated the number; however, this is unlikely in light of their sophisticated astronomical and mathematical systems. Another explanation is that they rounded their figure from 365 days to 360 to facilitate the interaction of the year with their base-twelve numerical system.

The problem with the Babylonian's five-day omission was that the months would not stay in line with the seasons of the year. Each year the beginning of each month would occur at least five days earlier in relation to the position of the sun. Eventually, the months would be completely dissociated with the seasons in which they originally occurred. To correct this problem, the Babylonians may have periodically added days, weeks, or months to the calendar—a process termed intercalation.

The Babylonians were not the only people to face the problem of keeping the months coordinated with the seasons. Even though the Egyptians calculated the length of the year more accurately, they too realized that their determination was not exactly perfect. In fact, the year cannot be divided into exact fractions that can be expressed in days.

The solar system affects the length of the year. Precise division of the year into days is impossible because the cycle of the seasons is determined by the earth's relationship to the sun *and* the moon. Unfortunately, the movements of these heavenly bodies do not neatly coincide with the mathematical systems of any human civilization.

The quest to discover the secrets of how the universe fits together has motivated astronomers throughout history. In the second century C.E., Ptolemy, a Greek astronomer formulated the theory that the earth was the center of the universe and that sun, stars, moon, and other planets revolve around it. In the fifteenth century C.E., the Polish astronomer Copernicus introduced the notion that the earth rotated on an axis and, along with the other heavenly bodies in the solar system, revolved around the sun. Shortly after the Copernican assertion, Galileo presented evidence from his observations using the telescope to support this view of the universe. It is the solar cycle—the relationship among the earth, moon, and sun—that determines the cycle of the seasons.

The crux of the dilemma is a gap between the lunar and solar cycles. Herein lies the difficulty of keeping the cycle of the months in line with the passing of the seasons: An 11.25-day difference exists between the 354-day lunar cycle on which the months are based and the 365.25-day solar cycle which determines the seasons. Three main ways of dealing with this discrepancy have been attempted. The first is to ignore the seasons and allow the lunar cycle to be the basis of the year as the Islamic calendar does. Another method is the lunisolar system like the Hebrew calendar which involves an elaborate system of calculations to add days or months to the lunar year until it coincides with the solar year. The third system is the pure solar calendar which originated with the Egyptians and allows the sun to determine not only the seasons, but the length of the months as well. In the following chapters, each of these systems will be explored.

Chapter 2

Lunar and Lunisolar Calendars: Western Traditions

The earliest system for constructing calendars was developed by Babylonian, Sumerian, and Assyrian astronomers living in the Mesopotamian valley hundreds of years before the birth of Christ. These calendars were based on the phases of the moon and were closely related to the religious life of the cultures that developed them. The influence of the Mesopotamian civilizations on the global art of calendar making was far reaching as many of the techniques they developed were adopted by future societies.

The Babylonian Calendar

Of the various cultures that thrived in the Mesopotamian valley, the Babylonians seem to have had the most significant influence on calendar making. Many details of the evolution of the Babylonian calendar have been lost over the centuries, but it is known that the calendar was lunar in nature, had a system of intercalation, had months divided into seven-day units, and had days with twenty-four hours.

Intercalation reconciles nature's incongruous cycles. Because these early calendar makers were pioneers in the field, they were among the first to be confronted with the discrepancy between the lunar and solar cycles–a problem that had the potential to render any calendar system ineffective. To reconcile the two natural courses, the Babylonians worked out a schedule whereby an extra month was periodically intercalated. The process of intercalation, termed *iti dirig*, seems to have been rather arbitrary at first, but by 380 B.C.E. a formal system had developed. The plan consisted of a 19-year (235 month) system in which an extra month was added in the third, sixth, eighth, eleventh, seventeenth, and nineteenth years. Many other cultures, including the Greeks, developed similar intercalation schemes which may have been based on the Babylonian model.

The Babylonians introduce the seven-day week. Although the origin of the week has been a subject of much research and debate among scholars since the time of Plutarch (46-119 C.E.), most agree that the Babylonians are the primary source for the week in the Western civil calendar. Many researchers also conclude that the Babylonians devised the week as a part of their religious practices. They have observed that years, months, and days are all based on natural cycles, but the week is not. This observation has led to some questions: Why does the week have seven days? Why are the days named after planets? Why are the days not arranged according to the order of the planets in the solar system? Many proposed solutions to these quandaries have surfaced over the course of time.

A different view of the universe may account for the structure of the week. Lawrence Wright articulates a theory on the origin of the week in his *Clockwork Man*, which may help a modern audience understand the ancient mind-set. Using available historical and archeological information, Wright has attempted to reconstruct the Babylonian view of the universe.

Wright proposes that the seven-day week was not based on any naturally occurring pattern, but was the result of other influences within Babylonian society. He suggests that the week may have been based on 168 hours rather than seven days.

Moreover, he suggests that the order of days may be explained by the Babylonian belief in the earth as the center of the astronomical cycles they observed. Thus, if one lines the planets up according to their distance from the earth (Saturn, Jupiter, Mars, Sun, Venus, Mercury, Moon) rather than their order in the solar system, an interesting pattern arises. If each hour of the day is assigned a planet, by the time all of the hours have been assigned, and each planet has been given the first hour of one day, a seven-day sequence has been completed. For example, beginning with the first day, assign the first hour to the farthest planet from the earth, Saturn. That day would be known as Saturn's day or Saturday. Assign each hour of the day to another planet so that the second hour would be assigned to Jupiter, the third to Mars, and so on, repeating the sequence of planets until each hour of the day has been assigned to a planet. A twenty-four hour period requires that each planet be assigned three times and three planets four times. The first hour of the second day is named for the next planet in the sequence, or the Sun (hence, Sunday). Although the Babylonians had different planet and day names, they occurred in the same pattern as the current Western calendar observes.

The week may be based on a type of astrological system. Another explanation for the order of the week may be that the Babylonians attached special significance to the days of the week and hours of the day. This suggests that the divisions may have been important to Babylonian religious practices.

Archeological evidence reveals that the Babylonian religion involved worship of the "visible gods," the seven lights in the sky that the Babylonians believed wandered against the background provided by the fixed stars—a type of astrological system similar to the Greek zodiac. Each day of the Babylonian month was sacred to one of these seven gods. Thus a seven-day pattern of gods' days would have emerged. This pattern would have offered a convenient division of the month.

Although in English the names of the week bear the influence of the Anglo-Saxons, the days in Latin and the Romance languages correspond to the ancient Babylonian "visible gods."

The sabbath may have its beginning in Babylon. The Sabbath is a common occurrence in many cultures. Historians suggest that the Babylonians may have been the first to develop this idea. In fact, the modern word "sabbath" can be traced to the Babylonian "shabattu" which means seventh. The Babylonians considered the days numbered 7, 14, 19, 21, and 28 "evil days" since the god of the underworld was the deity governing those days. Some scholars have proposed that the seven-day week was translated into other cultures by the ancient Hebrews, who adopted the concept when they were subject to Babylonian rule. From there, over a period of thousands of years, the Hebrews were diffused into nearly every culture on earth, taking their traditions with them.

Details of the Babylonian calendar are few, but some are known. It appears that the major festival of Babylonian society was the New Year celebration which took place in the spring of the year during the Babylonian month of Nisanu. On the first day of the festival, a ritual marriage was performed between the king and the high priestess, who symbolized the sovereignty of the land. On this day, the Babylonian creation myth (called *Enuma elish* from its opening words, "When on high") was read aloud. On the fifth day, Rites of Atonement were observed. During the Rites the king, as a representative of the people, endured a ritual of abasement to atone for the sins of the people against the gods. On the seventh day, the Festival of the Sun, or spring equinox, took place.

The Hebrew Calendar

Structural details of the ancient Hebrew calendar are fragmentary. The first written evidence of a Hebrew calendar is the Gezer Calendar, a stone carving which lists the tasks associated with the agricultural duties for each of a series of 12 yereah (the Hebrew word for lunation or month). Historians believe this early calendar was derived from the Canaanite cycle sometime before the establishment of the Jewish monarchy around 1050 B.C.E. References in the Old Testament to the Hebrews using Canaanite month names help to support this theory. The months that are recorded in the Hebrew scriptures (Aviv, Ziv, Etanim, and Bul) correspond to the modern Jewish months of Nisan, Iyar, Tishri, and Heshvan.

While many technical aspects of the Hebrew calendar remain a mystery, it is known that the lunar and solar cycles were reconciled in some manner because the Passover month always occurred in a specific season. This would be impossible unless the calendar also took the solar cycle into account.

Discovery of ancient manuscripts led to Hebrew reforms. According to the Biblical account in *II Kings 22*, participation in the religious feasts and festivals of Israel was mandated by King Josiah around 621 B.C.E. At that time, although these celebrations had been practiced earlier in their history, the Hebrews had not observed them for nearly 600 years. Apparently even the most rudimentary knowledge of the rituals surrounding the festivals had been lost until, during renovations of the Temple in Jerusalem, the High Priest, Hilkiah, discovered what he claimed were ancient manuscripts of the Law of Moses. These documents reportedly detailed the ceremonies necessary for observing the ancient Hebrew holidays. Hilkiah presented the discovery to King Josiah who required that all Hebrews observe its provisions.

Sweeping changes were made to the religious practices of the Hebrews as a result of the reforms. These included the establishment of Passover as a national festival and the designation of Jerusalem as the only acceptable site for observing the three Hebrew pilgrimage feasts: Passover, Pentecost, and Sukkot. Also, attendance of these feasts was made mandatory for all able-bodied men in Israel; they were required to bring their tithes, or religious taxes, to the Temple on these occasions.

Conflict over religious reforms splits the Judeans and Samaritans. These decrees angered many Hebrews who lived outside the region of Judea because they had been practicing their religious ceremonies in local houses of worship for hundreds of years. The distance and inconvenience of traveling to Jerusalem caused many of these people to break away from the reform movement and worship at their traditional sites.

This splinter group, located in northern Israel, became known as the Samaritans. As a result of the break in religious practices and the ensuing conflicts that arose, the Samaritans and Israelites developed slightly different practices regarding their calendars. The custom of the Samaritans was to figure the start of the month according to the absence of a moon while the Israelites defined the "new moon" as the evening on which the crescent of the waxing moon is first visible locally. A difference of one to three days is possible between these two systems. Both groups sought to impose their method over the other; each sect felt if they embraced the other method, they would break the law and offend God. This conflict was a source of division among Jews for centuries, but the Israelite method was the one which prevailed.

Exile in Babylon influences the Hebrew calendar. Around 586 B.C.E., the Babylonians conquered Jerusalem. They took the ruling class of the Israelites captive and deported them to Babylon where the Israelites lived in exile for fifty years. Some researchers have suggested that many elements of modern Judaism, such as monotheism, were formalized at this time.

Clearly, the Babylonians exercised an influence on the Hebrew calendar as is evidenced by many similar elements within both systems. Scholars surmise that the Hebrews adopted many elements of the Babylonian calendar because the Babylonian system was clearly established by the sixth century B.C.E., and there is no evidence to suggest that the Hebrew system was explicitly defined at that time.

Structurally the influence of the Babylonians on the Hebrew calendar was manifested in the adoption of the Babylonian month names, the establishment of Nisanu 1 as the point from which regnal years of the king were reckoned, and the incorporation of the seven-day week. As a result of these structural changes, the Hebrew calendar became a distinct entity with well-defined rules for calculating the passage of time.

Aside from technical elements, the Babylonian and Hebrew systems have other similarities. For example, both groups employ the wedding motif in various celebrations. One of the most important Hebrew celebrations, Passover, falls at the same time as the Babylonian new year, and both occasions incorporated some similar ceremonial rites. The Hebrews adopted some Babylonian rites into their own new year which occurs in the fall. Sir James Frazer argues in his *Golden Bough* that the account of Esther and Mordecai, the story at the center of the Purim celebration, is drawn from the Babylonian legend of Ishtar and Marduk.

In any case, the Babylonian-inspired calendar was used by the Hebrews until 70 C.E. except for the period during which Alexander the Great and the Ptolemies imposed the use of the Macedonian system (322-200 B.C.E.).

The Diaspora complicated the method of constructing the Hebrew calendar. The Babylonian and Israelite calendars both based the beginning of the month on the sighting of the new moon. In Hebrew society, the High Priest appointed watchmen to look for the new moon. When it appeared, the watchmen would report back to the High Priest who would proclaim the beginning of a new month. The Priests took great care to confirm the accurate proclamation of a new month because Hebrew religious practices prohibit the celebration of certain holidays on particular days of the week and require a specific number of days between festivals. Rosh ha-Shanah (New Year), for example, cannot fall on a Sunday, Wednesday, or Friday, but must fall 163 days after Passover.

The system of observing the new moon became impractical after the destruction of the Temple in 70 C.E. and the subsequent Diaspora of the Jews. The central system for proclaiming a new month could not adequately meet the needs of a dispersed population. As an attempt to solve this problem, a messenger system was instituted whereby a series of "runners" would travel from town to town bringing official word of the new month once it had been declared in Jerusalem.

An equation replaces the sighting system. By 200 C.E., Hebrew priests had developed an equation to replace the sighting method of determining the beginning of months. This formula was known only by a select group of priests in Jerusalem who continued to be the official voice to proclaim the new month. At the same time, many Hebrew communities were taking the matter into their own hands by appointing their own watchmen rather than waiting for the official word. This situation caused great strife and division among the Hebrews because, once again, the

start of the new month varied from region to region. This division became especially crucial on the point of the celebration of Passover.

In 358 C.E., the High Priest Hillel II recognized the potentially destructive nature of the problem and, to maintain the unity of the Hebrew people, he made the secret equation public. Hillel's decision has been hailed as one which helped preserve the Hebrew faith through ensuing periods of dire crisis. Even though individual enclaves of Jews were often completely isolated from one another, they were able to maintain a sense of unity and identity partly because of their common religious calendar and observances.

Days, weeks, months, and years in the Hebrew calendar. From the time of Hillel II until the present, the Hebrew calendar has evolved into one of the most intricate systems of time reckoning in existence. The calendar includes such elements as varying year lengths, varying month lengths, and leap years—all of which are designed to meet the requirements of Judaic law regarding the celebration of feasts, festivals, and holidays.

The structure of the modern Jewish calendar is lunisolar with the months based on the moon and the years on the sun (see Table 2.4 at end of chapter). The day is 24 hours long but each hour is divided into 1,080 parts each of which are approximately 3.3 seconds long. The day officially begins at 6:00 p.m., but for religious purposes, sunset is considered the beginning of a new day.

The 12 months of the Hebrew calendar alternate between 29 and 30 days with two months, Marheshvan and Kislev, that have variable lengths. Months containing 30 days are known as "full" and the 29-day months are called "defective." The calendar includes an intercalary month, We-Adar, which is 30 days in length.

To meet the requirements of the Jewish religious law and reconcile the lunar cycle with the solar cycle, the Hebrew calendar has years ranging in length from 353 to 385 days. First, to bring the 19-year lunar cycle into harmony with the 28-year solar cycle, the intercalary month, We-Adar, is added in years 3, 6, 8, 11, 14, 17, and 19 of the lunar cycle. Second, to ensure that their religious regulations are fulfilled, the months of Marheshvan and Kislev vacillate between 29 and 30 days. Years in which both months are full are called "complete" years (shelema). If it is a regular year, it will contain 355 days; a complete leap year (in which We-Adar is added) will contain 385 days. A "normal" (sedura) year is one in which Marheshvan is full and Kislev is defective and will contain either 354 or 384 days. "Defective" (hasera) years, totaling 353 or 383 days, occur when both Marheshvan and Kislev contain only 29 days.

Similarities between the Hebrew calendar and the Greek Metonic cycle are observed. The Hebrew calendar picks up a common thread with the Greek Metonic cycle (see below) for reconciling the solar and lunar cycles. Although We-Adar is intercalated in seven out of every 19 years like the Metonic cycle, the specific years to which the month is added is different from the most prominent of the Greek methods, the Athenian calendar. The reason for the difference in the patterns is that We-Adar is added whenever it is needed to push the 15th ("full moon") of Nisan after the spring, or vernal, equinox because the Passover cannot be held before the equinox.

The basis for naming years in the Hebrew calendar is a code indicating the characteristics of the year. The character of a year (qevi'a, literally "fixing") indicates the important technical details of the coming year. It is signified by three Hebrew letters: the first and third give the days of the weeks on which the New Year occurs and Passover begins, the second is the initial of the Hebrew word for defective, normal, or complete. There are 14 types of qevi'a, seven in common and seven in leap years. According to Hebrew scholars, the era used to number the years of the Jewish calendar (designated anno mundi or AM) had its epoch in the year of Creation which they believe was 3761 B.C.E.

Thus, beginning with the equation made public by Hillel II, the Hebrew calendar became schematic and independent of the true New Moon. In fact, if the dates of the Hebrew calendar are compared with the dates for astronomical full and new moons, the dates will often differ by several days. The "new moon" is defined as the evening on which the crescent of the waxing moon is first visible locally, not as the astronomical new moon, which will always be one to three days earlier. The "full moon" is defined as the fourteenth evening after the "new moon" (first crescent),

not as the astronomical full moon, which may occur up to three days earlier.

The Greek Calendar

Equally as ancient as the Hebrew calendar was the Greek system. The classical Greeks had calendar systems that varied among the city-states. The political powers of each city-state retained the right to intercalate months and days to reconcile the lunar and solar cycles. These intercalations were arbitrary and seem to have been more closely associated with political whimsy rather than natural cycles. The most influential calendar system was the Athenian.

The Athenian calendar consisted of twelve lunar months that alternated between 29 and 30 days in length, plus an intercalary month of 30 days. This extra month, Poseideion Deuteros or second Poseideion, was inserted into the calendar after the sixth month Poseideion. Also, an extra day could be added to the last month, Scirophorion, to keep the months in phase with the moon.

When the Athenians became rulers of the Delian League in the sixth century B.C.E., they realized the need to have an official calendar that could be used by all the League's members. Hence in 582 B.C.E. they regulated the intercalation of months by using an eight-year, or octennial, cycle in which a month was added to the third, fifth, and eighth years.

The Athenians divide months into three "decades." The Athenian calendar began in midsummer and comprised twelve months: Hecatombaion, Metageitnion, Boedromion, Pyanopsion, Maimactrerion, Poseideion, Gamelion, Anthesterion, Elaphebolion, Mounychion, Thargelion, and Scirophorion. These months were divided into three "decades" of ten days each. The first ten days were called the "waxing moon"; the middle ten days were called "full moon"; and the last nine or ten days were called the "waning moon." Dates were assigned according to these decades, and days within the last decade were numbered from the end of the decade. For example, the first day of the month was called the "first day of the waxing moon" of whatever month. The eleventh day would be "the first day of the full moon". The twentieth day was called "the tenth day of the full moon," but the twenty-first day was called "the tenth day of the waning moon" (or the ninth day, if the month had only 29 days).

Cleostratus constructed an eight-year cycle to reconcile the lunar and solar patterns. The Grecian concept of an eight-year cycle was devised by Cleostratus of Tenedos (ca. 500 B.C.E.) and advanced by Eudoxus of Cnidus (390 to ca. 340 B.C.E.). Called the octaëteris, the Greek cycle was based on a solar year of 365 days; thus, the eight-year cycle was composed of 2,920 days. The octennial cycle closely matched the length of 99 lunations (a total of 2920.5 days), which made it a promising link between lunar and solar calendars.

The actual length of a solar year is 365.24 days, and eight solar years have a length of 2921.93 days. Therefore, the calendar based on the octaëteris accumulated an error of 1.5 days every eight years. After about a century of use, the discrepancy had accrued to nearly 30 days. When the Greek scholars realized the problems with their calendar, some of them began to search for a more effective system to reconcile the lunar and solar calendars.

The Metonic cycle is developed. The most significant of all the early attempts to relate the lunar calendar to the tropical year was the Metonic cycle. First devised about 430 B.C.E. by the Athenian astronomers Meton and Euctemon, the system is based on a nineteen-year cycle which intercalates months in seven out of the nineteen years.

To determine the length for the tropical year, Meton and Euctemon made a series of observations of the solstices—the point at which the sun's noonday shadow cast by a vertical pillar, or gnomon, reaches its annual maximum or minimum. Assuming the value of the synodic lunar month to be 29.5 days, the two astronomers computed the difference between 12 lunations and the tropical year at 11 days. To accommodate the lunar cycle and create a rule that would be accurate on a long-term basis, Meton and Euctemon constructed a nineteen-year cycle. It consisted of twelve years of twelve lunar months each and seven years each of thirteen months for a total of 235 lunar months. The cycle contains 110 "hollow" months (of 29 days) and 125 "full" months (of 30 days), which comes to a total of 6,940 days. The difference between this lunar calendar and a solar calendar of 365

days amounted to only five days in nineteen years and, in addition, gave an average length for the tropical year of 365.25 days.

In practice, Meton's cycle is even more precise that he realized. The five-day difference that arose over the course of the cycle was based on a slightly inaccurate day count. Astronomers who came after Meton have discovered the actual length of 235 lunar months to be 6939.69 days and the number of days in nineteen solar years to be 6939.602. The actual difference between the two cycles accrues to less than one day in nineteen years—a discrepancy easily corrected by occasionally adding days to or subtracting them from the year.

There are two primary accomplishments of the Metonic cycle: it established a lunar calendar with a rule for intercalating months to keep it in step with the tropical year; and it gave a more accurate average value for the tropical year. Although none of the Greek calendars appear to have adopted the system, the Persians did around 380 B.C.E. The Metonic system then passed into the Hebrew liturgical calendar which is still based on the cycle, as are the formulas used by the Christian churches to calculate the date of Easter.

Callippus enhances Meton's system. The Metonic cycle was improved by Callippus of Cyzicus (ca. 370-300 B.C.E.). He developed the Callippic cycle which is a variation on the Metonic cycle. Consisting of four nineteen-year cycles, the Callippic system takes into account that 365.25 days is a more precise value for the tropical year than 365 days. The Callippic period encompasses 940 lunar months, but its distribution of hollow and full months differs from Meton's 440 hollow and 500 full months. Callippus adopted 441 hollow and 499 full months, reducing the length of four Metonic cycles by one day. The total number of days in the Callippic cycle, therefore, is 27,759. When this total is divided by 76 (the number of years in the cycle), the result is 365.25 days exactly. Thus, the Callippic cycle fits 940 lunar months precisely to 76 tropical years of 365.25 days.

Hipparchus' discovery of the Precession of the Equinoxes further improves the Metonic Cycle. Hipparchus, who flourished in Rhodes about 150 B.C.E., was probably the greatest observational astronomer of antiquity. He discovered that the equinoxes—where the ecliptic (the sun's apparent path) crosses the celestial equator (the celestial equivalent of the terrestrial Equator)—were not fixed in space but moved slowly in a westerly direction. The movement, now known as the precession of the equinoxes, is small, no more than two degrees of arc in 150 years. Yet, it was important to the development of the calendar because the tropical year is measured with reference to the equinoxes. The precession reduced the value of the year that was accepted by Callippus.

Hipparchus calculated the tropical year to have a length of 365.242 days, which was very close to the present 365.242199 days. He also computed the precise length of a lunation, using a "great year" of four Callippic cycles. He arrived at the value of 29.53058 days for a lunation, which, again, is comparable with the present-day figure, 29.53059 days. Hipparchus' adjustments made the Metonic cycle the most accurate long-range time keeping system available to scientists until well into the modern age.

The Metonic cycle was used for liturgical and astronomical calendars. Meton's innovative cycle fell victim to the political winds of the day and was not recognized by the political establishment of Greece during his lifetime. Fortunately, Greek religious leaders and classical astronomers did use Meton's cycle to calculate their calendars. The cycle has been passed down through the course of history as subsequent calendar makers, including the Julian and Gregorian reformers, have adapted its basic formula to fit their systems.

Religious holidays and the Greek liturgical calendar. The celebration of religious holidays in the Athenian months followed some consistent patterns. For example, the first and seventh day of each month was sacred to Apollo, and the first and fifteenth days were sacred to Selene. Festivals of other gods fell into consistent patterns as well. Dionysus tended to be celebrated on days 11 to 13; sacrifices to Zeus on day 14; the cycle of games on days 11-15. Therefore, by knowing the Greek pattern of religious celebration, scholars can accurately surmise the specific dates on which the festival of a deity was observed. By following these patterns, scholars have been able to reconstruct the Athenian calendar with a high degree of

accuracy (see Table 2.5 at end of chapter). Days in the Greek calendar began at sunset just as in the Hebrew calendar. Since the Renaissance, the religious practices of the Greeks have been studied with interest, and have been revived by various Neoclassic and Neopagan groups.

The Eleusinian Mysteries perplex modern historians. The most important Athenian festival was that of the Eleusinian Mysteries, which has intrigued scholars for centuries. Because the contents of the Mysteries were an Athenian state secret, the details of the festival are not known. The Mysteries fell into two periods. The earlier, in Anthesterion, was called the Lesser Mysteries, and probably involved a ritual or drama about the life, death, and resurrection of Dionysus. The later, in Boedromion, was called the Greater Mysteries, and was definitely centered on the myth of the Rape of Persephone, as told in the Greek poem called the Homeric *Hymn To Demeter*.

Some have surmised that initiation into the Lesser Mysteries was a prerequisite to participation in the Greater Mysteries. This may not be accurate, however, especially as the Romans began to influence the Greeks. Many Romans and other inhabitants of the Roman empire came to Athens in Boedromion to be initiated at the Greater Mysteries.

Preparation for the mysteries began formally on Boedromion 15. The Hierokeryx (sacred herald) would stand on the Painted Porch in Athens and, in the presence of the Hierophant ("high priest" of Eleusis), announce the assembly for the Mysteries. After several days of sacrifices and preparations, the Procession of the Mysteries would leave Athens on the morning of Boedromion 19, reaching Eleusis after sunset, which was then Boedromion 20 because the Athenian day began at sunset. Based on the known rituals, the celebration of the Mysteries probably lasted three nights. The festivities included a torchlit search for Kore and an initiation of the candidates who were sworn to secrecy as the key of the Hierophant was laid upon their lips. The agenda may have also included a ritual drama about the reunion of Demeter and Kore; evidence indicates that a ritual or mime of the Rape of Kore took place during the Thesmophoria. Finally, there was probably a ritual in the Telesterion. It is possible that the entire festival lasted nine days or longer based on the tradition of a nine-day fast which was clearly a part of the observation of this event. Therefore, the ending date of the festival can certainly be placed on or after Boedromion 23, nine days after the Proclamation of the Mysteries on Boedromion 15.

Evolution of the Christian Feasts

Clearly visible within the Christian liturgical calendar are elements of both the Hebrew and Greek time-keeping systems. Most immediately recognizable, however, are the influences of the Hebrew calendar.

The evolution of Christianity as a separate religion from Judaism is often misunderstood. The division between the two belief systems was not initially over the deity of Jesus of Nazareth and his position as the Messiah, as many people suppose; in fact, for the first fifty years that Christianity existed, it remained a movement within Judaism. Most Christians were Jews who believed that Jesus was the Messiah. Although many other Jews did not share the Christians' belief, the two groups continued to worship in the synagogues together.

Roman conquest of Jerusalem in 70 C.E. spurred division between Jews and Christians. The tolerant situation between Christians and Jews was initially maintained by the popular and diverse nature of Judaism during the development of the Church. Christians were only one of many sects within Judaism; others included the Sadducees, Pharisees, Essenes, Zealots, gnostics, the "God-Fearers" (a group composed of Romans who lived a Jewish lifestyle without formal conversion—perhaps up to 20 percent of the Roman population), and other groups. This richly diverse Jewish culture was shattered into fragments in 70 C.E. by the Roman war.

After the Roman destruction of the Temple at Jerusalem, the surviving Hebrew rabbis argued that the disaster had been caused by "factionalism" and decided that unity was more important than individual expression. Thus, they merged the sects, drawing mainly from the Pharisaic tradition to create what is now know as normative or Orthodox Judaism. Christian Jews were invited to join this new, unified group, but the Christians decided not to merge because they could not accept the conditions and constraints of Orthodox Judaism. Jews and Christians continued to meet together in the synagogue on the sabbath evening until about 80-85 C.E., when Christians began to form their own synagogues. At that point, they were no longer recognized as Jews under the Jewish and Roman law, and Christianity became illegal. More than two centuries passed before Christianity was legalized again.

How Christians established Sunday as their meeting day. While Christians continued to meet with other Jews in the synagogue for the Sabbath, they also observed their own special meetings, on Sunday at sunrise, to commemorate the resurrection of Jesus. Once they began to separate from the Jews, they slowly switched to Sunday mornings as their primary meeting time. The reasons for this change in meeting time were two-fold: First to remember the resurrection of Christ; second, to separate themselves more clearly from the Jews. This period marks the distinct point at which the two systems of belief moved in opposite directions, and it was here that the roots of longstanding resentments between the two groups began to grow. However, Christians continued to celebrate the Jewish Passover as the anniversary of the Last Supper, and the Jewish Pentecost (Feast of Weeks) as the anniversary of the New Covenant, when the Holy Spirit descended on the disciples. Sunday, Passover, and Pentecost are the only Christian feast days mentioned by the prominent church father, Origen, in the early third century.

Constantine's conversion resulted in official sanction of Christianity. By the fourth century Christians had become so numerous that the acts of persecution initiated by the Roman emperor Diocletian a century before could no longer seriously endanger the movement. With the conversion of Constantine the Great in 312 C.E., Christianity became the official religion of the waning Roman Empire. This formal sanction spurred a massive evangelistic effort by Christians which resulted in the conversion of most inhabitants of the Empire and many barbarian groups on its outskirts.

Christians incorporated the celebrations of other religions into their own traditions. To facilitate the acceptance of Christianity by pagans, the leaders of the Church instructed its missionaries to allow new converts to continue observing the festivals to which they were accustomed. Pope Gregory specifically instructed Augustine of Canterbury in the early seventh century that the only stipulation on the rule of acceptance was that a new meaning had to be assigned to the symbolism of the event which would bring it into line with Christian teachings.

One new festival the church established about this time was Epiphany. The Alexandrian Church of Isis had long celebrated the day which became Epiphany as the birthday of Osiris from the Virgin. The Mysteries of Isis originated under the Ptolemies as an Egyptian form of the Eleusinian Mysteries of Greece and had been imported into Rome by the first century B.C.E. For several centuries, the Alexandrian Church of Isis represented serious competition to the Christian Church in the Roman world. It was from the tradition of the Alexandrian Church that Christianity garnered the practice of having daily liturgical services in large ornate temples.

The worshippers of Mithras, a Persian god extremely popular among the Roman soldiers, had long celebrated December 25 as the "Birthday of the Invincible Sun." In 273 C.E., the Christian Church established December 25 as the date of the Virgin Birth of their Invincible Son, and apparently about this time began emphasizing Christ as the Sacrificial Lamb as a substitute for the sacrificial bull of Mithraism.

The celebration of the Resurrection of Christ caused a problem between East and West. At first, Christians celebrated the Feast of the Resurrection on the first Sunday after the beginning of Passover. By the second century C.E., the relationship between Judaism and Christianity had deteriorated so greatly that it became impossible for Christians to find out when Passover would be celebrated from year to year because the equation for this determination had not yet been made public. As a result, Christians began determining the celebration of Easter according to the rules of their individual communities.

The Christian churches east of Greece celebrated Easter on the fourteenth of Nisan, whether or not it was a Sunday. The Western Church, however, developed a more complex system to determine Easter's date to ensure that it was celebrated on a Sunday in the Passover week. To claim authority for the date of the Resurrection and Easter Day, both groups appealed to the authority of the Gospels. However, the Gospel of John gives a different date for the crucifixion than the other gospels give. This inconsistency coupled with the controversy over how the evening of the fourteenth day of the month should be calculated produced a major schism between the Eastern and Western churches.

According to the Jewish definition, the full moon was the fourteenth day after the new moon. Defining the evening of the fourteenth day would, therefore, determine the date on which the Passover was celebrated. A group called the Quintodecimans counted the evening of the fourteenth as the one after the fourteenth day. The Quartodecimans claimed that it meant the evening following the thirteenth day, since sunset was the beginning of a new day. Supporters of the two points of view tended to fall along geographical lines: the Eastern Church supported the Quartodecimans, while the Western Church supported the Quintodecimans.

The Nicaean Council established the date of Easter and divided the Eastern and Western church. In 325, Constantine summoned all the bishops to the first Ecumenical Council, in Nicaea, to settle the numerous differences that were cropping up and threatening the unity of the Church. It was also around this time that the seven-day week became common in the Roman Empire, and schoolchildren had to begin memorizing the names of the weekdays in order to know which day was Sunday—indicating how strong the influence of Christianity had become in a short period of time.

The Council of Nicaea passed policies on many issues facing the Christian Church; among the most pertinent of these was a system for determining the date of Easter. Even though disagreement has arisen over the interpretation of the rule, it has been used by Christians ever since.

Because Judaism and Christianity had become defined as mutually exclusive religions, the Christian authorities wanted to ensure that Easter would never coincide with Passover. The rule for the date of Easter which the Council of Nicaea declared was in agreement with the Quintodecimans. The Feast of the Resurrection should be celebrated on the first Sunday after (not on) the first full moon after March 21 (which was the date of the vernal equinox the year the council met). This full moon became known as Paschal. In addition, the Council ruled that if the designated Sunday coincided with either Passover or the Easter Day of the Quartodecimans, the festival should be held seven days later.

The decision of the Council delighted the Western Church. The Eastern church, on the other hand, decided to retain the Quartodeciman position, as did the church in England. During the sixth century, Roman missionaries to England introduced the Western system which was adopted and is still followed.

A formula for determining the date of Easter is devised. The provisions of the Council of Nicaea later allowed the Church to devise a formula to calculate the date of Easter. There were two parts to the formula: dominical letters and golden numbers. The first part, dominical letters, was a system that would determine the day of the week on which any date of the year would fall. The golden numbers provided a method for concluding the dates of the full moon in any given year.

In order to determine what dates the Sundays in any given year would occur, the Church adopted a system similar to the one that had been used by the Romans to determine market days. For ecclesiastical use, the code gave what was known as the dominical letter.

The first seven letters of the alphabet, A through G, are each assigned to consecutive days beginning with the first day of the year. January 1 appears as A, January 2 as B, and so on through January 7 as G, January 8 as A, January 9 as B, et cetera. The letter given to the first Sunday in the year will be the letter of all the Sundays thereafter in the year. For example, if January 5 is the first Sunday, E will be the dominical letter for the year. The only exception to this is leap year. In this case, no dominical letter is assigned to February 29, but because it appears on the calendar like any other weekday, the series of letters moves back one day after the intercalation. So if a leap year begins with the dominical letter E, it will change to the dominical letter F on March 1. In charts of dominical letters, leap years are designated with a double-letter notation such as EF.

To determine the date on which Easter will be observed, one would look at the dates between which Easter must be celebrated (March 22-April 25), determine which of these dates are Sundays by using the system of dominical letters, and determine which of these Sundays meets the requirements for Easter: that it falls after the Paschal moon and does not coincide with the Passover or Quartodeciman celebrations. To find out if it falls after the Paschal moon, the system known as golden numbers was developed.

Golden numbers determined the full moon. Golden numbers are based on a cycle much like the Metonic cycle. A nineteen-year chart was constructed that predicted the phases of the moon for each year in the period. The number cycle indicated which days within the range would be full moons on which of the nineteen years included in its calculations.

The chart of dominical letters was then consulted to find out which days after the first full moon following March 21 were Sundays. The first Sunday to meet all of the requirements for Easter as laid down by the Nicean Council was then officially declared as the holiday.

Although the golden numbers were introduced in 530 C.E., the chart was constructed as if they had been accepted in the fourth century at the Council of Nicaea. The designers of the golden number system determined that the epoch of the era should fall when the New Moon occurred on January 1. They determined this year to be the one preceding 1 C.E. Therefore to determine the golden number for any year one would divide the year by nineteen, then add one to the remainder of the quotient. If the result is zero, the golden number for the year is nineteen.

The origin of the name "golden numbers" dates to medieval times, but its exact derivation is uncertain. Some have suggested that they were named for the Greeks name of the numbers within the Metonic cycle while others have conjectured that they were named after the gold color used for them in manuscript calendars.

Christians disconnected their holidays from the Hebrew roots. The effort of the Church Fathers to avoid the coincidence of Easter with the Passover feast underscores how far Judaism and Christianity had diverged. The notion that the Last Supper was an extension of the Passover Feast seemed to have been forgotten. The Church Fathers also fixed Pentecost as the seventh Sunday (fiftieth day according to the Roman inclusive counting method) after Easter, just as the Jewish Pentecost is the fiftieth day after Passover. Since December 25 had already been established as the birthday of the Christ, the Council of Nicaea established March 25, nine months before, as the date of his conception or as the Feast of the Annunciation, the day when the angel Gabriel told Mary she had been chosen to be the mother of the Messiah. Similarly, the traditional date for the birth of Mary, September 8, determined the placing of the feast of Mary's Immaculate Conception on December 8. Each of these dates was originally a celebration of a Roman, Greek, or Egyptian deity.

Why Easter is a movable feast. The Feast of the Resurrection had already been a movable feast for so long by the time of the Council of Nicaea that it could not easily have been established as a fixed feast on the actual anniversary of the event. Another reason why Easter may be a movable feast is that although the official teaching of the Roman Catholic Church is that the actual date of the Crucifixion was April 7, 30 C.E., both modern scholarship and medieval tradition agree that the actual date was March 25, 29 C.E. In fact, the medieval tradition continues with the feast day of St. Dismas, the "good thief" who died on the cross next to Jesus, which is celebrated on March 25. To avoid further controversy, the Church authorities may have made the holiday movable as a compromise. A third possibility for the movable date of Easter may have been that the Church leaders wanted to avoid having the Annunciation and the Crucifixion fall on the same date. If March 25 falls during Easter Week, the Feast of the Annunciation is celebrated a week or two later.

Based on the date of Easter, a series of "movable Feasts" developed. They begin with Shrove Tuesday, end with Corpus Christi, and include Ash Wednesday, Palm Sunday, Maundy Thursday, Good Friday, Ascension Day, Whitsunday, and Corpus Christi.

There are three movable feasts that do not depend on the date of Easter. The Sunday after January 6 is the Feast of the Baptism of the Lord. The last Sunday of the Roman Catholic liturgical year (it will fall on the third or fourth Sunday in November) is the Solemnity of Christ the King. The Sunday within the eight day celebration period following Christmas (or December 30, if Christmas is on a Sunday) is the Feast of the Holy Family.

Dionysius Exiguus introduced the notion of numbering years from the birth of Christ. In 463 C.E., Victorius of Aquitaine, who had been appointed by Pope Hilarius to undertake calendar revision, devised the Great Paschal period, also referred to as the Victorian Period. The Great Pascal period was a combination of the solar cycle of 28 years and the Metonic 19-year cycle. This cycle brought the Full Moon back to the same day of the month every 532 years. In the sixth century, this period was used by Dionysius Exiguus to figure the date of Easter. Hence, it also became known as the Dionysian period.

Recognizing the profound impact of Christianity on the world, Dionysius used the cycle to define a new era: the Christian era, based on the birth of Christ. He took the year now called 532 C.E. as the first year of a new Great Paschal period and the year now designated 1 B.C.E. as the beginning of the previous cycle. In the sixth century it was the general belief that this was the year of Christ's birth, and because of this, Dionysius introduced the concept of numbering years consecutively through the Christian era. Some scholars adopted Dionysius' practice early, but the B.C./A.D. dating method only came into wide use after its popularization in *The Ecclesiastical History of the English People* by the Venerable Bede of Jarrow (?673-735).

British Traditions

Time-reckoning begins with Stonehenge. The first evidence of a time reckoning system in Britain is the monument of Stonehenge. Historians suppose that the construction was originally used to mark solstices and equinoxes, and was built over a fifteen hundred year period beginning around 3000 B.C.E. Although little is known about the builders of Stonehenge, scholars have discounted the popular notion that it was built by Druid priests because of the gap in time between the monument's construction and the Druids' arrival in Britain (c. 500 B.C.E.).

Druid priests bring new religious traditions to Britain. Originally hailing from northern Europe, the Celtic tribes migrated to Britain in the sixth century B.C.E., bringing with them their religious holidays and customs. The Druids, who were priests of the Celtic tribes, governed the rites observed in the celebration of festivals on the first day of February, May, August, and November. These holidays were based on the weather patterns in northern Europe, rather than the solar cycle that the earlier Britons formed their religion around. These two sets of holidays became a point of division between the Celts and Britons and have remained such throughout the history of the island until the present.

Traditionally, the days observed by the Britons were called quarter days and fell on the solstices and equinoxes (around March 22, June 22, September 22, and December 22); they also marked the date on which quarterly rent was due. The Celts' holidays became known as cross-quarter days and celebrated the changes in season. Almost all of these days have several different names, reflecting their long and complex history.

Celts worldview divides everything into equal and opposite halves. Aylwin and Brinsley Rees point out in their *Celtic Heritage* that the Celtic worldview saw everything that exists as divided into two joined but opposing halves and that the seam between the two halves represents danger or evil.

This helps explain some of the festivals and holidays of the Celtic people. For example, their year began on Nov. 1 with a festival, Samhain, marking the end of good weather. The Celts believed that ghosts and fairies could slip into this world from the netherworld on the eve of this festival because it was the meeting place between the good half and bad half of the year.

Similarly, the Celts believed twilight and dawn were perilous times because fairies were most likely to steal into this realm and carry people off at these times. The two halves of the year were divided by Candlemas and Lammas; the night and the day were divided in half by midnight and noon.

The practice of beginning a celebration on the evening before a holiday, such as All Hallows Eve, is derived from the structure of the Celtic calendar.

Like most other ancient societies, the Celts began their days at sunset. Therefore, like the Hebrews and others, their observation of festivals and holidays began at sunset.

The Saxon influence changes the calendar. During the Roman domination of the southern British Isles, the Roman calendar was adopted. The influence of the Roman system faded, however, under the subsequent barbarian rule. The most significant of the barbarian groups to affect the calendar was the Saxons. They brought a lunisolar system of time reckoning with them when they came to power in England in the seventh century C.E.

The calendar was composed of twelve lunar months with a thirteenth intercalated once every three years (see Table 2.1). The day began at sunset and was divided in half by noon and midnight. Yule, or the winter solstice, was the major festival of the year, and scholars have surmised that the summer solstice, Litha, was also an occasion of grand celebration.

Some variables affecting the months are uncertain and have been tentatively reconstructed as follows: The placement of the fall, or autumnal, equinox

Table 2.1

The Saxon calendar

Name of month	Alternative name	Western civil month
Afteryule	Wolfmonth	January
Sproutkale	Solmonth	February
Hlydamonth		March
Eostremonth		April
Threemilks		May
Forelitha	Shearmonth	June
(Threelitha)	Intercalated month	
Afterlitha	Meadmonth	July
Weedmonth		August
Harvestmonth	Holymonth	September
Winterfull	Holymonth	October
Bloodmonth		November
Foreyule		December

determined the name of certain months. For example, the month in which the fall equinox occurred was called Holymonth. If the fall equinox occurred in the month after Weedmonth, the order of months went Weedmonth, Holymonth, Winterfull. If the equinox did not occur in the month after Weedmonth, the order was Weedmonth, Harvestmonth, Holymonth, and Winterfull. The designation of the month containing the fall equinox was clearly pagan in origin because there were no significant Christian festivals observed near the fall equinox during the seventh century.

The two months called Hlyda and Eostre were named after goddesses. Although details about the Goddess Eostre are few, historians suggest that it is from her name that English-speaking people derive the name "Easter" for the Feast of the Resurrection, which other languages call "Pasch" or something similar derived from the Hebrew word for Passover. The notion of the Easter Rabbit is also derived from Eostre, for the rabbit was one of her sacred animals. Furthermore, this rabbit lays Easter eggs because in some of the Mystery religions of the Roman period, an egg dyed scarlet was the symbol of the reincarnation and immortality promised to the initiate. The mixture of Christian and pagan traditions is clearly the result of Pope Gregory's policy of temperance and toleration which was articulated in a letter to Augustine of Canterbury early in the seventh century C.E.

Religious conflict influences the calendar. In the second century C.E., Diocletian's persecution of Christians caused many believers to flee from the Roman Empire. Some of these people settled in Ireland and there established Christian communities and monasteries among the Celts.

Over the next four centuries, the Irish Church developed apart from the Roman Church which dominated the rest of the British Isles. In the sixth century, Irish missionaries began proselytizing in England and came into conflict with the previously established Roman Church. The two branches of Christianity competed with one another for official recognition and converts during the next hundred years, often engaging in heated debate over doctrinal issues. In 664 C.E., the Council of Whitby was called by Oswy,

King of Northumbria, to settle some of the differences–most significantly, the method of determining the date of Easter.

The conflict over the date of Easter centered on the method used to calculate the phases of the moon. By the seventh century, the Roman Church had adopted the 532-year Victorian cycle to regulate the calendar. The Celts, on the other hand, still used the eight-year cycle developed in Rome before Diocletian's persecutions; the Celts also used the Eastern method for determining the night of the full moon. Therefore, the two methods arrived at significantly different dates for the celebration of the most sacred of Christian holidays. Eventually, the Roman Church prevailed and was declared to be the official Church in England.

Bede popularizes the use of the Christian Era in dating. The most clear information about both the Celtic and Saxon calendars as well as the Church controversies is found in Bede's *Ecclesiastical History of the English People*. The work was extremely popular among those who could read in the eighth and ninth centuries, and used the dating system of Dionysius Exiguus (B.C./A.D.) for the first time. It is because of Bede's work that this method of dating was spread throughout the Christian world.

The Christian era is developed by Dionysius Exiguus. In 532 C.E. Dionysius Exiguus, Abbot of Rome, calculated that Christ had been born about 753 years after the foundation of Rome (A.U.C.), and made that year the beginning of a new chronology. This date was determined by taking average of the dates of 747 A.U.C. (according to events in the Gospel of Matthew) and 759 A.U.C. (as indicated by events recorded in the Gospel of Luke) as the date of Jesus' birth. The accuracy of this date is no longer accepted, but the Western civil calendar as well as several other systems use the Christian era for dating because of the complications involved in changing to any other method.

Under Dionysius's system, March 25 was New Year's Day. The English adopted this for the ecclesiastical year in the twelfth century and the legal and civil year in the fourteenth century. The only exception was if March 25 fell during Holy Week—especially on Good Friday. If this occurred, New Year's Day was moved to April 1. This move may be behind the origin of April Fool's Day.

Quarter and cross-quarter days become an outlet for protest. An interesting pattern related to the observance of quarter and cross-quarter days (see Table 2.2) became evident in England during the early middle ages. The major Christian festivals were tied to the quarter days—Christmas to the winter solstice, Easter and the Annunciation to the spring equinox, St. John's Eve and Whitsuntide to the summer solstice, Michaelmas to the fall equinox.

Therefore, pagan protestors of the Christian establishment embraced the cross-quarter days as occasions for rebellion and celebration of traditions associated with their own belief systems. This may be the reason May Eve and Hallowe'en are associated with witches; but, in fact, both the quarter days and the cross-quarter days are equally pagan in origin.

Pagan and Christian traditions are melded together. Through the course of time, the pagan agricultural and weather festivals have become so meshed with Christian movable feasts that depend on Easter that it is difficult to distinguish the pagan traditions from those of the Christians.

Of the cross-quarter holidays, Hallowe'en is the only one still observed in the United States; the British have switched the festivities to Guy Fawkes' Day. May Day has become laden with political connotations which have removed any religious meaning from the day. Candlemas is still a minor church festival, but is otherwise remembered only as Groundhog Day. Lammas is completely forgotten in America, although it is still the reason for the British bank holiday on the

Table 2.2

Cross-Quarter Holidays

Date	Christian Name	Gaelic Name
Feb 2	Candlemas	Oimbelg
May 1	May Day	Beltane
Aug 2	Lammas	Lughnasad
Nov 1	Hallowe'en	Samhain

first Monday in August, and is kept as a harvest festival in rural Ireland.

The Neo-pagan movement has revived some festivals around the world. Although Christianity became the official religion of the British Isles, some people continued to practice pagan rituals clandestinely. An interest in reviving ancient pagan practices began to grow during the Renaissance but did not blossom until the nineteenth century when the Romanticists in art and literature picked up the theme. Poets such as Percy Bysse Shelley, John Keats, and William Blake pursued the revival of classical themes and practices, including religious traditions.

In the twentieth century, the Neo-pagan movement has moved from the realm of literary esoterica into a more popular sphere. As a result, more open celebrations of the original pagan rites developed. Since the 1920s, the movement seems to have become a loosely knit association of covens and other worship groups that observe common holidays such as the quarter and cross-quarter days. These holidays are considered the Sabbats of the Neo-pagan movement and form an eight-spoked wheel of holidays throughout the year. The most familiar names for the celebrations are:

Brigid, on Feb. 1
Eostre, on Mar. 22
Beltane, on May 1
Litha, on June 22
Lammas or Lughnasad, on Aug. 1
Mabon, on Sept. 22
Samhain, on Nov. 1
Yule, on Dec. 22.

In the 1960s, the movement became more organized and open to the public, which led to a surge in popularity during the 1980s when regional and national festivals were held that attracted hundreds and sometimes thousands of participants.

The leaders of the Neo-pagan movement have designed the sequence of eight Sabbats to provide a new liturgical form comparable to that of the Christian Eucharistic celebration. The literary arm of the Neo-pagan movement has revived the myths of the gods and goddesses most favored by Neo-pagans, and sometimes the re-creation of ancient pagan rituals.

Table 2.3

Graves's Tree Calendar

Western Civil Date	Tree Calendar Month
Jan 21	First day of the Rowan
Feb 18	First day of the Ash
Mar 18	First day of the Alder
Mar 21	Day of the Furze
Apr 15	First day of the Willow
May 13	First day of the Hawthorn
June 10	First day of the Oak
June 22	Day of the Heather
July 8	First day of the Holly
Aug 5	First day of the Hazel
Sept 2	First day of the Vine
Sept 22	Day of the Aspen
Sept 30	First day of the Ivy
Oct 28	First day of the Reed
Nov 25	First day of the Elder
Dec 23	Day of the Yew and Silver Fir
Dec 24	First day of the Birch

For example, a ritual to commemorate the Eleusinian Mysteries is held annually at the fall-equinox Sabbat, and other ancient rituals are revived at the spring festival. The rituals of Inanna and Dumuzi (also known as Ishtar and Tammuz) have been reconstructed from Mesopotamian records and are reenacted annually.

Robert Graves develops the Tree Calendar in the 1950s. The movement adopted a calendar developed by Robert Graves in his *White Goddess*, a work in which he assumes the truth of the Neo-pagan foundational doctrines and proceeds to devise a plausible history for them. The calendar designed by Graves is called the Tree Calendar (Table 2.3), and it is based on the eighteen-letter Gaelic alphabet.

When the Celtic religions were outlawed by the Christian authorities, those who would have been priests in the pagan systems became poets and authors instead and maintained the religious system by developing elaborate codes to communicate with one another. These clandestine communication systems consisted of sets of eighteen trees, or birds, or animals, etc., which corresponded with the eighteen letters of the Gaelic alphabet.

Graves's calendar uses the thirteen consonants of the tree alphabet as names of months and the five vowels as markers of quarter days. This configuration creates a calendar of thirteen 28-day months, plus an extra day (two in leap years) to make up the 365 days of a year. Although there is no plausible evidence that any such calendar was ever in general use in ancient Britain, it has been adopted by the Neo-Pagan movement. Neo-pagan playwrights have composed special dramas based on the symbolism of the tree calendar for use in the celebration of their eight Sabbats.

Table 2.4

The Hebrew Lunisolar Calendar

Name of Month	Days	Holiday	Occurs on day
1. Tishri	30	Rosh ha-Shanah: Civil New Year	1
		Fast of Gedaliah	3
		Yom Kippur: Day of Atonement	10
		Sukkot: Feast of Booths	15-21
		Shimchas Toirah: Rejoicing in the Law	23
2. Marheshvan	29 or 30		
3. Kislev	29 or 30	First day of Hanukkah: Feast of Lights	25
4. Tebet	29	Last day of Hanukkah	2 or 3
		(depending on the length of Kislev)	
5. Shebat	30	New Year for trees	1
6. Adar	29	Fast of Esther	13
	(30 when We-Adar is added)		
		Purim	14-15
We-Adar	29		
	(added in leap year)		
7. Nisan	30	Liturgical New Year	1
		Pesach: Passover	14
		Feast of Unleavened Bread	15-21
8. Iyar	29	Lag ba'Omer: Harvest Offering and Feast of Scholars	18
9. Shivan	30	Shavout: Pentecost, commemorate gift of the Law on Sinai	6
10. Tammuz	29	Fast of Tammuz	17
11. Av	30	Tisha b'Av: Fast in memory of the Temple	9
	(29 if both Marseshvan and Kislev are full)		
12. Elul	29	New Year for the herds	1

Table 2.5

Athenian Lunisolar Calendar

Please note when using this and other calendars in this volume that ancient sources are often incomplete or misleading so dates contained herein are approximate.

Hekatombaion, "sacrifice of a hundred," 30 days.

1	Consecrated to the deities Selene and Apollo. This day always coincides with the appearance of the first visible crescent after the summer solstice.
4	Consecrated to the deities Aphrodite and Hermes, and the hero Herakles.
6	Consecrated to the deity Artemis.
7	Consecrated to Apollo. The *Hekatombaia* festival held, honoring Apollo. *Hyakinthia* begins.
8	Consecrated to the god Poseidon and to the Hero of Athens, Theseus.
9	*Hyakinthia* ends.
11-15	Nemean Games held in years two and four of each four-year cycle.
12	Consecrated to the Titan deity Kronos, the father of Zeus.
15	Consecrated to the moon goddess Selene.
16	"Federation Day." Consecrated to the goddess Aphrodite Pandemos, Peitho, and to the Horae, or season, Eirene, the personification of Peace.
21-28	*Panathenaea*, the "All-Greek Festival of Athena."
30	Consecrated to the fertility goddess Hekate.

Metageitnion, 29 days.

1	Consecrated to Selene and Apollo.
4	Consecrated to Aphrodite, Hermes and Herakles.
6	The deities Artemis and Kronos honored with the sacrifice of a scapegoat.
6-14	Pythian games held at Delphi in year three of each four-year cycle.
7	Consecrated to Apollo; *Metageitnia* held in honor of Apollo. The people of Salamis sacrificed a pig to each of the deities Apollo Patroos, Leto, Artemis, and Athena Agelaa.
7-15	*Karneia*, a festival honoring Apollo Karneus; festivities included feasts, footraces, and musical contests.
8	Consecrated to the god Poseidon and to Theseus (Athenian Hero).
10	Athletic contests held at Olympus in honor of the goddess Hera in year one of each four-year cycle.
11-15	Olympic Games, held in year one of each four-year cycle.
15	Consecrated to the goddess Selene.
29	Consecrated to the goddess Hekate.

Boedromion, "month of helpers," 30 days.

1	Consecrated to the deities Selene and Apollo.
4	Consecrated to the deities Aphrodite and Hermes, and to the hero Herakles.
5	Genesia = Nekusia = Nemesia, the clans' feast of the dead.
6	Consecrated to the goddess Artemis.
6-7	*Boedromia* held, honoring the deities Artemis and Apollo.
7	Consecrated to the god Apollo.
8	Consecrated to the god Poseidon and to the Hero of Athens, Theseus.
13	Commencement of preparations for celebration of the *Eleusinian Mysteries*.

Table 2.5 (continued)

Athenian Lunisolar Calendar

15	Consecrated to the goddess Selene. The advent of the *Mysteries* announced from the Painted Porch.
16	*Synoekia*, the sacrifice of two oxen to the god Zeus (in the form Zeus Phratrios) and the goddess Athena (in the form Athena Phratria), "of the clans."
19-23	The *Great Mysteries of Eleusis*.
30	Consecrated to the goddess Hekate.

Pyanopsion, "month of boiling beans," 29 days.

1	Consecrated to the deities Selene and Apollo.
4	Consecrated to the deities Aphrodite and Hermes, and to the Hero Herakles.
6	Consecrated to Artemis. *Proerosia* held at Eleusis, a pig being sacrificed to Theseus.
7	Consecrated to Apollo. *Pyanopsia* festival held with the expulsion of a scapegoat.
7-9	*Stepterion, Herois,* and *Charilla* festivals held in honor of Apollo, once every eight years, at Delphi. A boy, representing Apollo, was placed in a hut called the palace of Python. The hut was set afire, and the boy removed from it and "sent into exile." Then all the celebrants were purified at Tempe, and returned to Delphi in procession along the Pythian Way.
8	The *Oschophoria*, a celebration honoring the god Poseidon, held with footraces, feasting on beans, and carrying of grapes. Also, the Great Festival of Theseus.
9-13	The *Thesmophoria*, "bringing of treasures," honoring the deities Demeter and Kore celebrated by women.
9	*Sthenia* held, honoring Demeter and Kore.
10	*Anodos*, "ascent," procession to the Thesmophorion, a temple of Demeter.
11	*Nesteia*, "fasting," observed.
12	The women built bowers, squated on the ground, and ate roast pork.
13	*Kalligeneia*, "bearer of beautiful children," in which the rotting remains of the pigs sacrificed at the previous Skira were brought up and mixed with the seed corn to improve the crop.
11-13	*Apaturia* or *Koureotis,* festival observed by adolescent boys.
13	*Apaturia*, day three—children, young men who had just reached the age of maturity, and newly married women were enrolled in the phratries (clans) of Athens, with appropriate sacrifices.
14	*Anarhusis*, marked by the sacrifice of oxen to the god Zeus Phratrios and the goddess Athena.
15	Consecrated to the goddess Selene. The festival of Hera held at Olympia every four years.
16	Birthday of Homer, death of Demosthenes.
28	*Chalkeia* and *Hephaestia*: torch race for the goddess Athena and the god Hephaestus.
29	Consecrated to the goddess Hekate.

Maimakterion, sacred to the god Zeus Maimaktes, "stormy," 30 days.

1	Consecrated to the goddess Selene and the god Apollo.
4	Consecrated to the goddess Aphrodite, the god Hermes, and the hero Herakles.
6	Consecrated to the goddess Artemis.
7	Consecrated to Apollo.
8	Consecrated to the god Poseidon and the Hero of Athens, Theseus.
14	*Maimakteria* held, marked by the sacrifice of sheep to Zeus Maimaktes.
15	Consecrated to Selene.

Table 2.5 (continued)

Athenian Lunisolar Calendar

30	Consecrated to the goddess Hekate.

Posideon, sacred to the god Poseidon, 29 days.

1	Consecrated to the goddess Selene and the god Apollo.
4	Consecrated to the goddess Aphrodite, the god Hermes, and the hero Herakles.
6	Consecrated to the goddess Artemis.
7	Consecrated to Apollo.
8	The festival of *Poseidea* held, honoring the god Poseidon and the Hero of Athens, Theseus.
11-13	The Rural Festival of Dionysus.
12	The *Haloa,* honoring the "Green Demeter" (fertility goddess) and an agricultural Poseidon/Dionysus figure.
15	Consecrated to the goddess Selene.
29	Consecrated to the goddess Hekate.

Posideon Deuteros, "second month sacred to Poseidon," 30 days. This was the intercalary month in the Athenian system.

1	Consecrated to the goddess Selene and the god Apollo.
4	Consecrated to the goddess Aphrodite, the god Hermes, and the hero Herakles.
6	Consecrated to the goddess Artemis.
7	Consecrated to Apollo.
8	Consecrated to the god Poseidon and the Hero of Athens, Theseus.
15	Consecrated to Selene.
30	Consecrated to the goddess Hekate.

Gamelion, sacred to the goddess Hera Gamelia, "of marriage," 30 days.

1	Consecrated to the goddess Selene and the god Apollo.
4	Consecrated to the goddess Aphrodite, the god Hermes, and the hero Herakles.
6	Consecrated to the goddess Artemis.
7	Consecrated to Apollo.
8	Consecrated to the god Poseidon, and the Hero of Athens, Theseus.
10	*Lenaion* held on the island Mykonos, marked by sacrifices to the goddess Demeter and Kore.
12-14	The festival of *Lenaia* held, honoring the god Dionysus.
14	The *Gamelia* held, honoring the goddess Hera.
15	Consecrated to Selene.
30	Consecrated to the goddess Hekate.

Anthesterion, sacred to the god Poseidon, 29 days.

1	Consecrated to the goddess Selene and the god Apollo.
4	Consecrated to the goddess Aphrodite, the god Hermes, and the hero Herakles.
6	Consecrated to the goddess Artemis.
7	Consecrated to Apollo. Celebration of Apollo's birthday, at Delphi, and commemoration of his return to Delphi following a three-month absence in winter.

Table 2.5 (continued)

Athenian Lunisolar Calendar

8	Consecrated to the god Poseidon and to the Hero of Athens, Theseus.
11	The *Anthesteria*, "feast of flowers," a three-day festival of the god Dionysus and the dead which began with the *Pithoigia*, "opening of wine jars."
12	*Anthesteria*, day two, and *Choes*, "cups" or "jugs." Celebration included the blessing of new wine before the god Dionysus, the use of libations (a sacrifice performed by pouring a liquid onto the ground), and drinking contests. A ship-shaped wagon containing a statue of Dionysus was drawn in procession from the seashore to the Boukolion, the temple of Dionysus as Bull God, where the Basilinna (the wife of the Archon Basileus, or King Archon) underwent a ritual marriage to Dionysus. Dionysus' santuary in Limnae was opened.
13	*Anthesteria*, day three, and *Chytroi*, "pots". Pots of cooked fruit sacrificed to chthonian Hermes and the spirits of the dead.
15	Consecrated to the goddess Selene.
20-23	*Lesser Mysteries of Eleusis.*
23	The *Diasia* held, marked by a burnt offering of pigs made to Zeus Meilichios.
29	Consecrated to Hekate.

Elaphebolion, "month of shooting stags," sacred to the goddess Artemis, 30 days.

1	Consecrated to the goddess Selene and the god Apollo.
4	Consecrated to the goddess Aphrodite, the god Hermes, and the hero Herakles.
6	The festival of *Elaphebolia* held, honoring the goddess Artemis.
7	Consecrated to Apollo.
8	Consecrated to the god Poseidon and the Hero of Athens, Theseus.
9-13	The "Greater"—or "City Festival"—of Dionysus, when the dramatic contests were held.
14	The *Pandia* held , honoring Zeus.
15	Consecrated to Selene.
30	Consecrated to the goddess Hekate.

Mounichion, sacred to the goddess Artemis, 29 days.

1	Consecrated to Selene and Apollo.
4	Consecrated to Aphrodite, Hermes, and Herakles. The people of Salamis sacrificed to Herakles, Kourotrophos ("nourisher of youths"), Alkmene, and Maia.
6	Consecrated to Artemis. The *Brauronia* held at Brauron, and the *Tauropolia* at Halai, for Artemis.
7	Consecrated to Apollo.
8	Consecrated to Poseidon and Theseus.
11-15	Isthmian Games in years two and four of each four-year cycle.
15	Consecrated to Selene.
16	The *Munychia* held, honoring Artemis as Moon Goddess.
29	Consecrated to Hekate.

Thargelion, sacred to Apollo, 30 days.

1	Consecrated to Selene, Apollo.
4	Consecrated to Aphrodite, Hermes, and Herakles.

Table 2.5 (continued)

Athenian Lunisolar Calendar

6	Birthday of Artemis.
7	The *Thargelia*, birthday of Apollo, celebrated with the carrying of the eiresione; condemned criminals were dedicated as pharmakoi, "scapegoats," hung with figs, and driven out of Athens.
8	Consecrated to Poseidon and Theseus.
11-13	The *Agrionia*, a festival honoring the god Dionysus, associated with the myth of the daughters of Minyas, or of Proetus, in Boeotia, Rhodes, Sparta, Kos, and Byzantium.
15	Consecrated to Selene.
24	The *Kallynteria* held, sweeping out Athena's temple. Torch race for Bendis, the moon goddess of Thrace.
25	The *Plynteria* held, washing Athena's robe and statue in the sea.
30	Consecrated to Hekate.

Skirophorion, sacred to the goddess Athena, 29 or 30 days.

1	Consecrated to Selene and Apollo.
4	Consecrated to Aphrodite, Hermes, Herakles.
6	Consecrated to Artemis.
7	Consecrated to Apollo.
8	Consecrated to Poseidon and Theseus.
12	The *Skirophoria* or *Skira* held. Pigs sacrificed to Demeter by being thrown down into rocky chasms, where the scavenger birds could not get at them.
13	The *Arrhephoria*, "carrying secret objects," honoring Athena and Aphrodite. Two young girls of noble birth were given unidentified, wrapped objects which they then carried at night, through a secret tunnel, from the Acropolis to the Sanctuary of Aphrodite in the Gardens.
14	The festival of *Diipolia*, or *Buphonia*, held, and an ox sacrificed to Zeus.
15	Consecrated to Selene.
29/30	Consecrated to the goddess Hekate. *Diisoteria* held, honoring Zeus and Athena.

Chapter 3

Lunar and Lunisolar Calendars: Eastern Traditions

The development of calendars is largely based on the religious and philosophical direction of a people, which can often be traced to Eastern or Western traditions. For the purpose of this book, Islam will be considered under the Eastern traditions, although it is clearly not aligned with either Eastern or Western customs.

The Islamic Calendar

The *Qur'an* is the holy book of Islam, revealed through the Prophet Muhammad to his followers. Muslims believe that the Qur'an exists in Heaven with God, and that Muhammad transmitted a copy of it to his disciples. It is to this heavenly authority that the Muslims look for their calendar. In the *Qur'an* (IX, 36-37), Allah revealed to Muhammad that the calendar of Islam should be strictly lunar.

The Islamic lunar calendar is based on a thirty-year cycle. The Islamic calendar consists of twelve lunar months which alternate between twenty-nine and thirty days. The calendar operates on a thirty-year cycle in which an extra day is added to the last month of years 2, 5, 7, 10, 13, 16, 18, 21, 24, 26, and 29.

The eleven days which are added to the cycle compensate exactly for the .03059 days the moon gains in each average month of 29.5 days. Thus, the Islamic calendar stays perfectly in phase with the moon. However, because the Islamic year is 354 or 355 days long, it is about 11 days short of the solar year. As a result, there are about thirty-three Islamic years for every thirty-two solar years. This means that the months of the Islamic calendar pass through all the seasons every thirty-three years.

The emigration of Muhammad is the epoch of the Muslim Era. In 622 C.E., Muhammad fled from Mecca to Medina, an event which is known as the Hejira. The epoch of the Muslim Era is based on his arrival in the city of Medina. The era officially began at sunset on Muharram 1, 622 C.E. (which would have fallen on July 16 according to the Western civil calendar). In accord with the declaration in the *Qur'an*, the second caliph, 'Umar I, formally designated Muharram 1 to be the beginning of the year sometime during his reign (634-644 C.E.).

Throughout the Muslim world, the era of the Hegira (A.H.) or Muslim Era is used privately, and many nations use it as the authorized method for reckoning time. Countries which officially recognize the Muslim Era include Saudi Arabia, Yemen, and the principalities of the Persian Gulf. In Egypt, Syria, Jordan, and Morocco, both Muslim and Common Eras are sanctioned.

Still other Muslim countries use a combination of the two systems. Around 1088 A.H. (1677 C.E), Turkey, for example, designated March 1 as the New Year, adopted the solar year and Julian months, but kept the Muslim Era. In the nineteenth century, the Turkish Empire accepted the Gregorian calendar, and in the twentieth century, the Common Era.

Another country that adopted a combined system is Iran. During the reign of Reza Shah Pahlavi (1925-1942 C.E.), the solar year was incorporated into a calendar with Persian month names and the Muslim Era. March 21 is the beginning of the Iranian year. Thus, the Iranian year 1349 began on March 21, 1970.

Months, weeks, and days in the Islamic calendar. Like the Hebrew month, the Islamic month begins when two witnesses report seeing the crescent of the new moon. Their claim is verified by a qudi (judge) and a mufti (interpreter of Muslim law). The mufti declares the beginning of a new month. Also like the early Hebrews, Muslims faced the problems of cloudy nights and poor communications which posed a hinderance to the timely and efficient declaration of a new month. Each town or community would assume responsibility for declaring the beginning of the month. This caused confusion because the months would start on different days from one location to the next. Eventually, albeit reluctantly, the majority of Muslims agreed to accept the ruling of Cairo as the official beginning of the month.

All Muslim calendars are composed of seven-day weeks and twenty-four hour days. The names for the days vary from place to place except for the weekly holy day, Al Jumah, "the day of gathering." In terms of the Western civil calendar, Al Jumah falls on Friday and marks the beginning of the Islamic week. Days in the Muslim system run from sunset to sunset to commemorate Muhammad's entrance to Medina which took place at sunset.

Muslims observe a holy fast during the month of Ramadan. During the ninth month of the Islamic calendar, Ramadan, all faithful Muslims observe a dawn to dark fast. During this time (sunrise until the stars can be seen), they are not allowed to eat or drink anything except water. The month of Ramadan is declared in the usual manner unless the new moon is not visible. If this case occurs, the month of Sha'ban is assumed to have thirty days and Ramadan begins following the thirtieth day. The end of the month follows the same procedure. The fast of Ramadan is broken with a feast called Eed es Sagheer. The feast lasts for three days, Shawwal 1-3.

There is one more major feast in the Muslim calendar. It commemorates Abraham's attempt to sacrifice Isaac, his son. The feast is called Eed ed Keeber or Kurban and is observed during the Dhu al Hijjah—the last month of the Islamic year.

Minor fast and feast days in the Muslim calendar. The Muslim calendar also includes one minor fast and several minor feasts. The fast is called Yom and is observed for ten days during the month of Muharram. The minor feasts include: Muhammad's birthday on the twelfth day of the third month (Rabi I); el Hoseyn's birthday in the fourth month (Rabi II); and Muhammad's ascension to heaven in the seventh month (Rejab). Table 3.5 (see end of chapter) outlines the current Islamic calendar.

Bahá'í develops from Islam. Islam has not spawned many successful new religions because of its stern punishment for heresy. One of the most notable exceptions to this pattern is Bahá'-ísm, which began from the Shi'ite branch of Islam. Based on a new revelation, Bahá'í has evolved into a completely independent world religion, as the leaders of Islam officially recognized in 1925.

Bahá'ísm began in the late eighteenth century when Shaykh Ahmad started a journey in search of the Mahdi, or "Promised One." The *Qur'an* mentions this person whom the Shi'ite Muslims believe will be the legitimate successor of Muhammad as the leader of Islam. Ahmad did not find the Mahdi, but passed his quest on to his successor, Siyyid Kázim, who in turn passed the quest on to his students, along with a revelation that would enable them to recognize the Mahdi. Kázim's student Mullá Husain traveled to Shiráz, where he was the first to meet a young man, Siyyid 'Alí-Muhammad, who spontaneously proved to Husain that he fulfilled all the requirements of the revelation. After sunset on May 22, 1844, Siyyid 'Alí-Muhammad declared himself to be the Báb, the "Gate" of God. Followers of Bahá'í date their era from this event. Another 17 of Kázim's students arrived in Shiráz and spontaneously recognized the Báb, whereupon he authorized them to begin preaching his message publicly. He seems not to have claimed to be the Mahdi himself, but to be a messenger preceding the Mahdi, much as John the Baptist is portrayed in the Gospels as the forerunner of Jesus.

The Báb's disciples, or Bábis as they were called at first, were soon denounced as heretics by the Muslim authorities and severely persecuted. The Báb himself was imprisoned and executed on July 9, 1850. After his death, his student Mirzá Husain 'Alí, who assumed the name Bahá'u'lláh, took over leadership of the movement, and during the period of April 21 to May 2, 1863, revealed himself to be the Mahdi. Despite his repeated imprisonments, and the persecution of his followers, Bahá'ísm grew steadily under his leadership. After Bahá'u'lláh's death on May 29, 1892, leadership passed to his appointed successor, his oldest son, 'Abdul-Bahá, who had been born on May 23, 1844, the very night of the Báb's declaration to Mullá Husain. Under his leadership, Baha'ísm grew into a true world religion. He died on November 28, 1921, passing on leadership to his eldest grandson, Shoghi Effendi.

Bahá'í constructs its own calendar. The Báb instituted a great many reforms of Islamic culture in his revelations, laying the groundwork for Bahá'ísm's nature as a religion in its own right. One of these reforms that contributes greatly to the Bahá'í sense of identity is the Bahá'í calendar, which contains nineteen months of nineteen days each. A unique feature of this calendar is that the same nineteen names used to indicate the months are also used to delineate each day within the month. These names each represent a characteristic of God and the combination of month and day forms a phrase such as "the Splendor of Glory" or "the Mercy of Light." Table 3.6 (see end of chapter) details the months and days of the Bahá'í calendar. To these 361 days are added four intercalary days—five in leap years—to keep the calendar in phase with the solar year and the common calendar. On the first day of each month, followers of Bahá'í gather for the "Nineteen-Day Feast," which combines functions of community government, worship, and social life, usually including a large and joyous meal. Only registered Bahá'ís may attend these gatherings.

The Calendars of India

Throughout its history, India has used a plethora of calendars and dating systems of which there have been two basic types: a civil calendar which changed with each new regime (the current civil holidays are listed in Table 3.1), and a religious calendar maintained by the Hindus. Although each geographical region had its own Hindu calendar, most of the

calendars shared some elements that they gleaned from a common heritage. When India became a unified and independent nation in the mid-twentieth century, the differences among regional calendars included over thirty methods for determining the beginning of the era, the year, and the month. These variations in the Hindu calendar were the culmination of nearly 5,000 years of history.

Foreign calendars influence but never replace India's original calendar—the Kali Yuga. Around 2000 B.C.E., India's first time reckoning system, the Kali Yuga, emerged. It was based on astronomical observations similar to those used by Western calendar makers today.

Although in 1200 C.E, the Muslims brought the use of their calendar for administrative purposes, and the British introduced the Gregorian calendar in 1757, the Kali Yuga continued to be the basis for local calendars. Each separate state maintained a calendar which its citizens used in their daily interactions. Throughout India's colonial days, the entrenchment of these local calendars created havoc for the central government because any given date would have up to six different interpretations throughout the country. The difficulties continued as an indigenous government took control in 1947.

The regional Hindu calendars had common elements based on the Kali Yuga. Despite regional differences, all of the Hindu calendars did share

Table 3.1

Holidays on the Indian Civil Calendar

Western date	Holiday
Mar. 22	New Year's Day
Apr. 13	Vaisakhi (Old New Year's Day)
Aug. 15	Independence Day
Oct. 2	Mahatma Gandhi's birthday
Jan. 14	Pongal or Makar-Sankranti: three-day festival of sidereal entrance of the Sun into Capricorn
Jan. 26	Republic Day

some common components–elements which are associated with the Kali Yuga. They were based on a sidereal year (not the tropical year used in the West). The year began with the month of Chaitra–around April 13 in the Western civil calendar—and had six seasons: spring (vasanta), summer (grisma), the rains (varsa), autumn (sarad), winter (hemanta), and the dews (sisira).

Each season contained two months, the length of which were determined by the astrological constellations of the zodiac. These months, unlike months of the Western calendar which are based on the tropical year, perfectly corresponded to the signs of the zodiac. Month names among the Hindu calendars varied according to the dialects of the regions, but the names of the astrological signs were the same throughout the country. The months were based on the celestial movement of the sun and stars along the ecliptic. Each month and sign had an arc of 30 along the ecliptic, but because of irregularities in the earth's rotation, they varied in actual length between 27 and 32 days. Because the months were based on the stars and corresponded directly with the solar cycle, they were not defined by the phases of the moon. Instead, the month began when the moon entered a new celestial sign.

The seven-day week was another common feature of the regional calendars and had a structure similar to the Western week. Each twenty-four hour day was named for a planet. Interestingly, the planets occur in the same order in both the Hindu and Western calendars.

The Hindu calendar has a system of intercalation that takes place about every three years. Like many other religious calendars, the Kali Yuga had a lunar component from which the Hindus derived their lunar calendar. The Hindu calendar consists of twelve 30-day months with one month intercalated about every three years (see Table 3.7 at end of chapter). Whenever two new moons occur within one solar month (months based on the zodiacal signs), the intercalary lunar month is added. The normal month in which the two new moons occurred has "nija" added to the end of its name. The intercalated month is named for the normal month but "adhika" is added to the end. The normal months of the Hindu

lunar calendar are named for the solar month in which they begin.

Hindu sects define the month differently and cause confusion. The definition of the lunar month has caused a division in the Hindu religion. The boundaries of the contending groups seem to fall along geographical lines. In northern India, the lunar month begins with the full or waning moon, while Hindus in the south of India measure the month from the new or waxing moon.

The confusion caused by the use of two methods of measuring the month has resulted in the celebration of holidays on different dates by the Vishnu and Shiva sects of Hinduism. This happens because the waxing half of the month (from the new to the full moon) falls in the same month in both regions, but the waning half falls in different months. Therefore any festivals that take place in the waning half of the month can fall up to thirty days apart in the north and south.

To make the two systems as compatible as possible, Hindus number the two halves of the months separately. The months are divided into two periods of approximately fifteen days called pakshas, or "fortnights," in which the days are numbered from one to fifteen (see Table 3.2).

Hindu holidays are a rich mixture of theology and mythology. Hindu festivals are inextricably interwoven with Hindu mythology, which is as old as and similar to the Greek system. In theology, the most important Hindu gods form a trinity: Brahma, the Creator; Vishnu, the Preserver; and Shiva, the Destroyer. In practice, Brahma seems to have a less prominent continuing role as Hindu worship is shaped by the belief that Vishnu has been repeatedly incarnated as avatars or "savior figures," and that Shiva has appeared in many forms as well. The two primary incarnations of Vishnu were as Rama and as Krishna, although some Hindus also believe that the Buddha, Jesus of Nazareth, and Muhammad were incarnations of Vishnu, and in this way create a unification of all religions. Vishnu is almost always worshipped in the form of an incarnation.

The Hindu offshoots—Jains and Sikhs—have unique holidays. Two major offshoots of orthodox Hinduism are the Jains and the Sikhs. The Jains are an ascetic religious community that originated at the

Table 3.2

Days of Hindu "Fortnights"

Day	Name	Comparable Greek or Latin term	Deity to whom day is consecrated
1	Pratipada	proto	Brahma
2	Dvitiya	duo	Vidhatr
3	Tritiya	tri	Vishnu
4	Chaturthi	quatro	Ganesha or Yama
5	Panchami	penta	Moon
6	Shashti	sextus	Kartikeya
7	Saptimi	Septem(ber)	Indra
8	Ashtami	Octo(ber)	Shakti or the Vasus
9	Navami	Novem(ber)	Shakti or the Serpent
1	Dashami	Decem(ber)	Dharma
11	Ekadashi		Vishnu or Rudra
12	Dvadashi	duodecimal	Sun
13	Trayodashi	tridecimal	Shiva
14	Chaturdashi		
15	Purnima (if moon is full)		Devas
	Amavasya (if moon is new)		Devas

time of the Buddha. The Sikhs are an independent faith that resembles both Islam and Hinduism in some ways, but is not directly associated with either. The Sikhs, distinguished from other groups by their turbans, are largely concentrated in the Punjab area of northwestern India, which many members of the faith hope to turn into an independent nation. The most important holidays of the Jains and the Sikhs are shown on the Hindu calendar.

Indian festivals extend beyond the bounds of religion. In India, the celebration of spiritualism and religion overflows all social boundaries. Although India's fasts, festivals, feasts, and pilgrimages are deeply rooted in religious belief, they serve an important social function which brings together people from all over the nation regardless of religious background.

The Buddhist Calendar

Hinduism gave rise to Buddhist beliefs. Buddhism is derived from Hinduism in much the same way that Christianity is derived from Judaism. As a reform of Hinduism in India, Buddhism did not meet with great success. In fact, at one point, it became virtually extinct as a separate movement, only to be reintroduced into the country in the 1950s when the Dali Lama fled to India for sanctuary after the Chinese annexation of Tibet. However, Buddhism bears the marks of its Hindu ancestry in its time reckoning system. Similarities between the two calendars include the lunar and astrological base and intercalations.

Because the Buddhist calendar is not associated with a specific civil calendar, the variances among geographical locations are even more pronounced than differences in Hindu calendars. For example, the method for determining the date of the new year is not uniform among Buddhist sects. Some Buddhist calendars begin the new year, Wesak, with the full moon in Taurus, which is believed to be the date of the Buddha's birth, enlightenment, and passing on. In contrast, the Tibetan Buddhists, whose calendar has been heavily influenced by the Chinese calendar, begin their new year at the full moon nearest to the midpoint of the sign Aquarius.

Differences in Buddhist beliefs lead to division within the religion. The two major traditions within Buddhism, Myhayana and Theravada, developed as a result of a doctrinal dispute among followers of the Buddha (Siddhartha Gautama) after his death around 483 B.C.E. As Buddhism spread outside of India, the two traditions became prominent in separate regions. To the east of India the Theravada tradition predominated; to the west the Mahayana tradition was established by the fourth century B.C.E. Also around the same time, Alexander the Great, who ruled some parts of India where Buddhism was practiced, exported Buddhist teachings to the west. From the northwestern part of India, Buddhism spread into Tibet where it became amalgamated with the native magical and Tatric traditions. It also spread to China and Japan, becoming integrated with the existing systems of Confucianism, Taoism, and Shintoism.

Each of these regions developed different holidays and calendars. Holidays honoring diverse manifestations of the Buddha such as the Medicine Buddha, or the Buddha of Boundless Light, became a part of some calendars. Also, many religious festivals of the new host lands became incorporated into the Buddhist calendar. One such festival is the Chinese Ch'ing ming, or Festival of Pure Brightness. This ancient Chinese festival, held in honor of the dead, has become an established Buddhist holiday in China.

Buddhism also has a following in the West. Buddhism in the West has generally been of the Mahayana tradition, which emphasizes the universal presence of the "Buddha-nature" rather than the historical person of the Master himself. According to Robert S. Elwood in his *Religious and Spiritual Groups in Modern America*, the Buddha-nature is an "ontologizing of the Buddha's enlightenment experience. It is the true nature of reality, which he lets irradiate his being at that moment." Followers of this faith believe that the Buddha-nature can be realized whenever one lets go of the fear of separateness and allows him or herself to become one with all. To aid the believer in this release, followers are encouraged to envision the universe as filled with Buddhas and Bodhisattvas who are projections of the enlightened self. These figures are a psychological creation rather than individuals of historical actuality. The essential character of this group is reflected in the abstract quality of its holidays (see Table 3.8 at end of chapter). When these are contrasted with traditional Theravada holidays, which centers on the person of Buddha, the difference between the two groups is apparent.

Zen Buddhism, the Japanese form of the belief system, is another form of the faith familiar in the United States, and its holy days are observed among American Buddhist groups. Unlike the highly esoteric and ethereal Mahayana system, Zen advocates strict asceticism as a means to freedom from the individual self. The theory is that extreme self-denial builds a tension that can be used to break through to a revelation of Oneness.

Pure Land Buddhism, practiced in the United States, is the form that comes closest to the Western experience of religion. The basis for the Pure Land doctrine is that salvation comes from a transference of merit from the Buddha to an unworthy follower. Emphasis

is placed on the importance of family and community involvement. The Buddha of Boundless Light, or Amitabha, is honored by this sect and is celebrated on the fifteenth day of each month.

The Chinese Calendar

The Chinese calendar, which has been used widely throughout the Asian world over the course of history, is based on the longest unbroken chain of time measurement in mankind's history with its epoch believed to be 2953 B.C.E. Influences from the Hindu and Muslim have been introduced at various times, but none succeeded in changing the Chinese calendar. The traditional calendar has only diminished in its official use since the 1912 adoption of the Gregorian calendar for public use.

Part of the reason that the Chinese calendar has survived intact for nearly five millennium is that, until the middle of the twentieth century, the document was considered sacred. Any changes to the calendar were tightly controlled by imperial authorities, and the penalty for illegally tampering with the time keeping system was death. Therefore, although minor adjustments in the astronomical calculations have been made to the calendar, its essential structure today is the same as it was nearly five thousand years ago. Until the rise of Communism in China during the twentieth century, the official calendar was presented to the emperor, governors, and other dignitaries in an elaborate ceremony each year on the first day of the tenth month.

Three celestial "roads" provide the structure for the Chinese calendar. As most ancient time reckoning systems, the Chinese calendar is lunisolar. It is organized according to three paths or roads which map the movements of celestial bodies. The Red Road helps define the solar month and year by tracing the constellations in a line roughly corresponding with the equator. Each of the 28 constellations along the Red Road fall into one of 28 lunar mansions which vary in size from 1 to 34 degrees of the 360 degree circle in the sky around the earth. The earth's movement around the sun (or, according to a geocentric view of the universe, the sun's movement against the stars) is charted on the Yellow Road which also gives definition to the length of the solar year.

The White Road follows the phases of the moon and is the basis for the lunar aspects of the Chinese calendar.

The Chinese zodiac is based on the Big Dipper. The Chinese zodiac is not comparable to other systems. The "twelve branches" are derived from the twelve positions in the sky to which the seven stars of the Big Dipper point during the year. The Chinese use the zodiac in two different cycles to name their years. The first system matches the ten celestial signs with each animal of the zodiac (see Table 3.3). For example, the first zodiac sign is combined with the first celestial sign to form the year Kai-tsu. The second year is I-chaw, a combination of the second sign in each series. When all ten celestial signs have been paired, the eleventh zodiacal sign is matched with the first celestial sign. Thus the cycle continues through sixty years.

The Chinese use this system not only for counting years, but also for counting days. When it is used to enumerate days, it is known as the kah-chih system. The pattern of repeating the ten celestial signs probably led to the development of the hsun—the Chinese ten-day equivalent of the week.

The second cycle for naming the years is used less frequently and never in conjunction with the other.

Like the first system, it is a sixty year cycle, but instead of using celestial signs as counterparts to the zodiac, it uses the elements of the earth: wood, fire, earth, metal, and water (see Table 3.4).

The Chinese year is divided into twenty-four parts. The Chinese New Year takes place on the new moon nearest to the point which is defined in the West as the fifteenth degree of Aquarius—roughly February 4 or 5 according to the Western civil calendar.

Each of twelve months in the Chinese year is twenty-nine or thirty days long and is divided into two parts defined as the period of time covering 15 degrees of the sky—about two weeks. The Chinese calendar, like all lunisolar systems, requires periodic adjustment to keep the lunar and solar cycles integrated. Intercalation in the Chinese calendar takes place each time a month contains the beginning and end of only one of the 15 degree divisions. Beginning with the New Year the names for the divisions are: Spring Begins, the Rain Water, the Excited Insects, the

Table 3.3

The Chinese Zodiac and Celestial Signs

Celestial Signs	Zodiac Symbol	English Animal
Kiah	Tse	Rat
Yih	Chau	Ox
Ping	Yin	Tiger
Ting	May	Hare
Wu	Shin	Dragon
Ki	Se	Snake
Kang	Wu	Horse
Sin	Wi	Sheep
Jin	Shin	Monkey
Kwei	Yu	Rooster
	Siuh	Dog
	Hai	Pig

Table 3.4

Partial Cycle of the Chinese Zodiac and Elements of the Earth

Zodiac Symbol	English Animal	Element
Tzu	Rat	Wood
Chou	Ox	Wood
Yin	Tiger	Fire
Mao	Hare	Fire
Shin	Dragon	Earth
Ssu	Snake	Earth
Wu	Horse	Metal
We	Sheep	Metal
Shin	Monkey	Water
Yu	Rooster	Water
Hsu	Dog	Wood
Hai	Pig	Wood
Tzu	Rat	Fire
Chou	Ox	Fire
Yin	Tiger	Earth
Mao	Hare	Earth

Vernal Equinox, the Clear and Bright, the Grain Rains, the Summer Begins, the Grain Fills, the Grain in Ear, the Summer Solstice, the Slight Heat, the Great Heat, the Autumn Begins, the Limit of Heat, the White Dew, the Autumnal Equinox, the Cold Dew, the Hoar Frost Descends, the Winter Begins, the Little Snow, the Heavy Snow, the Winter Solstice, the Little Cold, and the Great Cold.

Table 3.5

The Islamic Lunar Calendar

Name of month	Duration in days	Festivals	Festival Days
Muharram	30	New Year Festival	Days 1-10
		'Ashura: Commemoration of God's Covenant with Noah	Day 10
Safar	29		
Rabi'al-Awal	30	Mawlid al-Nabi: birth of the Prophet	Day 12
Rabi'al-Akhir	29		
Jumada al-Aula	30		
Jumada al-Ukhra	29		
Rajab	30	Lailat al Miraj: Ascent of the Prophet into Heaven	Day 27
Sha'ban	29	Vision of the Prophet's Journey from Mecca to Jerusalem	Day 15
Ramadan	30	Month of fasting	
		First Revelation of the Prophet	Days 3-4
		Revelation of the *Qur'an*	Day 27
Shawwal	29	'Id-il-Fitr, Feast of Fastbreaking	Day 27
		Hajj (pilgrimage to Mecca) begins	
Dhu al-Qa'da	30		
Dhu al-Hijjah	29	Al-'id al-Kabir: Great Festival ending the Hajj season	
		Tabaski, or 'Id al-Adha: Feast commemorating Abraham's sending Ishmael into the Desert	Days 10-12

Table 3.6

The Bahá'í Calendar

Western calendar date	Name of month's first day	Event
March 21	Bahá, "Splendor"	Feast of Naw-Ruz (New Year)
April 9	Jalál, "Glory"	
April 22		Day 1 of Feast of Ridván or the Declaration of Bahá'u'lláh
April 28	Jamál, "Beauty"	
May 2		Last day of Feast of Ridván
May 17	'Azamat, "Grandeur"	
May 23		1. Declaration of the Báb
		2. Birthday of 'Abdul-Bahá
May 29		3. Ascension of Bahá'u'lláh
June 5	Nur, "Light"	
June 24	Rahmat, "Mercy"	
July 9		Martyrdom of the Báb
July 13	Kalimát, "Words"	
August 1	Kasmál, "Perfection"	
August 20	Asmá, "Names"	
September 8	Izzat, "Might"	
September 27	Mashíyyat, "Will"	
October 16	Ilm, "Knowledge"	
October 20		Birthday of Báb
November 4	Qudrat, "Power"	
November 12		Birthday of Bahá'u'lláh
November 23	Qawl, "Speech"	
November 26		1. Day of the Covenant
November 28		2. Ascension of 'Abdul-Bahá
December 12	Masá'il, "Questions"	
December 31	Sharaf, "Honor"	
January 19	Sultán, "Sovereignty"	
February 7	Mulk, "Dominion"	
February 26 to March 1	Ayyám-i-Há, intercalary days	
March 2	Alá, "Loftiness"	

Table 3.7

Festivals of the Hindu Lunar Calendar

("Shukla" is the bright or waxing fortnight, "Krishna" is the dark or waning fortnight.)

Chaitra Shukla

1   *Gudi Padva* (New Year's Day).

3   *Gangaur*, (Gauri is a form of Durga): Festival of Shiva and Parvati.

8   *Shitala Ashtami*, "Shitala's Eighth". Shitala is the goddess of smallpox, and resembles Devi or Durga.

9   *Rama Navami*, "Rama's Ninth": Birthday of Lord Rama.

13   *Mahavir Jayanti*: Birthday of Lord Mahavira, the founder of Jainism.

15   *Hanuman Jayanti*: Birthday of Hanuman, the monkey god and servant of Rama.

15   *Chaitra Purnima*: Festival of Chitra Gupta, the divine recordkeeper, in south India.

Vaisakha Shukla

3   *Akshya Tritiya*, "undecaying Third": Festival of Vishnu and Lakshmi.
         Also, *Parshurama Jayanti*: Birthday of Parshurama, the axe-bearing incarnation of Rama.
         Also, *Chandan Yatra*: Beginning a three-week festival of Lord Jagannath.

5   *Shankaracharya Jayanti*: Birthday of Adi Shankaracharya.

9   *Janaki Navami*, "Janaki's Ninth": Festival of Janaki, a goddess similar to Sita or Lakshmi.

14   *Narsimha Jayanti*: Birthday of Narsimha, the incarnation of Vishnu as "Man-Lion."

15   *Buddha Purnima*, "Full Moon of the Buddha": Festival honoring the birth, enlightenment, and death of the Buddha.

Jyaishtha Shukla

8   *Jyaistha Ashtami*: Festival of the goddess Khir Bhawani.

10   *Ganga Dussehra*, "Ganges washes away 10 sins": A festival of bathing in the Ganges.

11   *Nirjala Ekadashi*: A festival of Vishnu.

15   *Vata Savitri*: A festival celebrated only by married women.

15   *Snan Yatra* (in Orissa): Festival of Lord Jagannatha.

Ashadha Shukla

2   *Ratha Yatra*: Festival of Sri Jagannatha, Lord of the Universe, a Krishna-type deity.

3   *Teej*: Festival of Parvati, celebrated only by girls and women.

11   *Hari-Shayani Ekadashi*: Festival celebrating the beginning of Hari's annual "sleep".

15   *Guru Vyasa Purnima*.

Shravana Shukla

3   *Hariyali Teej* or *Hari*. Also, *Tritiya*: A women's festival for Hari.
         Also, *Nag Panchami*, "Nag's Fifth": A festival of snake worship.

7   *Tulsidas Jayanti*: Birthday of Tulsidas.

11   *Putrada Ekadashi*: Festival of Vishnu.

15   *Narieli Purnima*: End of the monsoon; offering to Varuna.
         Also, *Jhulan Latra* (in Orissa): "Swinging" festival of Lord Jagannatha.
         Also, *Raksha Bandhan*: Family festival of "protecting brothers."

Table 3.7 (continued)

Festivals of the Hindu Lunar Calendar

Also, *Avani Avittam*.
Also, *Shravani Mela*.
Also, *Onam* (in Kerala): Festival of Vishnu.

Shravana Krishna

11   *Kamada Ekadashi*, "wish-fulfilling Eleventh": Festival of Vishnu.

Bhadra Shukla

3   *Haritalika Teej*: A women's festival for Parvati and Shiva.
4   *Ganesh Chaturthi*, "Ganesha's Fourth": A festival of Ganesha.
5   *Rishi Panchami*: A women's festival.
5-13   *Partyshana Parva* is celebrated by Digambar Jains.
14   *Anant Chaturdashi*: Honors Vishnu slumbering on Anant.

Bhadra Krishna

6   *Hala Shashti or Balaram Shashti*, "plowing Sixth."
8   *Janamashtami*: Birthday of Lord Krishna.
    Also, *Radha Ashtami*, "Radha's Eighth": Birthday of Radha, an incarnation of Lakshmi.
13   *Partyshana Parva* is celebrated through the 5th day of Ashvina Shukla by Svetambar Jains.

Ashvina Shukla

1-9   *Durga Puja* or *Navrata*: The major festival of Durga.
1-10   *Vijay Dussehra*: Festival of Rama and Sita.
15   *Sharad Purnima*, "Sharad's Full Moon": Festival of Sharad, the Moon God.
    Also, *Kojagara*: Festival of Lakshmi.
    Also, *Valmiki Jayanti*: Birthday of Valmiki.

Ashvina Krishna

1-15   *Pitra Paksha:* Offerings to dead ancestors.

Kartika Shukla

1   *Govardhan Puja and Annakut*: Festival of Krishna.
2   *Bhaiya Duj* or *Yama Dvitiya*, "Yama's Second."
    Kartika Snan.
6   *Surya Shashti.*
    Also, *Skanda Shashti*: festival of Subramanya.
11   *Devathani Ekadashi*: Festival of Vishnu awakening from his annual "sleep".
    Also, *Tulsi Vivahotsava*: wedding of Tulsi and Vishnu.
    Kartika Purnima: Festival of Matsya Avtar, an incarnation of Vishnu, and of Shiva as Tripurari.
    Also, *Guru Parab*: Birthday of Guru Nanak, founder of Sikhism.

Table 3.7 (continued)

Festivals of the Hindu Lunar Calendar

Kartika Krishna

4   *Karwa Chauth*: Festival of Shiva and Parvati, celebrated only by married women.
13   *Dhan Teras* or *Dhanvantri Trayodashi*: Festival of Dhanvantri, the physician god.
14   *Narak Chaturdashi*: Festival of Yama.
15   *Deepawali* or *Diwali*: Festival of lights; festival of Lakshmi, Rama, and Krishna; festival of Kali (in Bengal).
         Also, *Kartika Amavasya*: Death of Mahavira, commemorated by Jains.

Margashirsha Shukla

11   *Vaikuntha Ekadashi*: Festival of Vishnu.
         Also, *Gita Jayanti*: Anniversary of the *Bhagavad Gita*.
15   *Dattatreya Jayanti*: Birthday of Dattatreya.

Margashirsha Krishna

8   *Bhairava Ashtami*: Festival of Shiva as Bhairava.
11   *Vaikuntha Ekadashi*: Festival of Vishnu.
         Also, *Vaitarani Vrata*.

Pausha Krishna

8   *Rukmani Ashtami*: Women's festival of Rukmani, the wife of Krishna.
12   *Swarupa Dwadashi*: Women's festival of Vishnu.

Magha Shukla

5   *Vasant Panchami*: Festival of Saraswati and Kamadeva.
8   *Bhishma Ashtami*.
15   *Magha Purnima*: Festival of Parvati and Shiva.
         Also, *Ravidas Jayanti*: Birthday of Ravidas.

Magha Krishna

4   *Sakata Chauth*: Birthday of Lord Ganesha.
15   *Mauni Amavasya*: Festival of Krishna.

Phalguna Shukla

11   *Amalaha Ekadashi*: Festival of Hari.
15   *Dol Purnima* (in Bengal): Birthday of Chaitanya Mahaprabhu.
15-16   *Holi*: Festival of Vishnu.

Phalguna Krishna

14   *Shivaratri*, "night of Shiva."

Table 3.8

Buddhist Holidays

The calendar outlined below is a composite of various Buddhist calendars. Aside from the holidays listed in the months, the eighth day of each lunar month is usually devoted to the Medicine Buddha, the fifteenth to Amitabha Buddha, and thirtieth to Shakyamuni Buddha. Many Buddhists also commemorate the consecration in 1940 of the fourteenth Tibetan Dali Lama on February 22 according to the Western civil calendar.

First month

1	Carnival begins, lasts until middle of second month.
1-8	*Yüan tan*: Chinese New Year.
9-15	Liturgy of Bhairava.
15	*Magha Puja*: Conception of the Buddha; feast of flowers in honor of his mother (Theravada). Also, *Teng Chieh:* Chinese feast of lanterns.

Second month

1	*Ch'ing ming*: Chinese Festival of Pure Brightness, a festival honoring ancestors and spirits of the departed.
9-15	Liturgy of the Medical Buddhas.
15	*Parinirvana*: Commemoration of the Buddha's passing into nirvana (Mahayana).
29	Chasing and expulsion of the Demon of Bad Luck.

Third month

15	The Kalachakra Revelation and sacred masquerades.
16-22	Celebration of Tu-K'or.

Fourth month

8	Birthday of the Buddha (Mahayana).
8	Celebration of the Great Renunciation, the Enlightenment of the Buddha (Theravada).
9-15	Worship of the Great Pitier.
15	Commemoration of the Buddha's birth, enlightenment, and death; Feast of the Dead (Theravada).

Fifth month

4-10	Liturgy of Sambhara.
5	*Tuan yang chieh*: Chinese Dragon Boat Festival.
10	Birthday of Padma-sambhava.
15	*Asalha Puja*, or *Dhamma Day*: Commemoration of the Buddha's first preaching (Theravada).

Sixth month

4	Celebration of Buddha's birth and preaching; the Picture Feast.
9-15	Liturgy of the White Tara.

Seventh month

7	*Chi hsi*: Chinese Festival of the Milky Way.

Table 3.8 (continued)

Buddhist Holidays

9-15	Liturgy of Mi-'krugs-pa.
14/15	*Chung yüan*: Chinese Festival of the Dead.
15	*Ullambana Day*: "Feast of the Hungry Ghosts"; last day of summer retreat for monks and nuns (Mahayana).

Eighth month

1	Beginning of Buddhist "Lent." During this period, Buddhist monks must remain inside the temple. This tradition came from India where this time of year marks the beginning of the monsoon season, thus the entire Indian population including Buddhist monks remain indoors.
9-15	Liturgy of the Nine Gods of Immortality.
15	Full-moon harvest festival; festival of dead ancestors (both Chinese and Buddhist).

Ninth month

1-15	The Kah-gyur scriptures are read.
9	*Ch'ung Yang*: Chinese Festival of High Places.
17-23	The service of the Dead Saints, the Svathira.
22	Shakyamuni's Descent from Heaven.

Tenth month

9-15	Worship of Guyakala.
25	Service of "the Five" at Guh-ldan monastery; ascension of Tsou K'apa; the feast of lanterns.

Eleventh month

1	New Year, old style.
23-29	Celebration of the Tor-gyak of the Lords of the Netherworld.
30	End of Buddhist "Lent" (monks may begin public begging again).

Twelfth month

8	"Bodhi Day," commemoration of the Buddha's enlightenment (Mahayana).
23	*Tsao chün*: Chinese Festival of the Kitchen God.
29	Beginning of carnival and masquerade; pantomime expulsion of old year (both Chinese and Buddhist).

Chapter 4

Solar Calendars

The previous sections discussed lunar and lunisolar calendars. Addressed here is the third system of reckoning time, the pure solar calendar, which disregards the phases of the moon and stays in step with the seasons. Most Western nations use this system as did the citizens of ancient Egypt and Rome.

The Egyptian Calendar

The Egyptians develop multiple calendar systems. The earliest Egyptian calendar was lunar and regulated by the cyclical (helical) rising of the star Sirius or Sothis, which coincided with the annual flooding of the Nile. This calendar was only twelve minutes shorter than the true solar year—a much more accurate system than most of its contemporaries.

In time, the inherent discrepancies between the lunar and solar cycles caused problems for the Egyptians. Although details of the difficulties are not known and while the lunar calendar was preserved for agricultural use, a second calendar was developed for civic purposes. In this civil calendar, the year was composed of twelve 30-day months and five days added to the end of the year for a total of 365 days. Its days, unlike those of other ancient calendars, began at sunrise. There was no intercalation to compensate for the one-quarter day difference between this year and the true solar year of 365.25 days; consequently, the Egyptian civil year gained one day on the true solar year every four years. Therefore, over the course of 1,460 solar years, or 1,461 Egyptian years, the months of the Egyptian calendar would move com-

pletely through the seasons. This 1,461 year period is known as the Sothic Cycle.

Egyptian legend explains the design of the calendar. Egyptian religious myths sought to explain the origin of the civil calendar. The legends of the Osiris-Isis cycle indicate that the Egyptian calendar originally incorporated a year of 360 days. To this calendar of twelve 30-day months, the god Thoth added five days—the birthdays of the gods Osiris, Isis, Horus, Nephthys, and Set. When this civil calendar was introduced, its first day—the first of the month Thoth—coincided with the helical rising of Sirius.

Egyptian months were arranged into three seasons. The importance of the Nile River to the survival of civilization near its delta was reflected in the Egyptian calendar. The months of the year were divided into three seasons of four months each, and these seasons were based on the flood stages of the Nile. The season of Inundation occurred when the river flooded its banks; Going Forth was the time of planting crops after the river had receded; and Deficiency was when the river was at its lowest point, but ironically, it was harvest time for the crops. Individual months within the seasons were indicated only by numbers: the third month of Inundation, the second month of Deficiency, and so on.

A second lunar calendar is designed to coincide with the civil system. Over the course of time, the Egyptians realized that the discrepancies between their two calendar systems caused problems as they tried to set the dates of holidays. They were accustomed to using the original lunar calendar, but this became confusing when the new civil calendar came into use. The best solution, they decided, was to create a third calendar—another lunar one—for use in planning religious activities. This calendar, however, was related to the civil year and not, as the agricultural one was, to the helical rising of Sirius. It was kept in sequence with the civil year by the addition of an intercalary month each time the beginning of the lunar year preceded the beginning of the civil year. Eventually, a twenty-five year intercalation schedule was adopted.

The Egyptian Sothic calendar was finally stabilized by Augustus Caesar. The Egyptian Sothic-cycle calendar remained in use and unchanged until Roman times. After Alexander the Great conquered Egypt in the fourth century B.C.E., his successor Ptolemy III declared a change to the calendar which added a day every four years beginning in 238 B.C.E. Egyptian priests, however, unwilling to give control of their sacred practices over to a foreign ruler, ignored the decree. Finally, in 30 B.C.E., Augustus Caesar enforced Ptolemy's order, stabilizing the calendar so that the first day of Thoth always fell on August 29.

The Roman Calendar and Julian Reform

The first Roman calendar is credited to legendary historical figures. According to writers during the Augustan period, the first Roman calendar was developed either by King Romulus, to whom the founding of Rome is attributed, or by King Numa, the supposed founder of the Roman religious system. Although there is no concrete evidence to support either of these theories, their existence attests to the importance the Romans assigned to their calendar. To have given it the honor of being developed by the leading figures in their history reflects the great need the Romans saw for the ordering of time.

Strict control over access to the calendar causes civil unrest in Rome. The first Roman calendar for which there is historical evidence dates to 450 B.C.E. It was a list of "named days"—holidays on which the legal system shut down—that was published by the Decemvirate. Access to this information was limited to the aristocracy of priests and magistrates which meant that the average citizen did not officially know when he could attend to his legal matters. This caused

such tension that in 304 B.C.E, Flavius was forced by plebeian outcry to post a calendar in the Roman forum that designated the legal days for conducting business. This calendar has become known as the pre-Julian calendar.

One interesting result of the popularization of the calendar in this manner was that many Romans began using the calendar as a decoration in their homes. Ornate renditions of Roman calendars (both pre-Julian and Julian versions) appear on the walls of Roman ruins which date as recently as the fourth century C.E. These pieces of artwork provide a great deal of the information about the Roman time reckoning system.

The structure of the pre-Julian calendar. The year, according to the pre-Julian calendar, was 355 days long, and roughly corresponded to a lunar year. It was divided into ten months which varied in length: Martius, Maius, Quinctilis, and October had 31 days; Januarius, Aprilis, Junis, Sextilis, September, November and December had 29 days; and Februarius had 28 days.

Each month was divided into three sections by special days: the Kalends was the first day of the month; the Nones was the fifth day of a short month or the seventh day of a long month; the Ides was the thirteenth day of a short month or the fifteenth day of a long one. All of the other days were designated in relation to one of these special days. For example, Martius (March) 10 would be called the sixth day before the Ides. (The Romans counted inclusively. While March 15 was the Ides, it was also counted as the first day of the set before the Ides. Thus, March 14 would be the second day before the Ides, and so on.) Apart from these dividing days, there were forty-five named days in the Roman calendar, most of which were significant for religious reasons.

Roman beliefs influence the structure of the calendar. The Romans seemed to be a highly superstitious people. One of the Roman superstitions, a mistrust of even numbers, affected the calendar in several ways. First, it may have been the reason for the alternation of the length of month between 29 and 31 days rather than using twelve 30-day months. Also, the one month that did have an even number of days, February, was considered unlucky. The second way in which the Roman aversion to even numbers affected the calendar was that festivals that were noted as three-day festivals would actually take place over five days because the Romans did not count the even days in between.

The Roman system of intercalation was different from other systems of the period. To keep the months and years of the calendar in line with the seasons and solar year, an extra month was intercalated every other year. The Roman method of intercalation was quite unusual compared with other methods. They reduced the month of February to 23 or 24 days and intercalated a 27-day month after the shortened February. Holidays that were normally observed on the 24th and 27th of the February were moved to the 23rd and 26th days of the intercalated month.

The problem with the Roman system of intercalation was that, over a four year period, a three to four day discrepancy built up between the calendar and the solar year. Instead of adjusting the length of the intercalary month, the Romans chose to omit it all together every time the man-made calendar accrued at least twenty-seven days more than the solar cycle.

The unusual nature of the intercalary schedule has long been a question among scholars. One highly plausible reason for the placement of the intercalation is that two holidays that fell at the end of February, the Regifugium and the Equirria, were significantly related to holidays in March and needed to fall in close proximity to them.

Celebrations of the Kalends, Nones, and Ides were related to the phases of the moon. According to the Roman writer Varro, who was a contemporary of Julius Caesar, the Kalends, Nones, and Ides were each celebrated in specific ways. On the Kalends, the pontifex maximus stood in the Curia Calabra on the Capitoline Hill and announced when the Nones would fall (thus indicating whether a month was long or short). The Nones was the day on which the festivals for the month were announced (all festivals took place between the Nones and the Kalends of the next month). The customs surrounding the Ides are less clear; it was apparently a day of ritual sacrifice (which adds to the poignancy of Julius Caesar's assassination on that date in 44 B.C.E.).

The origin of the customs surrounding the Kalends, Nones, and Ides dates to the time before the public had access to the calendar. According to Macrobius, a fifth century C.E. historian, the customs were developed while a lunar calendar was in place. A pontifex minor was assigned the task of watching for the crescent of the moon to be visible at night. When this occurred, he would inform the pontifex maximus (the most powerful religious leader of Rome) who would declare the Kalends the next day. The ceremony of declaration involved several sacrifices and a declaration of the day of the Nones. Word of when the Nones would occur was spread throughout the countryside and people traveled to Capitoline Hill for the announcement of which festivals would be celebrated during that month. The Nones occurred when the moon was at the first quarter. The sacrifice on the Ides coincided with the full moon.

These ceremonies, which served as a type of calendar for the people, would have become superfluous by the first century B.C.E. when the calendar was published openly. However, the traditions were maintained as part of the religious structure of Rome over which the pontifex maximus presided. There was also a strong political reason for the pontifex maximus to retain the official power of declaring months. Apparently even after the publication of the calendar, the pontifex maximus, as the most powerful religious leader, had a high degree of influence on its structure. This became significant because the pontifex maximus was an elected official and could manipulate the calendar to hasten or stall elections according to his popularity (or lack thereof). By the time Julius Caesar came to power, the Republican calendar was more than three months out of line because of political tampering. Julius Caesar was able to reform the Roman calendar, not because he had become the supreme military and political leader, but because he had been elected pontifex maximus in 63 B.C.E. when he was a relatively young man.

Julian reforms to the Republican calendar had a profound impact on history. During his campaigns in Egypt, Caesar realized that the Egyptian solar calendar was simpler and more efficient than the traditional Roman calendar. When he returned to Rome, he charged an Alexandrian astronomer,

Sosigenes, with the task of reforming the Roman system.

In 46 B.C.E., this plan was put into action: First, to reconcile the Roman year with the tropical year, 46 B.C.E. became, by decree, 445 days long. This was accomplished by lengthening most of the months, and adding two extra months. Caesar declared that this year was the "last year of confusion", but his constituents preferred to call it simply the "year of confusion."

Second, 45 B.C.E. marked the first year of the new system. New Year was moved from March 25 to January 1. January had 31 days, February 29, and, beginning with March, the rest of the months alternated regularly between 31 and 30 days. Every four years a second February 24 was added as the leap day. He thus produced the sequence familiar to the Western civil calendar of three common years of 365 days, and a leap year of 366 days. More importantly, he produced a calendar that required no intercalations, and that was therefore immune to political tampering. To commemorate this achievement, he had the month of Quinctilis renamed Julius.

Augustus added his own changes to the calendar. Several years after the assassination of Julius Caesar, a misunderstanding of his leap-year rule emerged. Because of the Roman habit of counting inclusively, they began to count the fourth year of each leap-year cycle as the first year of the next one. This meant that they were adding the extra day every three years. Augustus Caesar corrected this problem between 8 B.C.E. and 8 C.E. by declaring that the leap years would be left out during this time. The Western civil calendar traces its cycle of leap-year dates to this occurrence.

Augustus also made other changes to the calendar which seem to have resulted more from pride than practicality. The month Sextilis was renamed Augustus to honor his own reform of the calendar, and he took a day from February and added it to his own month. Then, to avoid having three 31-day months in a row, he switched the lengths of September, October, November, and December. Although the switch disrupted the pattern established by Julius, it produced the sequence the Western civil calendar still maintains.

Augustus also revived many of the old Roman religious festivals. These events, however, had little meaning to the majority of Roman citizens who had not practiced them for generations. A great deal is known about how these festivals were celebrated from Ovid's *Fasti*, which gives an account of the monthly practices of the Roman people. Unfortunately, only a portion of the manuscript exists.

The Gregorian Reform of the Julian Calendar

The changes Julius instituted were a vast improvement over any previous system, but they had one significant fault. The Julian calendar was based on a year of 365.25 days long, but the true solar year is 365.2422 days long. This error of 11 minutes 14 seconds per year amounted to three days every 400 years. In 45 B.C.E., when Julius Caesar established his calendar, the spring equinox fell on March 25. By 325 C.E., when the Council of Nicaea met to fix the Easter rule, the spring equinox was falling about March 21. This discrepancy had a greater impact on the dates of the Christian Movable Feasts than on agricultural or civil events.

Although the problem was noticed and considered by Church councils for 1200 years, the first action on the matter was not taken until 1545 when the Council of Trent authorized Pope Paul III to investigate the problem and find a solution. After nearly forty years of investigation, a proposal was submitted by Jesuit astronomer Christopher Clavius to Pope Gregory XIII. In 1582, the Pope issued a papal bull instituting an adjustment based on Clavius's plan.

The Gregorian reform instituted several significant changes: First, it subtracted ten days from the month of October 1582. By making the day following the feast of St. Francis (October 5), October 15, the date of the spring equinox was brought back to March 21.

Second, to bring the year closer to the true tropical year, a value of 365.2422 days was accepted. This value, which differed by 0.0078 days per year from the Julian calendar reckoning, amounted to 3.12 days every 400 years. It was therefore decided that three out of every four centennial years should be common years, and one a leap year. This resulted in the rule that a centennial year is a leap year only if it is divisible by 400. Therefore, 1700, 1800, and 1900 do not count as leap years, but the year 2000 does.

Third, the Gregorian reform set January 1 as the new year which was different, at least in Britain, from the old Julian system which had established December 25 as the new year. The Gregorian calendar, therefore, gained the title "New Style" as opposed to the Julian "Old Style".

Computing the date of Easter was also outlined in the Gregorian reform. At the time of the Gregorian reforms, the medieval system of golden numbers was rejected because it was astronomically inaccurate. The actual full moon could appear up to two days before or after the golden numbers indicated (see Chapter 2). Once again, the Church looked to Clavius and Lilius, whose calculations lay behind the Gregorian reform, for a more accurate system to calculate the date of Easter. Lilius used a method, the epact, that was already being used informally under the Julian calendar. The epact, which is derived from the Greek word meaning "to intercalate", is a system of numbers used to determine the age of the stage of the moon on the first day of the year.

The informal epact system was not completely accurate though, because it was based on the Metonic cycle, like the golden number system. This cycle occupied a period of 6,939.75 days, whereas to be accurate for the Moon, it should have lasted for 6,939.9 days. Although the difference is small, it amounts to one day in about 307 years; after this period, the New Moon would occur one day earlier than the epact table indicated.

Lunar and solar corrections are made to enhance the accuracy of the Gregorian calendar and the date of Easter. When the Gregorian calendar was adopted, the discrepancies in the epact system were taken into account. A correction (known as the lunar correction) was introduced which adjusted the age of the Moon, making it one day later on specific centennial years in a 2,500-year cycle. Seven of these adjustments were made, one every 300 years and an eighth time after a subsequent 400 years.

To keep the system of epacts in step with the other changes instituted by the Gregorian reforms, Clavius proposed another correction—a solar correction. The Gregorian calendar omitted most centennial

leap years to accommodate the more accurate length of the year. Clavius's plan maintained that in ordinary centennial years, the number of the epact should be reduced by one. These two corrections kept the lunar and solar cycles in harmony with one another in relation to the date of Easter.

The epact system facilitated long-range planning more effectively than the previous system of golden numbers. It simplified the method of determining the dates of new and full moons throughout the year. Also, since the dates of full and new moons could be determined into infinity, the date Easter could also be calculated to the same extent.

Religious differences slow the spread of the Gregorian calendar. Adoption of the Gregorian reforms seems to have been greatly based on religious similarities and differences. Roman Catholic countries carried out the reform promptly, but the Orthodox Christian countries did not. The disagreement is not over the facts of astronomy, but over community identity: the Eastern Orthodox Church seems to prefer to celebrate Easter on a date different from that chosen by Roman Catholics, in order to emphasize its independence from Rome.

There was also resistance to the changes in Protestant countries since the calendar revision was proposed in the wake of the Reformation.

France, Italy, Luxembourg, Portugal, and Spain adopted the New Style calendar in 1582, and most of the German Roman Catholic states, as well as Belgium and part of the Netherlands, adopted it by 1584. In Switzerland, the change took place over 229 years, between 1583 and 1812. In 1587, Hungary was the last country to adopt the New Style before a break of more than one hundred years after which Protestant nations began to accept the system. The first of these to adopt the New Style were Denmark and the Dutch and German Protestant states in 1699-1700. The Germans, however, maintained their tradition of determining Easter through the use of the Tabulae Rudolphinae (Rudolphine Tables), astronomical tables based on the 16th-century observations of Tycho Brahe. They adopted the Gregorian calendar rules for Easter in 1776.

From the mid-eighteenth century on, a steady stream

of countries embraced the New Style. In 1752, Britain and the colonies adopted the New Style, with Sweden following in 1753. In 1740, however, the Swedes had taken on the German Protestant astronomical methods for calculating Easter; they did not accept the Gregorian calendar rules for this practice until 1844. When Alaska became part of the United States in 1867, it adopted the New Style. Japan converted in 1873, Egypt in 1875. Between 1912 and 1917, there was a flurry of activity which resulted in its acceptance by Albania, Bulgaria, China, Estonia, Latvia, Lithuania, Romania, Turkey, and Yugoslavia. Soviet Russia embraced the New Style in 1918, immediately after the Revolution. Greece was the last major country to accept the calendar, doing so in 1923.

The change to a New Style calendar caused confusion in Britain. When the switch to the New Style was made in Britain, the discrepancy between the Old and New Styles had accrued to 11 days. The differ-ence was corrected in 1752 by a declaration that the day following September 2 of that year would be September 14. The legislators were faced with an unexpected response as many British citizens took to the streets demanding, "give us back our 11 days." The protest was not easily quelled even though the declaration had been passed with careful considera-tion given to make sure no one would suffer financial or other penalties.

Many British people continued to celebrate their holidays Old Style well into the nineteenth century— a practice revealing the deep emotional resistance to calendar reform. Even today, in western Ireland, the Celtic harvest festival of Lughnasad is celebrated more or less Old Style on the Sunday nearest August 13. George Washington, who was born on February 11, continued to celebrate his birthday Old Style after the calendar reform by moving it to February 22.

Chapter 5

Calendar Reform
Since the Mid-Eighteenth Century

Since the mid-eighteenth century, many proposals for calendar reform have been made. The objective of these reforms has been to develop a straightforward, universal, secular calendar. Three of these proposals have received significant attention in the Western world: the French Republican Calendar, the International Fixed Calendar, and the World Calendar.

The French Republican Calendar

Shortly before the French Revolution, calls for the secularization of the calendar began to be heard in France. The first rumblings for reform came in 1785 and 1788. The storming of the Bastille in July 1789 intensified the demands, and support swelled for the notion of a new calendar which would start from "the first year of liberty."

In 1793 the National Convention took notice of the demands and appointed Charles-Gilbert Romme, president of the committee of public instruction, to develop a new system. He delegated the technical matters to two eminent mathematicians, Joseph-Louis Lagrange and Gaspard Monge, and gave Fabre d'Eglantine the responsibility of renaming the months. Their proposal was submitted to the convention in September 1793. The delegates immediately ratified the new calendar which became the official system on October 5, 1793.

The new calendar, known as the French Republican Calendar, was retroactive to September 22, 1792, the day the Republic was proclaimed. (September 22 also

happened to coincide with the autumnal equinox in 1792.) September 22 was declared the New Year of the Republican calendar which had, in total, 365 days. The months were divided into twelve 30-day periods with the five extra days added to the end of the year (September 17 through 22 in the Gregorian calendar). The extra days were to be used for festivals and vacations in celebration and honor of virtue, genius, labor, opinion, and rewards. In a leap year the additional day was to be added to this period and was celebrated as the festival of the Revolution. Leap years continued to be inserted every four years, but the first leap year was inserted one year early so the Republican and Gregorian cycles would not coincide. Each four-year period was known as a Franciade.

The seven-day week was replaced with a ten day period called a *décade*. Each month, therefore, contained three *décades*, the tenth day of which was a rest day. The day was reorganized into portions divisible by ten, but this was too great a change for the whole society to adopt and was abandoned because of popular disapproval.

Fabre d'Eglantine renamed the months according to the meteorological characteristics of the periods. Table 5.1 lists the names and approximate Gregorian calendar dates.

The appeal of the French Republican Calendar was limited, for obvious reasons, to France. By September 1805, because of the difficulties of harmonizing the French system with the international standard, the Republican calendar had fallen into almost com-

Table 5.1

French Republican Calendar

French Month	English Translation	Approximate Gregorian Dates
Vendémiaire	Vintage	September 22-October 21
Brumaire	Mist	October 22-November 20
Frimaire	Frost	November 21-December 20
Nivôse	Snow	December 21-January 19
Pluviôse	Rain	January 20-February 18
Ventôse	Wind	February 19-March 20
Germinal	Seed-time	March 21-April 19
Floréal	Blossom	April 20-May 19
Prairial	Meadow	May 20-June 18
Messidor	Harvest	June 19-July 18
Thermidor	Heat	July 19-August 17
Fructidor	Fruits	August 18-September 16

plete disuse. On January 1, 1806, the Gregorian calendar replaced the French Republican system as the official calendar of France. The failure of the French Republican Calendar tended to discourage any further attempts at calendar reform for a long time.

Twentieth-Century Reform Proposals

In the 1930s, the Soviet Union made a brief attempt at calendar reform. By shortening the week to five days and giving workers a random day off within the week, the factories could operate continually which would, in theory, increase production. This experiment failed, however, because the social structure could not bear the stress of the change.

The two other prominent twentieth-century proposals for calendar reform have been the International Fixed Calendar and the World Calendar. Both of these calendars recognize that astronomically the current Western civil calendar is sufficient; however,

they offer slightly modified designs which would make its arrangement more convenient.

The International Fixed Calendar is a perpetual version of the Gregorian calendar. The International Fixed Calendar is divided into thirteen 28-day months, with one day added to the end of the year. All of the present month names remain the same with the thirteenth month named Sol and added between June and July. The extra day follows December 28, and is not included in any month or in any week. Leap day is treated in the same way and intercalated every four years after June 28. In this calendar, every month contains exactly four weeks, beginning on a Sunday and ending on a Saturday. (The tree calendar currently used by some Neo-pagans follows a similar pattern. See Chapter 2 for additional information.) The main criticism of the International Fixed Calendar is that it does not divide into four equal quarters and is therefore inconvenient for business purposes.

World Calendar creates four equal quarters. To answer the major criticism of the International Fixed Calendar, the World Calendar was devised. Its four quarters are composed of 91 days each, with an additional day at the end of the year. Each quarter is divided into three months: the first of 31 days and the second and third have 30 days each. The extra day and leap day are treated in the same manner as in the International Fixed Calendar, following December 30 and June 30, respectively.

Critics of this system argue that it is no better than the current Gregorian system because each month extends over part of five weeks, and each month within a given quarter begins on a different day. However, each of the four quarters is identical to the others, so a three month calendar could represent the entire year.

Both of these systems seem to be more convenient than the Gregorian calendar because of their streamlined detail. However, the problem with introducing reforms to the world community lies in the fact that the calendar has traditionally carried and continues to carry deep religious significance to all people. Thus, the success of any calendar reform will depend on its adaptability to the many different religious expressions of the modern world.

Part Two

Alphabetical Catalogue of
Religious Holidays

Abbey Fair
Movable date in early August

The Abbey Fair in Bethlehem, Connecticut, is a two-day monastic fair sponsored by the Abbey of Regina Laudis. The fair expanded significantly since its simple beginnings in 1952. Participants now enjoy a profusion of unusual events including performances of Gregorian chant, a variety of food, flowers, and crafts produced by the abbey, blacksmithing demonstrations, and a world-famous Neapolitan crêche situated in a horse stable once owned by an eighteenth-century Congregational minister. While many of the activities center around life in the abbey, other events include a fashion show, a basketball clinic, and various rummage sales.

Abbotsbury Garland Day
May 13

The trick-or-treating ritual in Abbotsbury, Dorset, England in which children bear garlands on poles and beg for gifts. The festival's date on "Old May Day" demonstrates that the roots of the celebration are found in English history prior to England's acceptance of the Gregorian reform in the eighteenth century.

'Abdu'l-Bahá
See **Ascension of 'Abdu'l-Bahá**
See **Birth of 'Abdu'l-Bahá**

Advent
Sunday closest to November 30 through December 24 in the Western Church; November 15 through December 24 in the Eastern Church

Advent is the beginning of the Western Christian liturgical year, and is the season of preparation for Christmas. In the West, it begins on the Sunday nearest St. Andrew's Day and ends on Christmas Eve. Because of the movable beginning date, the season can last from 22 to 28 days. The third Sunday of Advent is designated Gaudete Sunday by the Roman Catholic Church and the Anglican Communion. On this Sunday, the alter may be adorned with flowers and the purple vestments of the priests may be replaced by rose-colored garb.

The most common Advent customs in the United States have been imported from Germany and include the Advent calendar and the Advent wreath. Parents often give children an Advent calendar—which contains twenty-five flaps, one of which is opened each day between December 1 and December 24—to help them count the days before Christmas. The Advent wreath has become a part of many family devotional meditations during the season. It contains four or five candles which are lit in a special ceremony each Sunday of Advent and on Christmas day.

In the Eastern Orthodox tradition, the liturgical year begins on September 1, and Advent has a fixed beginning of November 15. A special name in the Eastern Orthodox Church for the Advent fast is Little Lent, because it is used as a time of meditation and preparation for Christmas like the Great Lent is for Easter.

African Methodist Quarterly Meeting Day
Last Saturday in August

This large annual gathering in Wilmington, Delaware, celebrates the establishment of the African Union Methodist Protestant Church (A.U.M.P.) in 1813, popularly referred to as the "Mother Church" for African-Americans. The A.U.M.P. Church had its origins in the congregation of Wilmington's Asbury Methodist Church which had denied its black members the right to fully participate in services. Under the leadership of Peter Spencer, 41 members of Asbury's congregation broke away from the Church in 1805, establishing Wilmington's first black congregation.

In the early days of the Big August Quarterly, participants from Delaware and surrounding states, many of whom were slaves, gathered together. They would hear and deliver revival messages, sing gospel hymns, and reunite with friends and family. Although the size of the gathering has diminished since its beginnings, the Big August Quarterly has recently enjoyed a resurgence of interest, and now offers an opportunity for participants to enjoy traditional cuisine and musical entertainment while mingling with fellow church members.

Akshya Tritiya
Third day of the waxing half of the Hindu month of Vaisakha (April-May)

Observance of Akshya Tritiya consists of both fasting and festivities. "Akshya" literally means undecaying or exempt from decay. The piety and devotions done on this day are believed to never decay and to secure permanency. This day is also believed to be the first day of Satya-Yuga, the "golden age."

On this day, a fast is observed and Vishnu, along with his consort Lakshmi, is worshipped with holy Ganges water, tulsi leaves (basil), incense, flowers, lamps, and new clothes. Brahmans are given food in charity.

Bathing in the holy Ganges or in other waters on this day is considered a sign of devotion. Also on this day, the passes of Sri Badrinarain in the Himalayas open after the long, snowy winter. Devotees worship Lord Badri on this day with food offerings in their homes and temples.

Aldersgate Experience
Sunday nearest to May 24

On May 24, 1783, John Wesley experienced a conversion while reading Martin Luther's preface to St. Paul's Epistle to the Romans with some friends in a house on Aldersgate Street in London. This event is commemorated by the Methodist Church on the Sunday nearest to May 24.

Al-'id al-Kabir
The 10th day of Dhu al-Hijjah

Al-'id al Kibar is the major Islamic festival marking the end of the Hajj or pilgrimage season.

See also **Hajj**.

All Hallows' Day
See **All Saints' Day**

All Saints' Day
November 1

All Saints' Day is observed by the Roman Catholic, Anglican, and many Protestant churches to honor all of the Christian saints, especially those who do not have their own feast days.

The celebration can be traced to the fourth century when groups of martyrs and other saints were honored on a common day, the first Sunday after Pentecost. Around 610 C.E., the Pantheon, a pagan temple at Rome, was consecrated as a Christian church for the honor of Our Lady and the martyrs. This event was celebrated annually on May 1. In 835 C.E., Pope Gregory IV combined the two celebrations and, in accordance with Pope Gregory I's policy of toleration for pagan tradition, moved the feast to November 1 to coincide with the pagan Festival of the Dead (see Samhain).

Observed as a religious and national holiday in 36 nations of the world, All Saints' Day is a Holy Day of Obligation for Roman Catholics in the United States.

See also **Samhain**.

All Souls' Day

November 2 in the West; three Saturdays prior to Lent and the day before Pentecost in the East

The dead were prayed for from the earliest days of Christianity. By the sixth century Benedictine monasteries were holding a service on Pentecost to commemorate deceased members of the order. In 998 C.E., St. Odilo of Cluny moved the date of this memorial to November 2, which became the standard throughout the Christian church. Although some Protestant churches observe All Souls' Day, it is essentially a Roman Catholic, Anglican, and Orthodox holy day.

On All Souls' Day, many Christians visit the graves of relatives to honor their ancestors. The evening of November 1 is often called All Souls' Eve and is observed by the decoration of family graves and lighting of candles as a remembrance of the dead.

Allen, Richard

See **Birthday of Allen Richard**

Amalaka Ekadashi

Eleventh day of the waxing half of the Hindu month of Phalguna (February-March)

Hindus believe in taking a respectful attitude toward all things, whether trees or beasts, rivers or deities, animate or inanimate, because the one Universal Spirit pervades all. It is this concept of God or Reality that underlies the worship of trees. On Amalaka Ekadashi the Alma tree (Emblica officinalis) is worshipped. Vishnu lives in this tree as well.

An Amalaka tree is ceremonially bathed and watered and then worshipped. A fast is observed and Brahmans are given gifts. Amalaka Ekdashi also marks the beginning of the Holi festival and its water-splashing tradition where people throw colored water on their friends, neighbors, relatives, and even passersby.

See also **Holi.**

Anant Chaturdashi

Fourteenth day of the waxing half of the Hindu month of Bhadrapada (August-September)

On this day, Vishnu—sleeping on the bed of Ananta (the serpent Shesha) in the milky ocean—is worshipped and meditated upon. While Vishnu slumbers on Ananta, his consort Lakshmi massages her feet.

On this day a fast is observed and fruits, sweets, and flowers are offered to Vishnu in worship. An unrefined thread colored in turmeric paste and having 14 knots is also tied on the upper right arm while meditating. Hindus believe that this ensures protection against evil and brings prosperity and happiness. The Pandava princes in exile observed this fast on the advice of Sri Krishna to regain their lost kingdom and prosperity. As a result, they defeated the Kauravas and regained their kingdom, wealth, reputation, and happiness.

Animals, Blessing of

See **Blessing of Animals**

Annakat

See **Govardhan Puja**

Annunciation of the Lord, Feast of

March 25

Formerly known as Annunciation of the Blessed Virgin Mary, this holiday commemorates the manifestation of the Archangel Gabriel to the Virgin Mary, announcing that she was chosen to be the mother of Jesus. Celebrated by the Roman Catholic, Anglican, Orthodox, and Lutheran churches, the Annunciation usually falls during Lent, but moves to April 1 if March 25 falls during Holy Week. Christians in the middle ages believed the coincidence of the Annunciation and Easter on the same date was a bad omen.

The feast was instituted about 430 C.E. in the East. The Roman observance dates from the seventh century, when celebration was said to be universal. It was traditionally called Lady Day in England and Ireland, where it was a quarter day, and a date for paying rent.

March 25 is also observed as St. Dismas Day in honor of the good thief who was crucified with Jesus. It was to St. Dismas that Jesus said "Today thou shalt be with me in Paradise." Some scholars have asserted that the date for commemorating St. Dismas may be the true date on which Jesus was crucified.

Antinmas

See **Up-Helly-Aa**

Archangels
See **Michaelmas**

Arrival of Roger Williams in the New World
February 5

American Baptists celebrate the coming of Roger Williams to North America on February 5, 1631, when he arrived in the Massachusetts colony from his native Wales. Williams and four other men were expelled from the colony for refusing to recognize the state's authority to prosecute religious offenses. The men and their families then established the colony of Rhode Island based on the principle of absolute religious liberty. The first Baptist congregation on the continent was established on Rhode Island.

Ascension Day
Between April 30 and June 3; forty days after Easter

Ascension Thursday. This holiday commemorates the ascension of Jesus back to Heaven after his resurrection from the dead. It is celebrated forty days after Easter Sunday because the Biblical account in the *Acts of the Apostles* indicates that Jesus spent forty days with his disciples after his resurrection, instructing them on how to carry out his teachings. Then, on the fortieth day, he took them to the Mount of Olives near Jerusalem and ascended to Heaven as they watched.

According to oral tradition, the observance of this day is one of the oldest celebrations of the Christian church, dating to 68 C.E. The first specific documentary evidence of the feast dates from early in the fifth century. Many churches traditionally observe the following Sunday as Ascension Sunday and structure their worship services around the Biblical account of Jesus' ascension.

Modern observances of this day reflect its roots in both pagan and Christian traditions. Processions are made, and, in some places, a chase of a "devil" through the streets symbolizes Christ's triumph over evil when he ascended to Heaven. Other traditions include "beating the bounds" where young boys are whipped with willow branch switches as they are driven along the boundaries of the parish. The two-fold purpose of this tradition on Bounds Thursday,

as the day is known in England, is to purify the boys' souls as well as teach them the edges of the parish.

See also **Rogation Days**.

Ascension of 'Abdu'l-Bahá
November 28

Bahá'í commemoration of the death of their third leader, Abbas Effendi, called 'Abdu'l-Bahá, the eldest son of the founder of Bahá'í, Bahá'u'lláh (Mirza Husayn Ali), on November 28, 1921. The Bahái use of the term "ascension" connotes the rising of the spirit rather than the body to its heavenly dwelling.

Ascension of Bahá'u'lláh
May 29

Each year, followers of the Bahá'í faith remember the death of the founder of the religion Mirza Husayn Ali, known as Bahá'u'lláh, by gathering together at 3:00 a.m. (the time of Bah'u'llah's death) for prayers and occasional readings from Bahá'í writings. This is one of the nine holy days during the year on which Bahá'ís do not work.

Ascension of the Prophet
See **Lailat al Miraj**

Ascension Sunday
See **Ascension Day**

Ash Wednesday
Movable observance, six and one-half weeks before Easter; occurs between February 4 and March 10

In the Western Church, Ash Wednesday marks the beginning of Lent, a season of introspection and penitence for Christians as they prepare for Easter. Ash Wednesday was designated as the first day of Lent by Gregory the Great (590-604 C.E.) who extended the traditional three-day Lenten season to a penitential period of forty weekdays of fasting. The length of Lent is in memory of the forty-day fasts of Moses, Elijah, and Jesus.

Ashes, symbolic of penance, are blessed and distributed among the faithful during the day. They are used to mark the forehead with the Sign of the Cross, with the reminder, "Remember, man, that you are dust, and unto dust you shall return," or "Repent, and believe the Good News."

In the Orthodox Church, Lent begins on the Monday prior to Ash Wednesday, and the observance of Ash Wednesday does not include the ceremonial application of ashes.

See also **Lent.**

Ashadha Purnima
See **Guru Purnima**

Ashokashtami
Eighth day of the waxing half of the Hindu month of Chaitra (March-April)

This car festival of Lingaraja at Bhubaneshwar is based on the Car Festival of Lord Jagannath at Puri, also known as Ratha Yatra. The Protege of Lord Lingaraja is taken out in a giant wooden chariot to the Rameshwar temple, about two kilometers from the Lingaraja temple, and returned after four days. Ashokashtami is a major local festival witnessed by thousands of devotees and spectators.

See also **Ratha Yatra.**

Ashura
10th day of Muharram

This festival is celebrated in the first month of the Islamic year and was derived from the Hebrew fast of Yom Kippur. There are several observances of this holy day which very among the sects of Islam.

Muhammad initially instituted and mandated its observance but later changed it to an optional fast. It is still observed in this manner by Sunni Muslims.

Shi'ite Muslims consider this day a major holy day as they mourn the death of Imam Hussein, the grandson and, according to Shi'ite belief, legitimate successor of Muhammad.

In Iran, some Shi'ite groups mourn the death by publicly scourging themselves as atonement for sin. During the days leading up to Ashura, the events of Hussein's last days are reenacted by various Shi'ite groups.

In Turkey, this day is celebrated in memory of Noah's departure from the Ark onto Mount Ararat and God's covenant with Noah never to destroy the earth by flood again.

Assumption of the Blessed Virgin
August 15

Assumption Day, called the Feast of the Most Holy Mother of God in the Orthodox Church, is observed in honor of the belief that the body of the Virgin Mary, the mother of Jesus, did not suffer decay, but was translated into heaven upon her death. The belief was not official dogma of the Catholic Church until 1950 when Pope Pius XII endorsed it. It is, however, one of the oldest solemnities observed by the Church, dating back to at least the seventh century, when its celebration was already established at Jerusalem and Rome.

It is possible that Assumption Day is a Christianization of an earlier pagan harvest festival and, in some places, it is still called the Feast of Our Lady of the Harvest.

Auditors' Day
Second Sunday in September

Observed by the Church of Scientology, this day allows auditors (a rank/profession within the church) to get together for a social and professional conference.

Autumnal Equinox
See **Quarter Days**

Avani Avittan
See **Ruksha Bandham**

Awwal Muharram
First day of the Islamic lunar month of Muharram

Awwal Muharram is the Islamic New Year celebration. It commemorates the flight of Muhammad from Mecca to Medina in 622 C.E. Muhammad's journey, or the Hejira, came about as a result of hostility toward his teachings and few converts in Mecca. He received an invitation from Medina to establish his new religion there. Thus, he migrated to the city where he was welcomed, and Islam was able to gain a solid following.

Because of the significance of this event, Muslims count their era from this date.

Ayyam-i-Ha
February 25 through March 1

The intercalary days inserted between the eighteenth and nineteenth months of the Bahá'í calendar. These days are a time of charity, gift-giving, rejoicing, and hospitality in preparation for the Bahá'í fast days during the nineteenth month.

B

The Báb
See **Birth of the Báb**
See **Declaration of the Báb**
See **Martyrdom of the Báb**

Bahá'u'lláh
See **Ascension of Bahá'u'lláh**
See **Birth of Bahá'u'lláh**

Baisakhi
April 13, the Hindu New Year

Also called Vaisakhi. The Hindu New Year, falling on April 13th, is celebrated by bathing in the Ganges or other holy waters, attendance at temple services, and exchanging of gifts.

The Baisakhi festival derives its name from the Hindu month of Vaisakha. On this day people bathe in the sacred rivers, pools, and wells early in the morning, dress themselves in festive clothes, and visit shrines and other places of worship to offer prayers.

This northern Indian festival is also observed in Punjab with special enthusiasm and fervor. The people of Punjab perform special dances, sing folk songs accompanied by rolling drums, exchange greetings, and enjoy feasts and merrymaking.

Baisakhi marks the beginning of a month-long bathing tradition held during Vaisakha. The pilgrimage to the only shrine of Badrinath, in the Himalayas, also commences from this day. Many Hindus believe that

charities done during Vaisakha are especially meritorious; thus, people generously give money, grains, and other items to the poor and the Brahmans. Observers of Baisakhi also fast, chant the glories of the Lord, and practice other pious activities.

Bakrid
See **'Id al-Adha**

Balaram Shashti
See **Hala Shashti**

Baptism of the Lord, Feast of the
January; Sunday following Epiphany

This feast was originally combined with Epiphany commemorating the manifestation of the divinity of Jesus at his baptism and the beginning of his public ministry. Although the Orthodox Church continues to observe this tradition, in 1961, the Roman Catholic Church set aside a separate holy day to recognize this event. The baptism of Jesus is observed by almost all Christian churches on some date in January.

At first, the date for the Feast of the Baptism of the Lord was January 13, but in 1969, the date was fixed on the Sunday following Epiphany. Since many countries have moved the celebration of Epiphany from the traditional date of January 6 to the Sunday between January 2 and 8, the two holidays sometimes coincide. In this case, the celebration of Epiphany takes precedence and the Feast of the Baptism is omitted.

Bara Wafat
See **Birthday of Muhammad**

Beating the Bounds
See **Rogation Days**

Beltane
May 1

Beltane is the Irish Gaelic name for the month of May. As a holiday, its celebration begins at sunset on the last day of April. One of the Greater Sabbats, it, along with the Lesser Sabbats, make up the eight Sabbats of the "Wheel of the Year"—the major holidays celebrated by members of Neo-pagan religions, such as the Gardnerian Witches, that have grown up in the United States since the mid-1960s. The Greater Sabbats of Brigid (February 1), Beltane (May 1), Lughnasad (August 1), and Samhain (pronounced "sa-oo-en," November 1) are the traditional holidays that seem to be specific to Celtic culture.

Beltane, or May Day, appears to have been a festival celebrating the beginning of the good weather season in northern Europe, when herdsmen could safely take the herds to the high summer pastures, and when wild fruits and berries began to grow and ripen. European folklore is full of May Day customs, a great many of them being divination methods apparently carried out by young women to determine who their future husbands would be.

May Day was also the traditional day for the Roman Catholic crowning of Blessed Virgin statues by a young girl chosen as May Queen. The month of May was dedicated to Mary as well. It is often claimed that Mary was substituted in the Middle Ages for the pagan goddess to whom May was originally sacred.

Bhairava Ashtami

Eighth lunar day of the waning half of the Hindu month of Margashirsha (November-December)

Bhairava is Shiva's inferior manifestation: a terrifying character worshipped to obtain success, prosperity, the removal of obstacles, and recovery from illness. One of the Bhairava's characteristics is that he punishes sinners with a danda (staff or rod); thus, he is also called Danda-pani. Another of Bhairava's names, Swaswa, comes from the legend that he rides a dog. "Swaswa" means "He whose horse is a dog."

On Bhairava Ashtami, people, after their daily morning baths, worship Bhairava and his mount with sweets and flowers. The dogs are fed with milk, sweets, and other such delicacies. At night, aspirants keep vigil and spend the time telling stories of Bhairavanath. Dead ancestors are offered oblations and libations in the morning after bath, and then Kal-Bhairava is worshipped.

Myth says that once a controversy arose among the Trinity of Brahma, Vishnu, and Shiva about who was the greatest. Each deity pleaded his case to the others, and ultimately the controversy took an ugly turn as they started maligning one another. A chance remark

of Brahma so enraged Shiva that he immediately produced Bhairava and ordered him to cut off one of Brahma's five heads. Bhairava did as he was told and Brahma became four-headed. It so terrified all the other gods, that they propitiated Shiva and Bhairava.

Bhaiya Duj

Second day of the waxing fortnight of the Hindu month of Kartika (October-November), the day following Govardhan Puja

Celebration of Bhaiya Duj symbolizes the deep affection between brothers and sisters. Married women invite their brothers to their homes, apply turmeric or sandal paste tilaks on the men's foreheads, tie a colored thread round their right wrists, pray for their prosperity and longevity, and then feed them sweets and other delicacies. In return the women receive valuable gifts. Unmarried girls do so at their parent's homes.

Bhaiya Duj is also called Yama Dvitiya, because this day also symbolizes the deep affection between Yama and his sister Yami. Sisters observe a strict fast and pray to Yama for their brother's longevity, good health, and happiness. The sun-born Yami, also known as Yamuna, the sister of Yama, is also worshipped.

Bhishma Ashtami

Eighth lunar day of the waxing half of the Hindu month of Magha (January-February)

On this day Bhishma Pitamaha, the son of Shantanu and Ganga, passed away, and his soul journeyed to heaven. He was called Bhishma, which literally means "terrible" and dreadful," because he had taken a vow of perpetual celibacy. Bhishma was renowned for his continence, wisdom, bravery, and fidelity to his word. On this day, Bhishma is offered libations with barley, sesame, flowers, and Ganges water.

The story of Bhishma is as follows. Shantanu, in his ripe old age, wanted to marry a beautiful, young maiden, but her parents would not allow it because Bhishma (Shantanu's eldest son, then called Devavrata) was heir to the throne; if the maiden bore sons they could not succeed. When it came to Bhishma's knowledge, he went to the girl's parents and vowed never to marry and have children, nor would he accept the crown. This satisfied the parents of the maiden Matsyagandha Satyavati. Shantanu then married Matsyagandha, and she bore him two sons.

During the great war of the *Mahabharata*, Bhishma took the side of the Kauravas, and he was made commander-in-chief of the vast army. In the war Bhishma was wounded so grievously by the rain of arrows discharged by Arjuna that not a space of two fingers breadth was left unwounded in his body. When Bhishma fell from his chariot he was upheld from the ground by the arrows and lay as on a bed of nails.

Bhishma remained on his deathbed of arrows for 58 days and during this period delivered many religious discourses. Having previously been allowed to fix the time of his death, he chose to die on the day when the sun had crossed to the north of the equator. Bhishma is held as a great example of self-denial, devotion, and fidelity.

Bhratri Panchami
See **Nag Panchami**

Bible Sunday
Last Sunday in November

Observed in many Protestant churches in America as a day honoring the Christian Scripture.

Birth of 'Abdu'l-Bahá
May 23

Bahá'í celebration of the birth of their third leader on May 23, 1844, the same night as the Declaration of the Báb. His birth on this date was significant because it fulfilled prophecies given by the Báb (Mirza Ali-Muhammad).

See also **Declaration of the Báb.**

Birth of Bahá'u'lláh
November 12

On November 12 Bahá'ís celebrate the 1817 birth of their Persian-born teacher and the Messiah of their faith. Born Mirza Husayn Ali, he was a follower of 'Ali-Muhammad, or the Báb, who founded the Bábi religion. Integral to the Babi belief was the coming of a messiah.

In 1863, Ali announced that he was the Messiah for whom they were waiting, changed his name to Bahá'u'lláh, and began teaching social and religious reform to his followers. These teachings were based on Islam, but some major teachings of the *Qur'an*, such as polygamy, slavery, and the notion of the holy war, were rejected, and a strong emphasis on the equality of the sexes was adopted.

The subsequent leader of Bahá'í, Abbas Effendi, spread the faith around the world through his missionary journeys. Followers of Bahá'í observe the Birth of Bahá'u'lláh as one of the nine holy days on which they refrain from work.

Birth of Mary
See **Nativity of the Blessed Virgin Mary, Feast of the**

Birth of the Báb
October 20

On October 20 Bahá'ís honor the birth of their founder, Mirza 'Alí-Muhammad, the Báb or "Gate" to God, in 1819. Bahá'í grew out of a sect of Islam, Shaikiya, which taught that a human intercessor between Allah and man was necessary. 'Ali-Muhammad claimed to be this intercessor, or gate, and began teaching a more moderate form of Islam that advocated toleration of other beliefs and fewer restrictions on its adherents.

Birthday of Brigham Young
June 1

Brigham Young, second President of the Church of Jesus Christ of the Latter-Day Saints and the leader who brought the beleaguered Mormons to refuge in Utah, was born on June 1, 1801, a date honored by Mormon churches worldwide.

Birthday of Joseph Smith
April 24

The birthday of Joseph Smith, founder and first President of the Church of Jesus Christ of the Latter-Day Saints, on April 24, 1805 is observed internationally by the six million members of the Mormon Church.

Birthday of L. Ron Hubbard
March 13

L. Ron Hubbard, founder of Dianetics and Scientology, was born March 13, 1911, at Tilden, Nebraska. This date is celebrated internationally by the Church of Scientology as the Founder's Birthday.

Birthday of Martin Luther
November 10

Martin Luther's birthday, November 10, 1483, is commemorated by Lutheran churches and German Protestants.

Birthday of Martin Luther King, Jr.
Third Monday in January

Observed as a holiday in most of the United States, usually on the third Monday in January. It is a political, rather than a religious, holiday; yet, its religious aspects cannot be ignored. King was a man of deep faith, and is regarded by millions as a modern-day saint much like Mahatma Gandhi. His accomplishments, and especially their foundation in King's Christian faith, are common topics for homilies in all Christian churches in the United States, including Roman Catholic churches, on the Sunday of that holiday weekend.

Birthday of Mary Baker Eddy
July 16

The birthday of Mary Baker Eddy (1821-1910), founder of Christian Science, is observed by Christian Science churches worldwide.

Birthday of Muhammad
Twelfth day of the month of Rabi al-Awwal

The feast of Mawlid al-Nabi, or Bara Wafat, is celebrated with enthusiasm by Muslims all over India. It commemorates the birthday of Muhammad, which in the Western calendar fell on April 12, 571 C.E. He was born at Mecca in Arabia, during a period of moral chaos and great corruption. Muhammad spent much of his time in prayer, meditation, and seclusion where he received revelations from Allah. For twenty-three years, from the time he was forty years old until his death, Muhammad succeeded in establishing a religion based on the revelations he had received, and brought a political cohesiveness to the Arab tribes that had not been previously experienced.

Around the twelfth century C.E., Muslims began celebrating his birth. On the day of Mawlid, the Prophet's teachings are repeated, the holy Qur'an is read and recited, and religious meetings are organized in the mosques. The devotees keep night vigil, spending their time in prayer and reading of the Qur'an. They invite friends and relatives to feast, and give donations to the poor.

Birthday of Richard Allen
February 11

Richard Allen, founder of the African Methodist Episcopal Church, is commemorated by members of that denomination on February 11, the date of his birth. Allen was born in 1760 and started the AME Church in 1816, serving as its first bishop.

Bi-Shevat
Fifteenth day of Shevat

The New Year for Trees is a minor Hebrew festival which is somewhat analogous to Arbor Day in the United States. The earliest reference to this holiday appeared late in the Second Temple period, at which time it was the final date for levying the tithe on the produce of fruit trees.

The observance of Bi-Shevat was revived in the 1940s with the return of Jewish colonists to Israel, the former Palestine. A massive reforestation program was undertaken by the settlers to reclaim barren land. It became customary to plant a tree for each newborn child—a cedar for a boy and a cypress or pine for a girl.

Today, Israeli children celebrate Bi-Shevat by planting trees and participating in traditional outdoor games. In other countries, the festival features the consumption of fruits from trees that grow in the Jewish homeland, such as oranges, figs, dates, raisins, pomegranates, and especially almonds—the first tree to bloom in Israel's spring.

Blavatsky, Helena Petrovna
See **Death of Helena Petrovna Blavatsky**

Blessing of Animals
Sunday nearest to January 17

The blessing of animals takes place in Catholic countries near the feast day of St. Anthony of Egypt, also known as Anthony the Abbot, the founder of monasticism and the patron saint of all four-footed beasts. (There are also some local blessings of animals on the feast of St. Francis of Assisi, whose love for animals is more well known.) Originally a day on which farm animals were blessed, the custom now extends to household pets, who are usually blessed at the church doors, but sometimes before the altar.

Blessing of the Shrimp Fleet
Last weekend in June

This traditional two-day gala in Bayou La Batre, Alabama celebrates the tiny town's major industries.

Bayou La Batre is one of the top seafood producers in the nation, bringing in about $300 million annually. Boat building is the other major industry, producing about $400 million each year.

On the day of this celebration, the two industries join in the blessing of the fleet by the priest of St. Margaret's Roman Catholic Church. Fifty to one hundred festively trimmed boats parade down the bayou (which serves as the main street of the town). The ceremony originated in the late 1940s and attracts up to 25,000 people annually.

Also included in the weekend's events are contests in oyster shucking, crab picking, gumbo making, and shrimp heading.

Bonfire Nights
Dates usually falling near each of the eight Sabbats of the Neo-pagan "Wheel of the Year"

In Britain there were many traditional nights during the year when a bonfire would be lit and danced around. Most of them fall on or near the dates for the eight Sabbats of the "Wheel of the Year," the major holidays celebrated by Neo-pagans in the United States, who have adopted the bonfire custom.

The specific list of bonfire nights is: Twelfth Night; Firebrand or Quadregesima Sunday; Holy Saturday night; Walpurgisnacht (May Eve); Midsummer Eve; Lammas Eve; Oidhche Shamhna, "vigil of Samhain," or All Hallow's Eve.

Booths
See **Sukkot**

Bounds Thursday
See **Ascension Day**

Brigid
February 1

The midwinter Sabbat of the Neo-pagans, this holiday is named for both the Irish goddess Brigid, patron of poets and daughter of the Dagda, and the Irish Saint Bridget, who, though certainly historical, shares many of the goddesses' qualities and attributes. Brigid is celebrated by Neo-pagans in the United States, and is considered one of the four Greater Sabbats along with Beltane (May 1), Lughnasad (August 1), and Samhain (pronounced "sa-oo-en," November 1). These are the traditional Celtic cross-quarter days, and according to tradition, are the days on which witches meet. The Sabbat is usually devoted to celebrations of light, poetry, and the overflowing bowl.

Buddha Purnima
Full-moon day of the month of Vaisakha (April-May)

Buddha Purnima, "Full Moon of the Buddha," is a most important Buddhist festival celebrating three events which all occurred on the same date—Siddhartha Gautama Buddha's birth at Lumbini near Nepal; his attainment of enlightenment at Uruvela, near Bodh Gaya, in Bihar; and his death at Kusinagar, in the country of Mallas, now Uttar Pradesh. It is celebrated the world over with immense piety, devotion, and fervor. Special celebrations are held at places like Sarnath, Sanchi, Kusinagar, Bodh Gaya, and at the Deer Park at Sarnath, near Varanasi, where the Buddha preached for the first time. At Sanchi, some of his sacred remains are enshrined under a magnificent stupa. Buddha images and portraits are taken out in a procession on this day. Buddhists read and recite their sacred scriptures, fast, worship Buddha at home and in temples, and practice charity.

See also **Wesak**.

C

Candlemas
See **Presentation of Jesus**

Carling Sunday
See **Mothering Sunday**

Carnea
August

This ancient Greek festival was one of the three principle religious celebrations observed in Peloponnesus, Cyrene, and Magna Graecia of antiquity. Dating as far back as 676 B.C.E., the festival honored Apollo Karneios, the god of fertility and herding. Carnea derived its name from the month of Carneus (August) and primarily celebrated a bountiful harvest. The ritual celebration featured young men called *staphylodromoi* ("grape-cluster-runners") who pursued other celebrants draped in garlands presumably made of grape vines. Successful capture of the garland-bearing participants indicated a good omen.

In addition to entreating the god Apollo to ensure a good harvest, the Carnea was intended to secure the god's aid in battle. Ironically, military engagement was prohibited during the Carnea. Some historians have suggested that the smashing defeat of the Spartan forces by the Persians at Thermopylae may have been prevented if the main Spartan army had not been immobilized in honor of the Carnea.

Carnival
Varying dates, beginning with Epiphany and ending with Shrove Tuesday.

In general, the carnival period is just before Ash Wednesday, the beginning of Lent; its name is said to be derived from the Latin carne vale, "farewell to meat," and is a time of revelry prior to the season of fasting during Lent.

Observed as a holiday in thirteen countries, Carnival varies in length from one to three days—usually the days just prior to Ash Wednesday. Some regions, however, begin the festivities soon after Epiphany, engaging in weekly or even daily parties, dances, and

festivities, as in the German Fasching customs. The celebration in Haiti is the biggest holiday of the year. A particular characteristic of the Haitian Carnival is the construction of "lamayotes" or wooden boxes decorated with paint and tissue paper. Boys in Haiti place a surprise inside the boxes—usually a mouse, lizard, or bug. Dressed in masks and costumes during Carnival, the boys roam the streets, trying to coax people to pay a penny for a peek inside the box. Brazil's Carnival is a major holiday as well, lasting five days and drawing participants from all over the world to Rio de Janeiro. Massive parades, dance competitions, and other merrymaking fill the days with joyous activity.

The most renown Carnival in the United States is the Mardi Gras festival held each year in New Orleans.

See also **Mardi Gras**.

Chaitra Parb
Eight days prior to the full-moon day of the Hindu month of Chaitra (March-April)

Chaitra Parb is a festival held by the tribes in Orissa, India. It starts eight days before the Purnima (full moon). Throughout the celebrations people fast, dance, and hunt. Heads of the families pay homage to their forefathers in the presence of the "Jani," or village priest, and every member of the family attends in festive new costumes. Animal sacrifice is a main feature of the festival, which also signals the beginning of the mango season.

Chaitra Purnima
Ten days in the Hindu month of Chaitra (March-April)

A great festival celebrating the Marriage of Lord Sundareswara with the fish-eyed Goddess Minakshi, Chaitra Purnima is observed with great religious enthusiasm in Madurai. It lasts for ten days and centers on the Minakshi Temple, an extraordinary example of Dravidian architecture said to have been founded by Indra. Representations of the deities are taken several times around the temple in chariots and thousands of devotees from all over India collect here on this occasion. The wedding anniversary is known as Minakshi-kalyanam, which is the most spectacular festival of Madurai.

In southern India, the full-moon day of the Hindu month of Chaitra (March-April) is also considered sacred to Chitra Gupta. On this day, Chitra Gupta, Yama's assistant, is worshipped. Some Hindus believe that it is Chitra Gupta who maintains the accounts of our good and bad actions in this world, and we are rewarded or punished accordingly hereafter. At Kanchipuram, near Madras, the image of Chitra Gupta is taken out in a procession, and the devotees bathe in the holy waters of the River Chitra, which flows from the nearby hills.

Chitra Gupta is invoked in a metal or earthen pitcher filled with water, and is offered worship and prayer in an elaborate ritual. Chitra Gupta literally means a "hidden picture," and his devotees believe that it is he who presents a true picture of one's actions after death.

Chandan Yatra
Twenty-one days beginning on the third day of the waxing half of the Hindu month of Vaisakha (April-May)

On each of this festival's twenty-one days, the images of the deities are taken out in grand procession to nearby water tanks, where they are rowed in decorated boats to the accompaniment of music and dance. This summer festival of Lord Jagannath is celebrated with religious zeal and passion at Puri and Orissa, and is also celebrated at Bhubaneshwar, Baripada, and Balanga.

Cheesefare Sunday
See **Lent**

Childermas
See **Holy Innocents' Day**

Children's Day
Second Sunday in June

Children's Day began as an observance in June 1856 at the Universalist Church in Chelsea, Massachusetts. It was adopted as the second Sunday in June by the Methodist Church in 1868, and is now placed on that date on the calendar of the National Council of Churches.

Christ the King, Feast of
Last Sunday in October in the Roman Catholic Church; last Sunday in August in the Protestant Church

Christians celebrate the kingship of Jesus over the earthly authority on this holiday. Pope Pius XI instituted the feast December 11, 1925; in 1937, the National Council of Churches designated the last Sunday in August for its celebration.

Christmas Day
December 25

Christmas is the day on which Christians celebrate the birth of Jesus Christ. The Roman Catholic Church designates it as a day of holy obligation on which members of the Church must attend services.

Originally, the birth of Jesus was commemorated in the East on the Feast of Epiphany (January 6) but by 354, the Christmas Feast had taken hold in the West and was observed on December 25. Since the fifth century, most Eastern Orthodox Churches have celebrated the Nativity on December 25; however, some Eastern congregations, called "Old Calendarists," still use the Julian calendar and honor the birth of Christ thirteen days later, on January 7. The Armenian Church continues to celebrate "Old Christmas" on January 6.

As with many traditions surrounding Christmas, the selection of December 25 as a commemoration of Jesus's birthday may be an example of the blending of Christian ideas and the pagan traditions they replaced. December 25 was the date of the Mithric observance of the "Birthday of the Invincible Sun." This also coincided with Saturnalia and the Winter solstice during the period when Mithraism was practiced in Rome. Since the day was already being kept as a holiday, Christians may have adjusted the symbolism of the day, declaring it the birthday of their "Invincible Son." According to events in the Gospel of Matthew, the date of Jesus's birth may actually have taken place much earlier in the year.

The word "Christmas" means "the mass of Christ," and originated in the 11th century as a name for this feast. It was one of the most popular and universally celebrated holidays in Europe during the Middle

Ages. During the Reformation, however, the celebration of Christmas began to decline in importance. Reformers engaged in complex doctrinal arguments in an attempt to prove the celebration of Christmas was unscriptural.

In some countries, the Protestant reforms brought about a ban of Christmas celebrations. By the time of the Restoration in 1660, however, the celebration of Christmas as a much more secular holiday was revived in these countries. In New England, Christmas remained outlawed until the mid-nineteenth century, and in Boston classes were held in the public schools on Christmas Day until 1870, with pupils who missed school that day being punished or dismissed. The mass immigration of Irish Catholics to New England brought about the reinstitution of Christmas celebrations.

In the calendar of the Roman Catholic, Lutheran, and Anglican confessions, Christmastide begins on Christmas Eve and continues until the Sunday after Epiphany. Christians generally attend services on Christmas Eve, and often on Christmas Day as well.

A vast number of non-religious customs are associated with Christmas in the United States. A traditional day of family gatherings, Christmas is often celebrated with a feast which typically includes such foods as turkey, goose or ham, yams, mince pies, and plum pudding.

The Christmas tree has become a standard symbol of the season in the United States. Each year, families decorate fresh cut or artificial evergreen trees in their homes. The tradition may have its roots in the sixteenth-century custom of decorating a "paradise tree" with apples in remembrance of Adam and Eve. Another theory about the origins of the Christmas tree date back to ancient pagan veneration of evergreen trees.

The Germans also brought the idea of Christmas lights or candles to the United States, although they were not placed on trees until perhaps the eighteenth century. This practice, combined with the Irish custom of putting lights in the windows, led to the lighting of houses and Christmas trees. At first, candles were used but they were a fire hazard. In the twentieth century, electric lights came into use and proved to be much safer.

Other plants are used in traditional Christmas decorations as well. Mistletoe, for example, was used by Druids for healing and as a symbol of peace and reconciliation (hence the kiss under the mistletoe). Holly's green leaves and red berries in the midst of winter make it another evergreen symbol. Ivy is associated with midwinter carousing. Laurel wreaths, worn as a victory symbol by the Roman, are hung on front doors as a symbol of Christ's victory over the forces of darkness and death. Poinsettia was introduced from Mexico in the nineteenth century and is especially appealing because of its red and green coloring.

In many American homes, Christmas presents are wrapped and placed under the tree to be opened on Christmas Eve or Day. The Christian practice of gift giving is associated with the gifts brought to Jesus by the three Magi and may have originally taken place during Epiphany. In Europe, Epiphany is still the usual day for gift-giving. In Italy, presents are said to be brought by *La Befana*, a Fairy Queen or "Mother Witch" figure whose name appears to be a worn-down form of "epiphany."

Gifts are traditionally delivered to American children by Santa Claus. The name "Santa Claus" is derived from the Dutch name, Sinter Klaas, for Saint Nicholas. The popular concept of Santa is based on the immensely popular verse, "The Night Before Christmas," by Clement Moore, first published in the mid-nineteenth century.

Very sophisticated theological arguments are possible over the question of whether Santa Claus is still really a Christian saint or not; he has certainly absorbed major characteristics of Hermes, Wotan, Thor, and various other pagan divinities. Another name for Santa Claus, Kris Kringle, was apparently derived from the German *Christkindel*, "Christ child," who is said to bring the presents on Christmas Eve in some families. Similar figures are Father Christmas (in England) and Knecht Rupprecht (Knight Rupert) in northern Germany.

Christmas Eve
December 24

The day before Christmas is a full or partial holiday in 29 countries, and in most of the United States. In central and northern Europe, Christmas Eve, rather than Christmas Day, is the occasion of the major family celebration, and some American families observe this custom as well.

A long-standing liturgical tradition of Christmas Eve has been the "Midnight Mass". Many parish churches hold the service much earlier in the evening, since it is intended to be an occasion on which entire families, including the very young children, can attend. Families that do not participate in the myth of Santa Claus then return home for a meal and the opening of the presents.

This day is celebrated in the Eastern Orthodox churches as the feast day of Adam and Eve, the parents of the human race. There are some especially interesting Slavic customs on this day. One is that on Christmas Eve the house must be clean, all borrowed items returned, all tools put away, no lint or unfinished work exposed to sight, and no task started that cannot be finished before nightfall. Another is that at the beginning of the evening meal, the father of the family breaks wafers and distributes them to the family members with a kiss and a wish for a joyous feast. The parallels to the Jewish customs associated with the Passover Seder are obvious, and are a reminder of the Jewish origins of Christianity.

Another Christmas Eve custom, that of being especially kind to animals, was instituted by St. Francis of Assisi, who also introduced his Franciscan monks to the concept of a joyful Christmas carol (as distinguished from the solemn Christmas hymns), and who began the custom of setting up a "manger scene," with statues or other representations of the Holy Family, the angels, the Magi, the shepherds, and the animals. Some families place the Magi with their camels far away from the manger scene. Each day of Advent, the children in the home move the figures closer to the manger scene until, on Christmas Eve, they reach the manger. The manger itself is left empty until Christmas morning, when the statue of the Christ child is put in place to complete the story.

Although Christmas is observed by the majority of Christians, there are a few sects of Christianity that make a point of not observing Christmas or most other Christian holidays, often opting instead to harken back to the Hebrew roots of Christianity for their holidays. Among these groups are Adventist churches, Jehovah's Witnesses, and various British Israelite communities. Since these groups usually use the Christian calendar, the dates of the holidays they celebrate are often different from the actual Jewish celebration of the same events.

Christmas, Twelve Days of
December 25 through January 5

The twelve days of Christmas are counted from Christmas to Epiphany. Epiphany was the traditional date for the visit of the Three Magi, and is still the traditional date for gift-giving in many parts of Europe, Mexico, and Latin America. Twelfth Night, the eve of the last day, marked the end of the Christmas season, usually by means of one last exuberant party (American practice is to consider New Year's Day to be the end of the "holiday season). Because of Shakespeare's play *Twelfth Night*, this night is generally observed as a festive occasion by actors.

Circumcision, Feast of the
January 1

This holiday is known by several different names throughout the Christian Church. Roman Catholics, who previously called it the Octave of the Birth of Our Lord, or the Circumcision of Jesus, now refer to the day as the Solemnity of Mary, the Mother of God. Episcopalians know the holiday as the Feast of the Holy Name of Our Lord Jesus Christ because it was on this day, according to Hebrew custom, that Jesus was given his name. Lutherans call it the Feast of the Circumcision and the Name of Jesus, while those in the Eastern Orthodox Church refer to the day as the Feast of the Circumcision of Our Lord. Some churches within the Eastern tradition continue to use the Julian Calendar for liturgical purposes and, therefore observe the holiday thirteen days later than the other branches of Christianity.

In the Roman Catholic Church, The Feast of the Solemnity supplants the former feast of the Maternity of Mary observed on October 11.

Close Sunday
See **Quasimodo Sunday**

Collop Monday
See **Lent**

Corpus Christi
Between May 21 and June 24; Thursday after Trinity Sunday

Also called the Feast of the Most Holy Body of Christ. In the Roman Catholic Church, this is a movable observance held in the United States on the Sunday following Trinity Sunday; elsewhere celebrated on the traditional day of Thursday after Trinity Sunday. This holy day has been celebrated in honor of the Eucharist since the thirteenth century C.E. Originating at Liege, France in 1246, Corpus Christi was spread throughout the Church in the West by Pope Urban IV in 1264. The Office for the feast was composed by St. Thomas Aquinas.

Although the exuberant public veneration of the Eucharist has waned in the United States since the Second Vatican Council, many other nations observe this day with public processions and liturgies in honor of the "Blessed Sacrament".

Counting of the Omer
Occurs between Passover and Shavuot

A minor Jewish festival, amounting to a custom in the traditional synagogue liturgy, of announcing the "counting of the omer (sheaf of wheat)," that is, of the days between Passover and Shavuot. This was traditionally a "lenten" period of abstinence and repentance; however, on the thirty-third day of the omer, these restrictions were relaxed for twenty-four hours. It is possible that this holiday may combine an ancient pagan festival day, with customs much like those of May Day, with Hebrew traditions.

Covenant, Day of the
See **Day of the Covenant**

Cross-Quarter Days
February 1, May 1, August 1 and November 1

The cross-quarter days are the four traditional Celtic festivals now celebrated in the United States by Neo-

pagans as their Greater Sabbats, which, with the four Lesser Sabbats on the quarter days, make up the "Wheel of the Year". Despite the traditional names, there is not much difference in the enthusiasm with which these holidays are celebrated. The most common names used by Neo-pagans for the Greater Sabbats are Brigid (February 1; see also Groundhog Day), Beltane (May 1, better known as May Day), Lughnasad (August 1), and Samhain (pronounced "sa-oo-en," November 1, better known as Halloween). These holidays "cross" the quarter days, the solstices and equinoxes, about halfway in between.

D

Dairy Sunday
See **Lent**

Dasain
The waxing half of Asvina (September-October)

This ten-day festival commemorating the *Ramayana* epic in which the benevolent gods overcome the evil demons is observed throughout the Hindu world. It is most elaborately celebrated in Nepal where it is the most important festival of the year.

The Nepalese participate in many special activities and ceremonies to commemorate the victory of the goddess Durga over the evil demon Mahisnasura. Houses are cleaned; swings and ferris wheels are set up in villages; joyful religious ceremonies are conducted daily; and hundreds of animal sacrifices are performed because Durga is believed to be a blood-thirsty goddess. In return, the people ask Durga to protect them through the following year.

The last day of the festival is a day of visiting older relatives to receive a blessing. In some towns, masked dances and processions consisting of priests carrying wooden swords symbolic of Durga's victory are held.

See also **Durga Puja** and **Dussehra**.

Dasara
See **Dussehra**

Dattatreya Jayanti
Full-moon day of the Hindu month of Margashirsha (November-December)

Celebrated all over India, especially in Maharashtra. On Dattatreya Jayanti people rise early in the morning and bathe in sacred streams, fast, and spend the day in meditation, prayer, and worship. They meditate on the life of Dattatreya and read his works, which include *Avadhuta Gita* and *Jivanmukta Gita*. The image of Dattatreya is worshipped with flowers, lamps, incense, camphor, etc., and the aspirants resolve to follow in the footsteps of Swami Dattatreya. Dattatreya is the son of Rishi Atri and Anusuya. Anusuya, the jewel among devoted and virtuous wives, did a severe penance to beget a son equal in merits to the Hindu Trimurti of Brahma, Vishnu, and Shiva. Anusuya's penance aroused the jealousy of Lakshmi, Saraswati, and Parvati, who sent their husbands Vishnu, Brahma, and Shiva to test her virtue by asking her to give them alms while nude.

They approached Anusuya in the guise of three mendicants, and asked her to give alms with an uncovered body. She was on the horns of dilemma for a while, but then she, reciting a mantra, sprinkled a little water over the three sanyasis (beggars); they were instantly transformed into babes, and her breasts at once swelled with milk. She took up the three babies and suckled them. In the meantime, her husband Atri returned from his morning bath and was told what had transpired during his absence, although he already knew through divine vision. He fondly embraced the three children, and they turned into one child with three heads and six hands.

Lakshmi, Saraswati, and Parvati got worried when their husbands did not return. They hurried to Anusuya and asked her to give them their husbands back and also begged her forgiveness. Anusuya acceded to their request and the Trimurti of Vishnu, Brahma, and Shiva appeared immediately in their actual forms. They blessed the Rishi couple and the child Dattatreya. Thus, Dattatreya came to possess three heads and six hands. In him, portions of Brahman, Shiva, and particularly Vishnu, were incarnated; therefore, Dattatreya is worshipped as a Triad. He had three sons, Soma, Datta, and Durvasa, to whom also a portion of the divine essence was transmitted.

Day of Atonement
See **Yom Kippur**

Day of the Covenant
November 26

On this date each year, Bahá'ís celebrate the Covenant set forth in Baha'u'llah's last will and testament. The Covenant established religious freedom for followers of Bahái by insisting that the kingdom of God depends on the freely given assent of Bahá'ís to the doctrines of their faith and the authority of Baha'u'lláh's legitimate successor (whom he designated as his son, Abdu'l-Baha).

Death of George Fox
January 13

The death on January 13, 1691, of George Fox, founder of the Society of Friends, is observed worldwide by all Quaker churches and Meetings.

Death of Helena Petrovna Blavatsky
May 8

In 1895, Helena Petrovna Blavatsky founded the Theosophical Society which was dedicated to increasing Western understanding of the Hindu religion.

The basic beliefs of the Society are that there is only one Universal Spirit behind all that exists and that the universe is cyclical in its development, reaching a zenith then diminishing into quiescnece. All souls, or Monads, emanate from the Universal Spirit and are thus eternal and divine, but each must be enlightened once they become encased in matter—animal, vegetable, or mineral. Reincarnation is believed to be the method by which eventual perfection for each soul is achieved.

On May 8, 1891, Helena Petrovna Blavatsky died. Theosophists around the world remember her on this day each year.

Death of Imam 'Ali
A holiday for Shi'ite Muslims, commemorating the death of the man whom they believed to be the true successor to the Prophet Muhammad.

Declaration of the Báb
May 3

On May 23, 1844, 'Ali-Muhammad revealed that he was the Báb, or gate, to the Coming One of all religions. With this declaration, the Bahá'í faith was started. The Báb based his teachings on the *Qur'an*, but adopted a moderate interpretation of its meaning. Although the Báb maintained that he was simply the forerunner of one who would be greater to himself (similar to John the Baptist as the precursor to Jesus), he attracted a significant following. His disciples were known as Bábis and among them was Mirza Husayn Ali. In 1863, Ali revealed himself to be the Messiah of whom the Báb had spoken and assumed the title Bahá'u'lláh.

The Declaration of the Báb is one of the nine holy days on which Bahá'ís suspend trade, commercial, industrial, and agricultural work.

See also **Ascension of Bahá'u'lláh, Birth of Bahá'u'lláh, Birth of the Báb,** and **Martyrdom of the Báb.**

Dedication of St. John Lateran
November 9

This Roman Catholic observance is classed as a feast and commemorates the first public consecration of a church, that of the Basilica of the Most Holy Savior, by Pope Sylvester on November 9, 324. The church and the Lateran Palace were the gift of the Roman Emperor Constantine. Since the 12th century it has been known as St. John Lateran, in honor of John the Baptist, after whom the adjoining baptistery was named. It was rebuilt by Pope Innocent X (1644-55), reconsecrated by Pope Benedict XIII in 1726, and enlarged by Pope Leo XIII (1878-1903). This basilica is highly regarded throughout the Roman Rite.

Deepvali
See **Dewali**

Devathani Ekadashi
Eleventh day of the waxing half of the Hindu month of Kartika (October-November)

Hindus believe that Vishnu's eventually triumphant battle with the great demon Shankhasura was so exhausting that he and the other deities went to sleep for a period of four months. Each year, Vishnu slumbers from the 11th day of the waxing half of Ashadha (June-July) till the tenth day of the waxing half of Kartika (October-November), then awakes on the 11th day, which is known as Devuthani Ekadashi. During those months, ceremonies like marriage or the thread ceremony are not observed.

On this day, Hindu women fast, worship Vishnu, and sing hymns in praise of various gods and goddesses around a fire. This day also marks the eating of the new products of the fields for the first time in the season, including sugarcane and waternuts. A rural festival, it is observed with much jollity in the countryside. From this day onward marriages and other ceremonies can be held, as it marks again the beginning of an auspicious time.

Dewali
Fifteenth day of the waning half of Kartika (October-November)

Dewali or the Festival of Lights is an important and popular festival which marks the New Year and is celebrated throughout India. Hindus believe that this great festival of lights symbolizes the human urge to move toward the light of truth from the darkness of ignorance and unhappiness. The climax of this five-day festival falls on the last day of the waning half of Kartika (October-November).

The customs observed during Dewali are associated with several legends. One myth says that on this day Lakshmi, the goddess of wealth and good fortune, roams about and visits the houses of people. Therefore people clean their homes and businesses, decorating them lavishly as they prepare to welcome the goddess. It also commemorates the triumph of Lord Rama over Ravana, the ruler of Sri Lanka who had stolen Rama's wife. Also on this day, Krishna is said to have killed the demon of Narkusura.

A few days before the festival, houses are whitewashed and cleaned. The courtyards, the gates, and the place of worship are decorated with flowers and intricate colored paperwork, and at night people place earthen lamps and candles in every nook and corner of their homes, and fireworks are displayed.

On the day of Dewali, sweets are prepared and exchanged, and people ask forgiveness of one another for any wrongs committed. In the evening, ceremonies in worship of Lakshmi are performed.

Dewali also marks the advent of new season and the sowing of new crops. On this day begins the new Vikrama Era and new account books are opened. The famous King Vikramaditya, whom this era is named after, was crowned on this day. In Bengal Kali is worshiped with great fervor on this day.

The Jains celebrate Dewali as a day of final liberation of Lord Mahavira and the anniversary of Swany Sayananda Saraswati's salvation experience. Also commemorated on this day is the entrance of the great swami Rama Tirtha into his final jal-samadhi. At great Jain shrines like Pavapuri in Bihar, and Girnar in Gujarat, special puja (worship) festivals are held, sacred scriptures read and recited, and Lord Mahavira worshiped.

Dhan Teras

Thirteenth day of the waning half of the Hindu month of Kartika (October-November)

Two days prior to Dewali, Dhan Teras, or Dhanvantri Trayodashi, is observed with great mirth and rejoicing. Dhanvantri, the physician of the gods, who appeared at the churning of the ocean, is worshipped on this day, especially by physicians. He is the father of Indian medicine, and Ayurveda is attributed to him. He is also called Sudhapani, because he appeared from the ocean carrying nectar in his hands.

People rise at dawn and bathe, don new robes, and fast. In the evening, an earthen lamp is lit before the door of every house and the fast broken. New utensils are bought on this day because it is regarded as very auspicious.

Dhanvantri Trayodashi
See **Dhan Teras**

Divali
See **Dewali**

Dol Purnima
Full moon day of the Hindu month of Dol

In Bengal, Holi is celebrated as Dol Purnima (full moon). This festival is dedicated to Sri Krishna. On this day, an image of Krishna richly adorned and smeared with colored powder is taken out in procession in a swinging palanquin decorated with flowers, leaves, colored clothes, and papers. The procession proceeds forward to the accompaniment of music, sounding of conch shells, trumpets, and shouts of "Jai!" (victory).

Dol Purnima is also significant because it is the birthday of Chaitanya Mahaprabhu (1485-1533), the great Vaishnava saint who popularized modern Sankirtana. He elevated the passion of Radha and Krishna to a high spiritual plane and underlined emotion at the cost of the ceremonial side of devotion. Followers of the Chaitanya School of Vaishnavism believe Chaitanya himself was a manifestation of Krishna. Chaitanya Mahaprabhu believed that the essence of sadhana is always the loving remembrance of Hari (Vishnu).

Durga Puja

This Hindu festival of the Divine Mother is a ten-day holiday in India honoring the ten-armed Durga, wife of Shiva. Also known as the Navrata or Festival of Victory, Durga Puja honors Durga's conquest of the demon Mashishasura.

Navratras are observed twice a year, once in the Hindu month of Chaitra (March-April), preceding Rama Navami, and then in the month of Ashvina (September-October), preceding Dussehra. This nine-day Navratra commences with the new moon of Ashvina, and terminates with Mahanavami, on the ninth day of the waxing half of the month. During these nine days, devotees keep a strict fast, and Durga is worshipped. The style of observing Navratra in different parts of India may be different, but its sole aim is to propitiate Mother Durga and to seek her blessings.

On the first lunar day of the waxing half of Ashvina, an earthen pitcher, filled with water and its mouth covered with green leaves and an earthen lid, is installed with an invocation of Ganesha, the god of learning and wisdom. A clarified butter lamp is always kept burning before the installed pitcher during the celebration. Durga is then invoked and worshiped in with ceremonial rites. Daily readings of the *Durga-saptashti, Devi Bhagvat Purana,* and *Devi*

Mahatmya sections of the *Markandeya Purana* are part of the celebrations as well. Unmarried girls below the age of ten are also worshiped and given gifts during these nine days. The aspirants sleep on the ground and keep a strict fast all these days. On the final day of the festival, people wear young barley sprouts in their hair and visit older relatives seeking a blessing.

In Bengal, Durga Puja is celebrated with great excitement and festivity. Huge puja (worship) pavilions with ten-armed Durga are constructed for this purpose. Durga, the beautiful but fierce goddess, rides her lion, killing the demon Mahishasura. She holds in her hands the gods' special weapons: Vishnu's discus, Shiva's trident, Varuna's conch shell, Agni's flaming dart, Vayu's bow, Surya's quiver, Indra's thunderbolt, Kubera's club, and a garland of snakes from Shesha. A fierce battle raged between Durga and Mahishasura, but finally she killed him with a spear.

Durga Puja surpasses all other festivals of Bengal in its popularity and mass appeal. During the celebrations music, dance, drama, and poetry are performed before the enthralled audiences. The earthen images of the goddess Durga are taken on the final day in triumphal processions to the river, where they are ceremonially immersed. Durga Puja is more than a ritual, as it invests the lives of every one, and produces a feverish literary and artistic activity. On these days, Durga traditionally visits her parents, Himavan and Mena, for the only time in the year. The final day marks the end of this brief visit when she leaves for Mount Kailash, the abode of her lord and husband Shiva. Bengali women give an emotional and affectionate sendoff to Durga, and the ceremony is described like a daughter's departure to her husband's house.

Dussehra

Tenth day of the waxing half of Ashvina (September-October)

Hindu festival celebrating Rama's victory after a ten-day struggle against Ravana, king of the demons, reenacted in puppet shows and in traditional plays. Dussehra or Vijay Dashami is very popular, being celebrated throughout India. It is a ten-day celebration during which the *Ramalila*, which is based on the epic story of the *Ramayana*, is staged in most of the cities and towns in northern India with elaborate rituals. During the performance of the *Ramalila*, the *Ramayana* is constantly recited accompanied by music. In addition, elaborate and joyous processions depicting various scenes of the *Ramayana* in the form of tableaus take place through bazaars and main streets.

On the last day of the festival, huge mannequins representing Ravana, his brother Kumbhakrna, and his son Meghnatha are stuffed with brilliant fireworks, raised at various open grounds, and set fire to. This climactic event marks the termination of festival.

On Dussehra, Lord Rama is worshipped, prayed to, and meditated upon to obtain his blessings and favor. In the past, kings often marched their forces on this day against their enemies, the day when Rama routed Ravana.

E

Easter

Between March 22 and April 25 in the West and April 4 and May 8 in the East; first Sunday after the first full moon on or following the vernal equinox

Easter, the most important holiday of the Christian faith, celebrates the Resurrection of Christ from the dead (Mark 16:1-7). One of the earliest observances of the Church, the ceremonies, customs, and rituals surrounding this mystery extend from Easter Sunday until the feast of Pentecost fifty days later.

The week preceding Easter is called Holy Week and is the culmination of Lent, the period of introspection and penance. Holy Week begins with Palm Sunday, commemorating Christ's triumphal entry into Jerusalem one week before his crucifixion. Maundy Thursday is the traditional date of the Last Supper and Jesus' arrest. On Good Friday, Christians mourn the crucifixion and death of Jesus; and on Holy Saturday, his Resurrection is anticipated.

The determination of Easter's date has been a subject of continual debate and revision for most of the history of the Church. Since the date of Easter determines the dates of most movable feasts throughout the Christian year, variances in the celebration of these feasts that occur between different branches of the Church are often due to disagreements in the way Easter is designated.

Easter Sunday itself concludes the observances of Holy Week, which begins on Palm Sunday, and specifically completes the liturgical observances of the Easter Triduum, which begins on Holy or Maundy Thursday.

In Roman Catholic parishes, the Easter Vigil mass on Saturday night has become the liturgical focus of the Easter Triduum. The Vigil often begins with the church plunged into total darkness, the congregation listening to solemn, sometimes mournful music. Suddenly the rear doors are flung open, and the celebrant (the bishop, at a cathedral) enters, bearing the lit Paschal candle, and singing "Christ, our Light, the light of the world." The candles of those next to the aisle are lit from the Paschal candle, and the light is passed from one candle to the next, until the church is filled with light. It is on this night that new adult converts are received into the Church, baptized, and receive their first communion.

Easter ends the forty-day fast of the Lenten season, which explains the fare of the feast after church on Easter Sunday.

Many traditions have grown up around the celebration of Easter. One of these is the Easter egg. Long a symbol of new life, resurrection, and immortality in much of Europe, the egg was easily adopted by Christians as a part of the Easter iconography. The origin of coloring eggs is unclear because the practice is present in many traditions.

Another Easter tradition is the Easter Bunny. Each year, the Easter Bunny visits the homes of children, bringing colored eggs, candy, and gifts. The first record of a rabbit being associated with Easter dates to sixteenth-century Germany, although the custom may be even older. It is possible that both the Easter egg and Easter Bunny may have come from the ancient Teutonic goddess of spring and fertility, Eostre, from whom the English holiday derives its name. Another possibility is that the ancient Germanic goddess Ostara who was always accompanied by a hare inspired the tradition of the Easter Bunny.

Eddy, Mary Baker
See **Birthday of Mary Baker Eddy**

Ekadashi
Eleventh day of each waxing and waning moon

Ekadashi is the Hindi word for "eleventh." In all, 24 Ekadashi (eleventh-day) fasts are observed during the course of a year, but some are of relatively greater importance. Each Ekadashi is held in honor of a different Hindu legend and has specific religious duties associated with it.

On all Ekadashi, however, rice eating is prohibited because a demon is said to dwell in rice grains on this day.

According to Hindu legend, a demon was born of the sweat that fell from Brahma's head on this day. Brahma sent it to inhabit the rice grains eaten by people on Ekadashi and to become worms in their stomach.

See also **Amalaka Ekadashi, Devathani Ekadashi, Hari-Shayani Ekadashi, Kamada Ekadashi, Nirjala Ekadashi, Putrada Ekadashi, Putrada Ekadashi,** and **Vaikuntha Ekadashi.**

Ember Days
Four times a year

These solemn observations occur at the beginning of each of the natural seasons. Traditionally marked by three days of fasting, Ember Days are the Wednesday, Friday, and Saturday following the first Sunday in Lent, Whitsunday, Holyrood Day (September 14) and St. Lucy's Day (December 13). The weeks in which these days occur are called Ember Weeks, and the Friday in each of these weeks is known as Golden Friday.

The word "ember" derives from an old English word referring to the revolution of time. Some historians have suggested that the Ember Days originated with pagan purification rituals that occurred at the seasons of planting, harvest, and vintage. The notion of fasting on these days was instituted by Pope Calixtus I in the third century, but the dates of the fast varied until 1095 when they were fixed at their current times.

In 1969, the Roman Catholic Church replaced these days with days of prayer for various needs. The Anglican Communion dedicates these day to prayer for those in formal ministry and for contemplation of one's own role in lay ministry.

Eostre

Near the vernal equinox, at or about March 22

Eostre is the spring-equinox holiday, a Lesser Sabbat of the Neo-pagans. The Lesser Sabbats comprise the English quarter days, that is, the solstices and equinoxes. With the four Greater Sabbats, which comprise the Celtic cross-quarter days, the Lesser Sabbats make up the eight Sabbats of the "Wheel of the Year." The other Lesser Sabbats are Litha (summer solstice, about June 22), Mabon (fall equinox, about September 22), and Yule (winter solstice, about December 22).

Epiphany

January 6; Sunday between January 2 and January 8 in the Roman Catholic Church in the United States

A church festival observed by observed by Roman Catholic, Anglican, Lutheran, and Eastern Orthodox Churches on January 6 or, by Roman Catholics in the United States, on the Sunday between January 2 and 8. This feast, commemorates the manifestations of the divinity of Christ. It is one of the oldest Christian feasts, originating in the Eastern Church in the second century and antedating the Western feast of Christmas. Originally it commemorated the manifestations of Christ's divinity in his birth, in the homage of the Magi, and at his baptism by John the Baptist. Later, the first two of these commemorations were transferred to Christmas when the Eastern Church adopted that feast between 380 and 430. The central feature of the Eastern observance now is the manifestation or declaration of Christ's divinity in his baptism and at the beginning of his public life. The Epiphany was adopted by the Western Church during the same period in which the Eastern Church accepted Christmas. In the Roman Catholic service, commemoration is made in the Mass of the homage of the Magi, or astrologers, from the East, and of Jesus's first public "miracle" or "sign," the changing of water into wine at the wedding in Cana.

In the Orthodox Church, Epiphany is also associated with the Blessing of the Waters. On this day, in honor of the baptism of Christ, the baptismal water in each church is blessed and small bottles of holy water are distributed to the congregation. In the United States, a service is often held at the banks of a local stream or river which the priest blesses. All around the world, the tradition of diving into the river to retrieve crosses thrown there by the priest has been practiced for centuries. It is believed that those retrieving the crosses will be especially blessed.

It is also called the Feast of Kings, Twelfth Day, Twelfthtide, Three Kings' Day, or Day of the Three Wise Men.

See also **Old Christmas Day.**

Epiphany Eve

January 5; the Saturday between January 1 and January 7 in the Roman Catholic Church in the U.S.

Also known as Twelfth Night or Old Christmas Eve. One myth associated with this day is that of the Glastonbury Thorn. According to the Grail cycle of Arthurian legend, there is a blackthorn tree in Glastonbury, England, that grew from the staff of Joseph of Arimathea (the man who owned the burial site of Jesus). Each year on January 5, the Glastonbury Thorn is said to bloom.

This legend gave rise to an annual pilgrimage to Glastonbury and lent an illusion of credence to England's claim as the cradle of Christianity. King Henry II of England used the legends of the Grail cycle to assert the authenticity of England's apostolic succession as independent of Rome.

Esbats

Full or new moon evening of each month; may be held on both evenings according to the custom of each particular coven

The regular meetings of modern Neo-pagan covens. Held on the most convenient evening nearest the full and/or new moon, these meetings are usually open only to initiates, because they are specifically intended to develop members who are in training for the priesthood of the religion.

See also **Sabbats.**

F

Fall Equinox
See **Mabon**

Family Week
Begins on the first Sunday in May

Protestantism, Roman Catholicism, and Judaism all observe National Family Week. Although each faith celebrates this holiday in a manner unique to its own expression, the focal point for all three is the importance of religion in fostering strong familial bonds. Each congregation's members are encouraged to examine the manner in which they contribute to their family's religious life. Group discussions focus on social conditions having adverse effects on family life.

National Family Week begins on the first Sunday in May and ends on Mother's Day. Some Christian families observe the Festival of the Christian Home.

A Family Day is also observed in many nations, but finds particular importance in some African nations. In Angola, the holiday falls on December 25 and in Nambia, December 26. South African families observe Easter Monday as Family Day.

Fasching
Between February 2 and March 8; the three days preceding Ash Wednesday

This Shrovetide festival is celebrated in Austria and Germany (especially in Bavaria) with costumed balls and parades on Fasching Sunday, Rose Monday, and Shrove Tuesday, the three days before Ash Wednesday, but usually preceded by several weeks of parties. It is similar to the Mardi Gras celebrations around the world.

Fast of Gedaliah
The first day following Rosh ha-Shanah

In 586 B.C.E., the Babylonian King Nebuchadnezzar destroyed the Jerusalem and its first Temple. He enslaved most of the city's Hebrew inhabitants, but allowed a number of farmers and their families to remain in Jerusalem under the supervision of a He-brew governor named Gedaliah ben Ahikam. Eventually those people who had fled to the hills during Nebuchadnezzar's attack and thus escaped slavery returned to Jerusalem, joining with the farmers who had been left behind.

Distrustful of Gedaliah, some members of the community accused him of traitorous collaboration and assassinated him, along with the small garrison of soldiers Nebuchadnezzar had stationed there. Subsequently, many of the farmers fled with their families to Egypt; those who remained were either killed or taken to Babylon. These events triggered Judah's final collapse. The Jewish Fast of Gedaliah commemorates the tragic consequences of Gedaliah's assassination.

See also **Jewish Fasts.**

Fast of the First-born
Nisan 14

The Fast of the First-born is the only Jewish fast which is observed for reasons other than atonement for sin or petition. Practiced symbolically by firstborn males on the day before Passover, the fast appears to serve as a reminder of how the firstborn sons of the ancient Hebrews were miraculously spared while the Egyptians lost their firstborn sons to the Angel of Death. The obligation to fast, however, may be avoided by participating in a *síyyum*–the study of a particular passage of the *Talmud*.

Fat Tuesday
See **Lent**

Festa de Serreta
September 8-15

The Festa de Serreta that takes place each fall in Gustine, California, is based on a similar festival held on the island of Terceira in the Azores. Many of Gustine's residents emigrated from there and, since 1932, have held the Festa de Serreta in honor of *Nossa Senhora dos Milagres* (Our Lady of Miracles). The week-long festival attracts thousands of visitors who participate in song contests, processions, and a traditional bullfight in which a bull with padded horns is held on a leash and men take turns in the arena playing rather than fighting with him.

Festival of Goodwill
See **World Invocation Day**

Festival of Lights
See **Dewali**

Festival of the Dead
See **Obon Festival**

Festival of the Giving of the Law
See **Shavuot**

Floating Lantern Ceremony
August 15

A Buddhist ceremony held in Honolulu, Hawaii, the Floating Lantern Ceremony, or Toro Nagashi, commemorates the end of World War II. This festival is part of the annual Buddhist Bon season during which the spirits of dead ancestors are entreated and welcomed back to earth with prayers, dances, offerings, and the ceremony of setting afloat several thousand colorful paper lanterns bearing the names of the dead.

Footwashing Day
Sunday in early summer

The practice of footwashing as a Christian observance has its origins in the account in the *Gospel of John* of Jesus washing the feet of his disciples before the Last Supper. Through his actions, Jesus entreated his disciples to show a similar love and humility to one another.

In some modern churches, footwashing has become a significant feature of the Eucharist. Congregations in the mountainous regions of Kentucky are particularly noted for this practice. Footwashing Day takes place only once a year, but is preceded by several weeks of preparation. When the day arrives, an elaborate ritual is practiced in which men and women are segregated and wash the feet of the members of the same sex. Children enjoy refreshments during the ceremony and, at its conclusion, all are invited to partake of a traditional meal.

Although originally performed during the Maundy Thursday services, many American Protestant de-

nominations practice the footwashing ceremony more frequently.

Founding of the Church of Jesus Christ of the Latter Day Saints
April 6

On April 6, 1830, Joseph Smith and the first five followers he had converted organized the Church of Jesus Christ of the Latter Day Saints under New York state law. This date is celebrated annually by the six million members of the Church of Jesus Christ of the Latter Day Saints, by the Reorganized Church of Jesus Christ of the Latter Day Saints, and by the many small offshoot Mormon sects.

Fox, George
See **Death of George Fox**

Freedom Day
December 30

Celebrated by all Churches of Scientology in the United States (and some other countries) on December 30 to commemorate the Federal court decision in 1974 that gave official recognition to the Church of Scientology as a religion.

Full Moon of the Buddha
See **Buddha Purnima**

G

Gabriel
See **Michaelmas**

Ganesha Chaturthi
Fourth day of the waxing half of the Hindu month of Bhadrapada (August-September)

Ganesha, or Vinayak, Chaturthi is one of the most popular Hindu festivals, celebrated all over India as the birthday of Lord Ganesha, the elephant-headed God, on the fourth day of the waxing half of the month of Bhadrapada (August-September). This lively Hindu festival honors Ganesha, the god of prosperity, especially around Bombay, where a spectacular week-long festival ends with the immersion of Ganesha's sculpted likeness in the waters at Chowpatty Beach to ensure well-being on both land and sea. Clay figures of Lord Ganesha are worshipped during this festival and then immersed in sea, river, pool, or some other water. Ganesha is the God of wisdom, learning, prudence, success, and power. As Vighnesha or remover of obstacles, he is propitiated at the start of every activity, whether it be a journey, marriage, initiation, house construction, writing of a book or even a letter.

Hindus generally believe that he is a great scribe and learned in religious lore and scripture. It was Ganesha who, at the dictation of the seer Vyasa, wrote the *Mahabharata.* He is also the Lord of Ganas, Shiva's hosts. He bears a single tusk; holds in his four hands a shell, a discus, a goad, and a lotus; and is always accompanied by his mount, the rat. Ganesha is a great lover of sweets and fruits.

On Ganesha Chaturthi, the images of Ganesha are worshipped with sweet balls, water, new clothes, incense, flowers, scent, betel leaf, and naivaidyas (food offerings). His mantra is repeated, he is meditated upon and worshipped, and the offerings of food are distributed as charity. Brahmans are fed and given gifts. In Maharashtra this festival is observed with great religious fervor, pomp, and gaiety, and Ganesha statues are taken out in grand processions before immersion in the sea.

Ganga Dussehra

Tenth day of the waxing half of the Hindu month of Jyaishtha (May-June)

On this day the Ganges descended to earth in Hashta Nakhsatra. Literally Dussehra means "that which takes away ten sins". People get up early in the morning and go to the Ganges to bathe in holy waters. When the Ganges is inaccessible, they bathe in some nearby tank, pool, river, or the sea, chanting "Har Har Gange! Har Har Gange!" thus invoking the Ganges and offering her prayers and worship. At places where the Ganges flows, such as Rishikesh, Hardwar, Garh Mukteshwar, Prayag, Varanasi, its banks are overcrowded with worshipers. Many Hindus believe that a bath in the Ganges on this day is of great religious merit and washes away all sins.

The very name of the Ganges is sacred to Hindus. Samples of its waters are kept within sealed pots in Hindu homes where, some believe, the water remains unpolluted even if it is kept for many years. Holy Ganges water thus kept is used on sacred days to sanctify places and is given to a dying person with tulsi leaves (basil) to facilitate the soul's peaceful separation from the body.

Gangaur

Chiatra (March-April); Two weeks after Holi

Gangaur is primarily a Hindu women's festival that culminates two weeks after Holi (see below). It is a great local festival in Rajasthan, but is also celebrated in many parts of northern India. Gangaur is an eighteen-day festival that takes place during the Hindu month of Chiatra and climaxes on the third day of the waxing moon of that month—the last day of the festival. The official celebrations start on the day after Holi with worship and prayers to Gauri, the most fair and benign aspect of the goddess Durga, the consort of Shiva.

Both married women and unmarried girls worship the goddess every day during the festival with durva grass, flowers, fruits, and bright brass pots filled with fresh water. The married women seek Gauri's blessings for conjugal happiness, while the unmarried pray for a suitable handsome husband and future marital prosperity.

The *Ramcharitra Manas* relates the story of Sita coming to the shrine of Girija or Gauri early in the morning, accompanied by her companions and attendants singing glad songs. After bathing Sita approaches the goddess with a cheerful heart and a contemplative mind, and after adoration paid with much devotion, she begs Gauri for a handsome and well-matched bridegroom. And finally her wish is fulfilled when Rama wins her hand in marriage.

On the final day of the Gangaur festival, Hindu women keep a strict fast, worship the goddess, wear colorful clothes and ornaments, and exchange sweets. The wooden or earthen images of Gangaur (also called Parvati) are taken through the main streets and bazaars in procession with decorated elephants, camels, horses, chariots, dancers, and musicians.

Ganjitsu
January 1

This Japanese New Year's Day celebration is also known as the "festival of festivals," and is actually celebrated for several days. Government offices, banks, museums, and most businesses are closed from January 1 through January 3.

In early December, cities prepare for the holiday by decorating the streets with pine and plum branches, bamboo stalks, and ropes festooned with paper. Small pine trees with bamboo stems attached, representing longevity and constancy, are traditionally placed in the home. For weeks before the New Year celebration, people clean house and purchase new clothes for their children, exchange gifts and pay off personal debts.

On New Year's Eve, many people don traditional kimonos and walk through the streets as they visit shrines. The ancient tradition of tolling the great bells in the Buddhist temples at midnight ends the day of celebration. Priests strike the bells 108 times as a reminder of the 108 human frailties or sins in Buddhist belief. At the end of the bell tolling ceremony, the impure desires of the old year have been driven away.

New Year's Day traditions include saying prayers at the household alter and eating specially prepared food. Often the New Year's Day repast includes such specialties as *mochi*—steamed rice pounded into small round cakes—herring roe, black beans, dried chestnuts, porgy, and prawns.

Gedaliah
See **Fast of Gedaliah**

Gita Jayanti
Eleventh day of the waxing half of the Hindu month of Margashirsha (November-December)

Birthday of the Bhagavad Gita. Some texts assert that on this day Lord Krishna taught Arjuna the sacred lore of the *Gita* on the battlefield of Kurukshetra, and thus made available to the whole of human race the

Song Celestial. It forms a part of the famous epic *Mahabharata*.

At the beginning of the great war between the Pandavas and the Kauravas, Arjuna, touched with pity for the possible slaughter and bloodshed of friends and relations, appealed to Krishna for guidance. Krishna had refused to take up arms on either side, but agreed to become Arjuna's charioteer. Krishna urged Arjuna to follow his dharma, or duty, as a soldier and a Kshatriya, forgetting all other considerations. It immediately dispelled all of Arjuna's doubts and gloom, and he engaged himself wholeheartedly in the performance of his dharma.

The *Gita* has been a great source of strength, inspiration, and wisdom to Hindus through the centuries. Many Hindus believe that the *Gita*, as a voice of the Supreme, is not merely scripture, but a great song of universal spiritual uplifting, always to be studied and pondered, for it illumines the path to perfection and purity, which can be followed even while doing one's worldly duties. It urges all to perform actions while remaining united with God at heart. On Gita Jayanti, the *Gita* is read and recited, and discourses are held on its various philosophical aspects. People fast, worship Krishna and the *Gita*, and resolve to study and imbibe the spirit of the *Gita* with far greater efforts.

Good Friday
Between March 21 and April 23; the Friday before Easter

The Friday before Easter is a major observance for all Christians; for Roman Catholics it is a privileged feast of Holy Week. Liturgical elements of the Roman Catholic ritual observance commemorate the Passion and Death of Christ by a reading of the Passion (according to the Gospel of John), special prayers for the Church and people of all ranks, the veneration of the Cross, and a communion service. The Solemn Liturgical Action takes place between noon and 3 p.m. This is the only day in the year on which the Eucharistic Liturgy is not celebrated in the Roman Rite.

Although Protestant denominations allowed observance of this day to wane, a recent emphasis on the holy day has brought back its nearly universal acceptance. Between noon and three p.m., many churches hold special services called "Tre Ore" from the Italian for "Three Hours." During the service, the seven last words of Christ are meditated upon, and Jesus' procession to the cross may be acted out.

Govardhan Puja and Annakut
First day of the waxing fortnight of the Hindu month of Kartika (October-November)

Govardhan Puja is celebrated on the day following Dewali (in northern India). Annakut is also observed on the same day. This day is associated with an event of Krishna's life where he lifted the Govardhan Mountain (in Vrindavana) on his little finger for seven days to protect the cows and people of Vrindavana against the deluge of rain sent by the enraged Indra, god of the heavens and rains. People by the thousands from all over India visit, worship, and circumambulate Mount Govardhan on this day. Those who cannot come to Vrindavana worship at home with great devotion and give gifts to Brahmans. Cows and bulls are also decorated and worshipped on this day.

See also **Dewali.**

Guardian Angels
October 2

A feast observed by Roman Catholic churches, classed as a memorial. Commemorates the angels who protect people from spiritual and physical dangers and assist them in doing good. A feast in their honor celebrated in sixteenth-century Spain was extended to the whole Church by Pope Paul V in 1608. In 1670, Pope Clement X set October 2 as the date of observance. Earlier, guardian angels were honored liturgically in conjunction with the feast of St. Michael.

See also **Michaelmas.**

Gudi Parva
First day of the month of Chaitra (March-April)

Gudi Parva, or Padva, marks the beginning of the Hindu New Year, and is mainly celebrated in Maharashtra on Chaitra Pratipada. People arise early in the morning, tidy up their houses, have baths, and wear festive and new clothes. Women decorate their houses, a silk banner is raised and worshipped, and then greetings and sweets are exchanged.

Gule of August
See **Lammas**

Guru Govind Singh, Birthday of
See **Guru Parab**

Guru Nanak's Day
See **Guru Parab**

Guru Parab
Full-moon day of the Hindu month of Kartika (October-November)

The festival celebrates the birth of Guru Nanak, the founder-guru of Sikh Dharma (Sikhism), and is also known as Guru Nanak's Day. Hindus honor God in the form of Matsya Avatar on this day which they call Kartika Purnima. Guru Nanak was born in 1469 at Talwandi (about 45 km away from Lahore), now known as Nankana Sahib. At Nankana Sahib there is a beautiful shrine and a holy tank. On Guru Parab, a grand fair and festival is held there, and Sikhs by the thousands congregate from India and abroad to honor Nanak.

Nanak was a great reformer, preacher, and saint. In Sikhism he tried to harmonize Hinduism and Islam. He never believed in caste distinctions and liberalized social practices. He preached the name of God as a potent means of spiritual realization. Many of Nanak's hymns, which form part of the Guru Granth Sahib, clearly reflect the supremacy of God's sight and his love.

Nanak travelled widely in India and abroad, and his life and teachings serve as a great source of inspiration. He was followed by nine other Gurus, in succession, under whom Sikhism gradually developed. On Guru Parab, the holy scripture Guru Granth Sahib is continuously read and recited in the shrines, processions are taken out, free meals are arranged, and food is distributed. The festival is observed with great enthusiasm all over India.

Similarly, other Gurus are also commemorated on other Guru Parabs. For example, the second Guru Parab, commemorating Guru Govind Singh, is celebrated in the month of Pausha (December-January).

See also **Kartika Purnima.**

Guru Purnima
Full-moon day of the Hindu month of Ashadha (June-July)

Recognized throughout India as Guru Vyas Purnima or Ashadha Purnima (full moon), this day is set apart for the veneration and worship of the Guru. In ancient days the students used to get their education in Ashrams and Gurukuls. The students would worship their teachers on this day, pay their fee, and give them presents according to their means and capacity. Devotees and disciples fast on this day and worship their gurus to seek their blessings.

It is also known as Vyasa Purnima because Rishi Vyasa was a great guru. Vyasa or Veda-Vyasa, the son of Rishi Parashar and Satyavati, is also known as Krishna Dwaipayna, because he was dark complexioned and was born on an island or dwipa. He is said to have compiled the four Vedas, the *Mahabharata*, and the 18 Puranas.

Guru Vyas Purnima
See **Guru Purnima**

Hajj
Begins on the first day of Shawwal and ends on the tenth day of Dhu al-Hijjah in the Islamic calendar

The Muslim season of pilgrimage to Mecca, which is one of the five great pillars of Islam. The end of the pilgrimage season is signaled by the festival of Al-'id al-Kabir.

See also **Al-'id al-Kabir**.

Hala Shashti
Sixth day of the waning half of the Hindu month of Bhadra (August-September)

Hala Shashti is also known as Balarama Shashti. Balarama, the elder brother of Krishna, was born on this day. The Hindu scriptures say that Vishnu took two hairs, one white and one black, and these became Balarama and Krishna, the sons of Devaki. As soon as Balarama was born, he was carried away to Gokula to preserve his life from the tyrant Kansa, and he was brought up as a child of Rohini. He and Krishna grew up together and took part in many adventures which included killing many demons. He was a preceptor both of Bhima and Duryodhana. He had refused to side either with the Pandavas or the Kauravas. Balarama died as he sat under a banyan tree near Dwaraka just before the death of Krishna.

Balaram's weapon was a plough, so this day is called Hala (plough) Shashti. On this day, Hindu women fast to ensure happiness, prosperity, and longevity to their sons, and only buffalo milk and curds are eaten. The plough is also worshipped on this day. This fast, primarily a rural affair, is observed with much enthusiasm in northern India.

After morning baths, a small piece of ground is sanctified and plastered with cow dung, and a tiny water pool is dug in it and then branches of ber (jujube plum), gular (a kind of fig tree), and palash (Butea Frondosa) are planted therein and worshipped. Unmarried girls observe the Chandra Shashti on this day, and their fast is terminated by the rising of the moon.

Hallowe'en
October 31

All Hallows' Eve, or the evening before All Saints' Day, is one of the most popular holidays in the United States because of the custom of "trick-or-treating," in which costumed children go from house to house begging for treats. The tricks and practical jokes once associated with this date are no longer a part of the tradition.

This holiday is a relic of the Celtic festival of Samhain, or New Year. The children dressed as ghosts, witches, and monsters reflect the spirits of dead ancestors, fairies, and other supernatural beings whom the Celts once believed could slip into this world through the seam in time on this day.

Hamishah Assar Bi'Shevat
See **Bi-Shevat**

Hanukkah
Eight day festival beginning on Kislev 25

Hanukkah is the Jewish festival of lights, celebrated for eight days, starting on the twenty-fifth day of the month Kislev. It is said to commemorate the Maccabean recapture and rededication of the temple in Jerusalem in 165 B.C.E.

The best-known custom associated with Hanukkah is the lighting of the eight-candle menorah, one additional candle being lit on each day of the festival, until all are lit on the last day. This is said to commemorate the miraculous burning of an oil lamp in the temple for eight days at the time of its recapture.

Many Jewish families today have adopted the practice of gift-giving at this time of year. It is supposed that this is a crossover from the Christmas celebrations of Christians. Some families also have decorated Hanukkah bushes in their homes and choose to celebrate the holiday on December 25. Other families celebrate Hanukkah on its traditional dates and sometimes observe a custom of presenting gifts to each family member on each of the eight days of Hanukkah.

Hanuman Jayanti
Full-moon day of the Hindu month of Chaitra (March-April)

The monkey-god Hanuman is worshipped everywhere in India, either singularly or together with Lord Rama. Hanuman temples dot the entire length and breadth of India and every temple dedicated to Rama also has a statue of Hanuman. Other temples also have Hanuman statues.

The birth anniversary of Hanuman, the son of the wind god Marut and Anjana Devi, is celebrated in India with great religious fervor. People visit Hanuman's shrines, fast, offer prayers and puja (worship), and read the *Ramayana* and the Hanuman *Chalisa*. On this occasion the statue of Hanuman is given a new coat of vermillion mixed with clarified butter and then richly decorated. Fairs are sometimes held at some places near the shrines.

On Hanuman Jayanti, Vaishnavites observe a strict fast, meditate on him and his lord Rama, practice charity, read the Hanuman *Chalisa*, and spend the day in repeating his glories and adventures.

Hanuman is regarded by Vaishnavites as one of the greatest embodiments of strength, speed and agility, learning, and selfless service to Lord Rama. He could fly at the speed of wind, uproot mountains and trees, assume any size and shape at will, and make himself invisible. In battle he was a terrifying figure as colossal as a mountain, as tall as a tower, and ever invincible. His face is red like a ruby, his yellow skin and coat shine like molten gold, and his mighty tail is of immense length. He shattered the enemies on the battlefield with his fierce roar and was granted immortality by Rama so that he could serve devotees in distress. His great adventures have been described in great detail and with much reverence and delight in the *Ramayana*.

Hari-Shayani Ekadashi
Eleventh day of the waxing fortnight of Kartika (October-November)

Hari-Shayani Ekadashi is the day when Lord Hari (Vishnu) retires to sleep on the bed of Shesha Nag in the Kshirsagar. According to a popular Hindu religious belief, Hari slumbers during the four months of the rainy season, which begins on the 11th of the waxing fortnight of Kartika (October-November). The rainy season is known as "Chaturmas," and during this period such activities as marriage and the thread ceremony are prohibited, and the sages, rishis, and munis confine their meditation to indoors.

Hari Tritiya
See **Hariyali Teej**

Haritalika Teej
Third day of the waxing half of the Hindu month of Bhadrapada (August-September)

Observed by Hindu women, the Haritalika fast (vow) honors the goddess Parvati and her consort Shiva, and their statues are worshiped ritually. Parvati, the daughter of Himalaya and Mina, desirous of having Shankara (Shiva) as her husband, performed extraordinary feats of magic and thereby married him. From that day onward married women have worshiped the divine couple, keeping a strict fast to ensure their conjugal happiness and prosperity. Unmarried girls fast to gain suitable husbands of their choice. Brahmans receive charity, unmarried girls are fed, and aspirant women tell the story of Haritalika among themselves and break their fast in the evening. The next morning the sun is worshipped and offered water.

Hariyali Teej
Third day of the waxing half of the Hindu month of Shravana (July-August)

Primarily a women's festival, Hariyali Teej is also known as Hari Tritiya. On this day women of all ages make merry, and daughters and daughters-in-law are given gifts. Swings are hung in the houses and gardens, and the women enjoy them throughout the day. The preparation of sweets is also a highlight in each home. Hariyali Teej is celebrated on a large scale in Uttar Pradesh and especially in Braj Mandal.

Hemis Festival
Usually in June or July

This three day Buddhist festival occurs at the Hemis Gompa (monastery) in the mountainous northern Indian state of Ladakh. The festival celebrates the birthday of Guru Padmasambhava, the Indian Buddhist mystic who introduced Tantric Buddhism to Tibet in the eighth century. Tradition says he was a native of Swat (now in Pakistan), an area noted for magicians.

The ceremonial aspects of the day include dancers in elaborate robes and heavy masks swirling to the music of symbols, drums, and pipes as they enact the battle between good and evil spirits. Fairs are set up around the monastery where local artisans sell their crafts.

Hill Cumorah Pageant
July

The Hill Cumorah Pageant revolves around a Mormon play performed in July at Cumorah Hill, near Palmyra, New York. The work recounts Joseph Smith's finding of the book engraved on golden plates that, Mormons believe, he translated as the *Book of Mormon.*

The Pageant takes place over a nine day period (excluding Sunday and Monday) beginning on the third weekend in July. The event involves as many as five hundred participants, attracts thousands of spectators, and is billed as the largest outdoor pageant in the United States.

Holi
Fourteenth day of the waxing half of Phalguna (February-March)

A Hindu festival celebrating the burning of Holika, an evil sorceress who once tormented all of India. Holi is one of the four most popular festivals of India, observed by all Hindus without any distinction of caste, creed, status, or sex. It marks the end of winter and the advent of the spring season. This two-day festival is most notable for the freedom and loss of inhibition practiced by the people of India.

On the first night of the festival, a bonfire is constructed in the evening. Before the fire is lit, a worship ceremony is performed in which water and grains are offered, then people dance around the fire. Throughout the evening, images of Holika are burned in the fire, drums are pounded, horns are blown, and people shout.

The next day many people interact by splashing colored water and throwing colored powder on their friends, relatives, neighbors, and even passersby. Noisy and colorful processions are taken out through the bazaars and streets. Other people celebrate the day with songs, music, floral decoration, and splashing of perfumed water. Sweets and visits are exchanged, and cold drinks prepared at home are served liberally. People forget all enmity and embrace each other, with warmth and love, and renew their friendship. New corn is baked and eaten on this day for the first time in the season.

There are several myths about the origin of the festival of Holi. According to one Puranic myth, an evil king, Hiranyakasipu, had a good son, Prahlad, who was sent by the gods to deliver the people from the oppressive rule of the king. This angered the king so greatly that he ordered the death of the child. The sister of the king was an evil witch named Holika, who claimed to be impervious to fire. So to kill Prahlad, Holika snatched the child and jumped into a great bonfire. Prahlad, however, was rescued from the flames by Lord Krishna and it was Holika who was destroyed. The burning of Holi commemorates this event. It symbolizes the triumph of good over evil.

Holocaust
See **Yom Ha-Shoah**

Holy Family, Feast of the
Sunday after Epiphany

The Roman Catholic Church commemorates the Holy family of Jesus, the Virgin Mary, and St. Joseph on this day each year. As the model of the perfect family, they represent perfect holiness and virtue.

The devotional background of the feast was very strong in the 17th century. In 1921, Pope Benedict XV extended the Divine Office and Mass of the feast to the whole Church.

Holy Innocents' Day
December 28

Also called Innocents' Day or Childermas, this day is dedicated to the memory of the male children in Bethlehem who were slaughtered by King Herod in his attempt to kill the infant Jesus. The day has come to be considered unlucky; therefore, among those who observe it, few marriages or important ventures are consummated on that day.

Holy Saturday
See **Easter**

Holy Thursday
See **Easter**

Homstrom
Usually the first Sunday of February

A Swiss festival celebrating the end of winter, usually by burning a straw man symbolizing Old Man Winter; occasionally observed by Swiss-American communities on the first Sunday in February. Reminiscent of the February 1 Celtic mid-winter festival of Brigid.

Hubbard, L. Ron
See **Birthday of L. Ron Hubbard**

Hungry Ghosts, Feast of the
Fifteenth day of the seventh or eighth lunar month (varies according to local tradition)

On this night, many Asian cultures believe that their ancestors return to visit their gravesites and descendants. To welcome the ghosts, people offer gifts at tombs, burn incense, and light fireworks.

Hussein Day
See **Ashura**

I

'Id al-Adha
Days 10-12 during month of Dhu al-Hijjah, the twelfth Islamic month

This three-day festival commemorates Abraham's obedience to God in nearly sacrificing his son Ishmael. Muslims maintain that it was Ishmael, not Isaac, who was the son of promise and thus it was Ishmael who was nearly sacrificed but saved by God at the last moment. Ishmael is believed to be the ancestor of all Arabs. In India and Pakistan the festival is also known as Bakrid.

To commemorate the miraculous provision of a sacrifice in Ishmael's place, goats and rams are offered to Allah at this time. The sacrifice of a ram or goat also symbolizes that man's position in the creation is far more high than any beast, and any sacrifice, however great, is a small thing for the sake of Allah.

In India and Pakistan, Bakrid is observed by Muslims who go to the mosques in the morning to offer prayers to Allah, and then return home to sacrifice the animal at home. The cooked meat becomes part of the family meal which ensues. The holiday is traditionally a time of peace, charity, and goodwill. As part of this, many people reach out to the poor, needy, and sick with money and gifts. Hindus also participate in the tradition and offer their good wishes to their Muslim friends.

'Id al-Fitr
First day of the month of Shawwal

This three-day festival, also known as "Breaking of the Fast," marks the end of the month-long fast of Ramadan.

'Id al-Fitr is a festival of great cheer, rejoicing and festivity. Throughout India it is observed with great enthusiasm, fervor, and preparation. On this day Muslims wear their new or best clothes and shoes, and offer mass prayers in mosques. After prayers there is a religious lecture from an Imam, and then they greet and embrace one another warmly. Hindus also greet and embrace their Muslim friends in a fraternal spirit.

In India and Pakistan the whole day of Id is spent in festivities and exchange of sweets, good wishes, and visits. Sewayyan, a sweet dish, is specially prepared on this occasion and distributed among friends, neighbors, and relatives. In the spirit of benevolence that characterizes the celebration, the poor and needy are given food, money, clothes.

Muslim women also celebrate it with great zest and enthusiasm. They wear their finest clothing and jewelry, and apply henna to their feet and hands. The traditional Muslim greeting on this day is "Id mubarak!"

Imam 'Ali
See **Death of Imam 'Ali**

Imbolg
See **Brigid**

Immaculate Conception of Mary, Feast of the
December 8

This Roman Catholic observance on December 8 is holy day of obligation on which church attendance required, and is classed as a solemnity. It celebrates the belief that Mary, in view of her calling to be the Mother of Christ and in virtue of his merits, was preserved from the first moment of her conception from original sin and was filled with grace from the very beginning of her life. She was the only person, aside from Jesus, believed to be so preserved from original sin. The present form of the feast dates from December 8, 1854, when Pope Pius IX defined the dogma of the Immaculate Conception. An earlier feast of the Conception, which testified to long-existing belief in this truth, was observed in the East by the eighth century, in Ireland in the ninth, and subsequently in European countries. In 1846, Mary was proclaimed patroness of the United States under this title.

Immaculate Heart of Mary, Feast of the
Saturday following the second Sunday after Pentecost

This Roman Catholic memorial is observed as a day to honor Mary and obtain her intercession for "peace among the nations, freedom for the Church, the conversion of sinners, the love of purity, and the practice of virtue," according to Pope Pius XII's 1944 decree. Two years earlier, he consecrated the entire human race to Mary under this title. Devotion to Mary under the title of her Most Pure Heart originated during the Middle Ages, but was given great impetus in the 17th century by the preaching of St. John Eudes. A feast, celebrated in various places and on different dates, was authorized in 1799.

Ingathering, Feast of the
See **Sukkot**

Innocents' Day
See **Holy Innocents' Day**

J

Jamshed Navaroz
Month of March

Jamshed Navaroz is the Parsi or Zoroastrian New Year festival, and is also known as Patati or the Day of Repentance. Adherents visit their fire temples and offer prayers and sandalwood, begging pardon for any misdeeds committed knowingly or unknowingly.

On this festive day they exchange greetings, good wishes, visits, and presents. This is also a day of charity, so Zoroastrians give food, money, and clothes to the sick, needy, and poor.

The Parsi New Year festival dates to the reign of Emperor Jamshed in Persia, where their ancestors lived. But later on they fled to India to escape the religious persecution by Muslims. They took shelter in India with their fire of Ahura-Mazda. Although in India, where they live under a covenant not to proselytize and their numbers are dying out, Parsis are expanding rapidly in the United States where they are free to attract converts.

Janaki Navami
Ninth day of the waxing half of the Hindu month of Vaisakha (April-May)

Sita, which means "furrow", is supposed to have sprung on this day from a furrow plowed by King Janaka in a field. Janaka took her up and raised her as his own child. She is also called A-Yonija, "not born from the womb." She was actually the goddess Lakshmi in human form, incarnated in the world to bring about the destruction of Ravana and other demons. Many Hindus believe that she reflects the idealized Indian woman as an embodiment of self-sacrifice, purity, tenderness, fidelity, conjugal affection, and other virtues. Some believe that Sita appeared in the field of Janaka on the eighth day of the waning half of Phalguna (February-March), and fast on that day.

Janamashtami
Eighth day of the waning half of the Hindu month of Bhadrapada (August-September)

Si Krishna, the eighth avatar, or incarnation, of Vishnu, was born on this day, which is known as Janamashtami or Krishna-Janamashtami. This birthday of Krishna, the direct manifestation of Vishnu himself, is celebrated in all parts of India with great enthusiasm. In the *Bhagavad Gita* Krishna declared: "All this Universe has been created by me; all things exist in me." Arjuna addresses him as "the supreme universal spirit, the supreme dwelling, the eternal person, divine prior to the gods, unborn, omnipresent." His life is celebrated in great detail in the Puranas.

The Janamashtami celebrations start with the early morning bath in sacred waters and prayers. The climax occurs at midnight with the rising of the moon, which signifies Krishna's divine birth. On this day, a strict fast is kept and broken only after the birth of Krishna at midnight. The temples and homes are decorated, and scenes depicting Krishna's birth and his childhood pranks are staged with both animate and inanimate models. The Krishna child's image is put into a richly decorated swing and rocked with tender care all day. At night, after the birth, a small image of toddling Krishna is bathed in the Charnamrita, amidst the chanting of hymns, blaring of the conches, ringing of bells, and joyous shouting of "Victory to Krishna!"

In Braja Mandala, especially in Gokula and Mathura, this festival is celebrated with great religious fervor and enthusiasm, and the special deliberations of the day are broadcast over the airwaves. People from distant places congregate in Mathura and Vrindavana on this day to participate in the festival. The piety and fast observed on this day is to ensure the birth of many good sons, and salvation after death.

Jesus
See **Baptism of the Lord, Feast of the**
See **Christ the King, Feast of**
See **Christmas**
See **Easter**
See **Most Precious Blood, Feast of the**
See **Presentation of Jesus**
See **Sacred Heart of Jesus**
See **Transfiguration of Jesus**
See **Triumph of the Holy Cross**

Jewish Fasts
There are four traditional days of fasting in the Jewish calendar, all associated with the destructions of Jerusalem.

The fast on the tenth day of the month Tebet remembers the beginning of the siege of Jerusalem by the Army of Nebuchadnezzar. On the 17th day of the month Tammuz, a fast recalls the first breach of Jerusalem's walls. The ninth day of the month Av marks the date on which both the First and the Second Temples were destroyed, in 586 B.C.E. and

69 C.E. This fast also commemorates the fall of Judaea to the Romans after the Bar Kochba rebellion, in 135 C.E. The fast on the third day of the month Tishri honors the assassination of Gedaliah, Nebuchadnezzar's viceroy in Jerusalem, and so is known as the Fast of Gedaliah.

Some scholars have suggested that these feasts are also a combination of Hebrew and pagan tradition. For example, there may have once been a feast of the god Tammuz on the 17th day of his month observed by the Hebrews prior to the advent of monotheism in the culture. The translation of this feast into a fast might have been a way to adjust the tradition to a new belief. Currently, the fasts are only observed by conservative Jews, as part of the synagogue liturgy.

See also **Fast of Gedaliah.**

Jhulan Latra
Full moon of the Hindu month of Shravana (July-August)

In Orissa, a festival of Lord Jagannath is celebrated. In a lavishly decorated swing, Lord Jagannath is asked to relax to the accompaniment of music and dance. The celebration is particularly observed in the Jagannath temple at Puri and other shrines for a week preceding the Shravana Purnima (full moon). The full-moon day of the month marks the festival's culmination.

Jyaistha Ashtami
Eighth day of waxing half of the Hindu month of Jyaishtha (May-June)

Jyaistha Ashtami is celebrated at Khir Bhawani in Kashmir as a festival of the goddess Khir Bhawani. To celebrate this goddess's birthday festival, people from the adjoining hill areas assemble at the shrine, offer prayers and worship at the foot of the goddess, and sing hymns and songs in praise of Bhawani. Khir (rice boiled in milk) is prepared on this day as a food offering. Khir Bhawani is the personal goddess of Kashmiri Hindus, hundreds of which visit the shrine daily. This beautiful marble shrine stands amidst a pool formed by spring waters, which change color from rosy red, turquoise green, lemon pale, sky blue, milky white, or pure white on occasion. It is 25 kilometers from Srinagar, and 5 kilometers from Ganderbal.

K

Kalpa Vruksha
Hindu New Year

Hindu village New Year celebration at which children receive gifts around a tree just beginning to show its leaves. New trees are also planted.

Kamada Ekadashi
Waning half of the Hindu month of Shravana

The Kamada Ekadashi is observed in a similar manner as Putrada Ekadashi. Kamada Ekadashi is known as the wish-fulfilling Ekadashi.

See also **Putrada Ekadashi**.

Kartika Purnima
Full moon in the Hindu month of Kartika (October-November)

Hindus celebrate Kartika Purnima as a day when God incarnated himself as the Matsya Avatar in Fish form. The aim of the Fish incarnation was to save Vavaswata, the seventh Manu and the progenitor of the human race, from destruction by a deluge. Charities done and piety observed on this day are believed to earn high religious merit. Bathing in the Ganges, or in other holy water, is considered of special religious significance. People fast, practice charities, and meditate on the gods.

It is also believed that Shankara killed the demon Tripurasura on this day, for which he is also called Tripurari. Shiva is worshipped on this occasion and giving a bull (Shiva's mount), as a gift to a Brahman is thought to be of great religious significance. Big cattle fairs are also held on this day at various places.

Sikhs also have a holiday on Kartika Purnima, but it is called Guru Parab and celebrates the birthday of the founder of Sikhism, Guru Nanak.

See also **Guru Parab**.

Kartika Snan
Hindu month of Kartika (October-November)

Among the 12 months of the year, some are regarded as especially holy and sacred, and as such they are most suitable for acts of piety. These are Vaisakha (April-May), Kartika (October-November), and Magha (January-February).

Throughout the month of Kartika, the early morning bath in a sacred river, stream, pond, or at a well is considered highly meritorious. On the sacred rivers like the Ganges and Yamuna, a month-long bathing festival is held. Some people set up their tents on their banks for this purpose, and at the termination of the festival return to their distant homes. During the month, aspirants observe strict continence, have regular early morning baths in the sacred streams, take a single simple meal every day, and spend their time in prayer, meditation, and other acts of piety and devotion.

Hindu women in villages and towns get up early in the morning and visit the sacred streams in groups, singing hymns, and after their baths visit the nearby temples. They fast and hang lamps in small baskets from the bamboo tops at their homes or on the river banks. These sky lamps are kept burning through Kartika to light the path of departed souls across the sky.

The Tulsi plant is sacred and cultivated specially in homes and temples. It is considered the wife of Vishnu and shown according respect. It is offered daily puja (worship) by Hindu women in the evening with lamps. Tulsi leaf is put in the mouth of a dying person along with Ganges water to facilitate an easy departure. Hindus believe that watering, cultivating, and worship of the Tulsi plant ensures happiness. When its leaves are put into any water, it becomes as holy as Ganges water. Tulsi leaves offered to Vishnu in Kartika (October-November) are said to please him more than the gift of a thousand cows.

Since Tulsi is Vishnupriya (beloved of Vishnu), their marriage is celebrated on the 11th day of the waxing half of the month of Kartika (October-November).

On this day the image of Vishnu is richly decorated and then carried to the place where the Tulsi plant is grown, and the marriage ritually solemnized. Fasting is also observed on this day.

Karwa Chauth
Fourth day of the waning half of the Hindu month of Kartika (October-November)

Karwa Chauth is observed by married Hindu women in order to ensure prosperity, sound health, and their husband's longevity. The married women keep a strict fast and do not take even a drop of water. They get up early in the morning, perform their baths, and wear new and festive clothes.

Shiva, Parvati, and their son Kartikeya are worshipped on this day along with ten Karwas (the small earthen pots with spouts) filled with sweets. The Karwas are given to daughters and sisters along with gifts. At night, when the moon appears, the women break their fast after offering water to the moon. The story of Karwa Chauth is told and heard among the women. Sometimes a Brahman priest tells this story and receives gifts in return. Married women receive costly gifts from their husbands, brothers, and parents on this occasion. They touch the feet of their mother-in-law and other elderly women of the family and seek their blessings.

King, Martin Luther, Jr.,
See **Birthday of Martin Luther King, Jr.**

Kojagara
Full moon in the Hindu month of Ashvina (September-October)

The word "Kojagara" is a combination of two terms, "Kah" and "jagara", which means "who is awake?" It is an exclamation of the goddess Lakshmi, who descends to the earth this night, and blesses with wealth and prosperity all those who are awake. Hence, the night is spent in festivity and various games of amusement to honor the goddess. It is a harvest festival and is celebrated throughout India. Lakshmi is worshipped and night vigil is observed. According to a folk-tale, a king once fell on evil days and was in dire financial straits, but his queen observed the fast and night vigil to worship Lakshmi, the goddess of wealth. Consequently, they were blessed by the goddess and their prosperity renewed.

Krishna, Birthday of
See **Janamashtami**

Kwanza
December 26-January 2

A seven-day festival celebrated by African-Americans, beginning on December 26. Based on a composite of African Harvest Festivals, Kwanza is offered as an expression of African religious heritage.

L

Lady Day
See **Annunciation of the Lord, Feast of the**

Laetare Sunday
See **Mothering Sunday**

Lailat al Miraj
Twenty-seventh day of the month of Rajab

Muslim commemoration of Muhammad's ascension into heaven to receive instructions from Allah regarding the five daily prayers observed by all Muslims. The holiday is also called the Night Journey or the Ascension of the Prophet.

Lammas
August 1

One of the four great pagan festivals of Britain, Lammas is the precursor of Thanksgiving in America

and Canada's Harvest Festival. Originally celebrated as the Gule of August, the festival came into the Christian realm by way of the blessing of loaves of bread made with the first grain of the season. Lammas is a shortened form of "loaf mass."

Lammas is important to the Neo-pagan calendar and is the source of the Neo-pagan tradition of "handfast marriages" or "craft marriages" in which either party can end the arrangement without any social stigma after one year.

Lantern Festival
Fifteenth day of the first month in the Chinese lunar calendar

The lantern festival, which originally may have been a celebration of spring's return, makes the culmination of the festivities attending the Chinese New Year. The presence of the lanterns is attributed to the traditional belief that, with the aid of light, the celebrants could better view heavenly spirits traversing the first full moon of the new year. Regional variations exist with respect to the lantern's use during the festival. In northern China, the lanterns are hung and remain stationary outside doorways, whereas in the south, the lanterns are mounted on poles and carried in processions.

Las Posadas
December 16-25

This feast of "The Lodgings" is celebrated in Hispanic communities to commemorate the journey of St. Mary and St. Joseph to Bethlehem. Folk plays in which children perform the roles of Mary and Joseph take place through the town. The children knock on doors and are turned away repeatedly until they finally find shelter in the parish church, at which point the community party begins. Another highlight of the celebration for the children is the breaking of the piñata which scatters gifts to those standing nearby.

Latter Day Saints
See **Founding of the Church of Jesus Christ of the Latter Day Saints**

Leap Year Day
February 29

This date, occurring only once every four years, is sometimes wrongly referred to as the bisextile day, because, after Julius Caesar reformed the Roman Calendar, the leap day was added as the "second sixth" day before the first day of March.

The date is also associated with an apocraphyl story about Saints Patrick and Bridget, who lived before celibacy was made mandatory for priests or nuns. Bridget one day complained to Patrick about the unrest amongst the women because of the custom that prohibited them from taking the initiative in proposing matrimony. Patrick offered to let women propose during one year out of seven, but Bridget convinced him instead to allow the leap years to be for this purpose, and immediately proposed to Patrick herself. Patrick declined, having already taken a vow of celibacy himself, but he softened his refusal by giving her a kiss and a silk gown, a gesture which continued to accompany a man's refusal until the custom's demise in the nineteenth century.

Lent
Between February 2 and March 8; forty days before Easter in the West, seven weeks before Easter in the East

Lent is a period of introspection and penitence observed by Christians in preparation for the celebration of Easter. The tradition of prayer, fasting, and self-denial was initially practiced only for three days before Easter, beginning with Good Friday. In the late sixth century, however, the Lenten season, or Great Lent in the East, was established at forty weekdays by Gregory the Great (590-604 C.E.). The significance of the length of days may reflect the importance of the number forty in the *Bible*: Moses fasted for forty days on Mt. Sinai, the Israelites had wandered for forty years with few provisions, Elijah's fast lasted forty days, and Jesus went forty days without food after his baptism and the onset of his public ministry.

Because of the tradition of abstinence during the Lenten season, festivals such as Carnival and Mardi Gras became popular as the last opportunity Chris-

tians had to engage in restricted activities and consume forbidden foods. Customarily, the three days beginning with the Sunday before Ash Wednesday are designated as the last day to eat a specific forbidden food. Sunday is Dairy or Cheesefare Sunday in the Eastern Church; Monday is Collop or Shrove Monday when the last of the meat in the house is eaten; Tuesday is Fat or Shrove Tuesday on which special very rich pastries are baked and consumed.

See also **Ash Wednesday, Carnival, Good Friday, and Mardi Gras.**

Litha
Summer solstice, on or about June 22

Litha is one of the Lesser Sabbats that, with the four Greater Sabbats, make up the "Wheel of the Year," the major holidays celebrated by the Neopagans. The Lesser Sabbats comprise the English quarter days, that is, the solstices and equinoxes. The most common names used by Neo-pagans for the Lesser Sabbats are Eostre (spring equinox, about March 22), Litha (summer solstice, about June 22), Mabon (fall equinox, about September 22), and Yule (winter solstice, about December 22).

Loi Krathong
Full-moon night in the twelfth lunar month of the Thai calendar; usually mid November

Often considered the loveliest of Thailand's festivals, Loi Krathong is held under the full moon throughout the country. On the evening of the festival, people gather at the water after sunset to launch small lotus-shaped banana-leaf or paper boats, each holding a lighted candle, a flower, and a small coin to honor the water spirits and wash away the past year's sins.

Losar
Determined by Tibetan astrologers in Dharmsala; usually occurs in February

Tibetans observe a form of Buddhism known as Lamaism, Lama Buddhism, or Tibetan Buddhism, which involves belief in evil spirits, magic, and the spirits of nature. Many of the traditions surrounding the celebration of Losar, or the New Year, are associated with these beliefs.

Prior to the new year, houses are whitewashed and thoroughly cleaned to chase away bad memories from the old year; a little dirt from the house is saved and thrown in a crossroads where spirits are believed to dwell. On the last day of the old year, the monks ceremoniously drive out evil spirits. In one such ritual, the monks dressed in grotesque masks, wigs, and exotic robes, perform a dance portraying the struggle between good and evil.

On the first day of the new year, people place water and offerings on their household shrines early in the morning. The three-day celebration is a time of hospitality and merrymaking, with feasts, dances, and archery competitions. Although much of the Tibetan culture has been suppressed since the Chinese invasion in 1950, the festivals are still observed in a modest way in Tibet and by Tibetans in exile.

Low Sunday
See **Quasimodo Sunday**

Lucia Day
December 13

Lucia Day is a festival of Swedish origin which falls on the day of the winter solstice before the Gregorian reform. It is observed by Swedish-American communities in honor of the Lucia, the Queen of Lights. Traditionally, the youngest daughter in the family dons a crown with lighted candles and wakes her parents to a breakfast in bed of Lucia buns, while the other children sing a hymn to Lucia.

Lughnasad
July 31

Lughnasad, which begins at sunset on July 31, is one of the eight Sabbats of the "Wheel of the Year" that constitute the major holidays celebrated by the various Neo-pagan religions (especially the Gardnerian Witches). It is usually celebrated outdoors during a weekend campout, if possible. The ancient "games of Tara" are reenacted or, alternatively, an appropriate

ritual drama is performed as part of the major ritual of the weekend.

Luther, Martin
See **Birthday of Martin Luther**

M

Mabon
Autumnal equinox, on or about September 22

Mabon is the fall-equinox Sabbat of the Neo-pagans. When the autumnal equinox does not exactly coincide with a date that is convenient for the pagan festival, Mabon is displaced from its traditional date and observed at another time. For example, the Eleusian Mysteries in Greece were celebrated just after the full moon that fell closest to the fall equinox; hence, if September 22 falls midweek, many covens that favor the Greeks will move their Mabon Sabbat to a weekend nearer the full moon.

Magha Purnima
Full moon day of the Hindu month of Magha (January-February)

Known as a great bathing day as important as Kartika Purnima for piety and devotion. On this day fasting is observed and charities are done. Early in the morning, dead ancestors are offered libations, and the poor are given clothes, food, and money. Then Brahmans are fed and given dan-dakshina according to one's means and capacity.

Magha is one of the four most sacred months and Hindus believe that bathing in the Ganges on this day is of high religious merit. When the Ganges is not accessible, one may bathe in any holy stream, river, tank, or pond.

Bathing in India is a ritual, ceremony, festival, and a great purifying act, a bath on Purnima is most significant. On this day great bathing festivals are held at various places along the banks of holy rivers like the Ganges, Yamuna, Sarayu, and Narmad. People walk for miles to have a holy bath on this day. Baths in the sea at Kanyakumari and Rameshwaram are also highly prized, as is a bath at Pushkar. At Kumbhkonam, near Madras, there are the great shrines of Sarangpani, Kumbeshwara, and Nageshwara. There is a large sacred tank where devotees take a holy bath on this day. Hindus believe that the Ganges flows into the tank on this day, and that every 12 years, Kumbha Mela is held here.

Magha Mela is held at Prayag (Allahabad) on this day, and more than a million devotees take a holy bath here. People fast and give to charity on this day.

Magna Carta Day
June 15

Magna Carta Day commemorates the signing of England's "great charter" on June 15, 1215 by which King John ensured certain rights to his noble subjects, one of which was the freedom of the Church of England from royal domination. Thus, although Magna Carta Day is not cited in any official church calendar, it is nonetheless a day of great significance for, among other individual rights, the notion of religious freedom.

Mahashivaratri
Fourteenth day of the waning half of the month of Phalguna (February-March)

The "Great Night of Shiva," or the Shiva Chaturdashi of Phalguna, is a major Hindu festival marked by worship services at all temples where Shiva is honored. It is celebrated by Hindus of all faiths and castes throughout India. Devotees spend the entire night in meditation, and in reading and reciting Shiva scriptures. The lingam (phallic) symbol of Shiva is worshipped with Ganges water, milk, curds, honey, and clarified butter. Betel leaves, dhatura fruit, aak, and flowers, are also offered to Lord Shiva.

Devotees by the thousands collect at Shiva shrines and spend the entire night practicing devotion and piety. Special puja (worship) celebrations are held at Varanasi, Tarkeshwar, Baidyanath, Walkeshwar,

Rameshwaram, and Ujjain. At Pashupatinath in Nepal a grand celebration is held and adherents keep a strict fast and do not take even a drop of water. As Mahadeva, Shiva is worshipped by various gods including Brahma and Vishnu. He can easily be pleased to grant a desired boon. He is a great and powerful god, one of the Hindu Trinity. He is Mahakala the destroyer dissolving everything into nothingness, but also, as Shankara, restores and reproduces that which has been destroyed. His lingam (phallus) symbolizes this reproductive power. As a Mahayogi, or great ascetic, he combines in himself the highest perfection of austere penance and abstract meditation. In this form he is a naked ascetic, digambra "clothed with the elements." He is also called Chandrashekhra, "moon crested"; Girisha, "mountain lord"; Mahakala, "great time"; Pashupati, "lord of the beasts"; and Vishwanath, "lord of the universe".

Mahavir Jayanti
Thirteenth day of the waxing half of the Hindu month of Chaitra (March-April)

Birthday of Lord Vardhamana Mahavira, the founder of Jainism, ca. 600 B.C.E. The Jains' celebrations begin with the new moon in Aries.

India has produced many saints and spiritual leaders and the days commemorating the birthdays or the incidents in the lives of these great sons of the soil are considered especially holy. This birth anniversary is celebrated in India, but observed with special charms in Rajasthan and Gujarat, where the Jains live in relatively greater numbers than in the other states. Jain pilgrims from all over India congregate at the ancient Jaina shrines at Girnar and Palitana in Gujarat and at Mahavirji in Rajasthan. Pawapuri and Vaishali in Bihar are the other such centers. A grand festival is held at Vaishali, Mahavira's birthplace, and it is known as Vaishali Mahotsava.

On this auspicious day, grand chariot processions with the images of Mahavira are taken out, rich ceremonies in the temples are held, fasts and charities are observed, Jaina scriptures are read, and at some places grand fairs are held.

Mahavira, the great teacher and the twenty-fourth Tirthankara of Jainism, was a contemporary of Lord Buddha. Mahavira's mother Trisala, also known as

Priyakarini, had a series of miraculous dreams heralding his birth. Vardhama achieved enlightenment
under an Ashoka tree after two-and-a-half days of
fasting and meditation. Then he stripped himself of
all his clothes and wore none thereafter, but Svetambras
(white-clad Jains) believe that Indra presented him a
white robe. After his enlightenment, Mahavira gave
away all his wealth and possessions and owned nothing, underlining the importance of austerity and
complete nonviolence as the essential means of spiritual evolution and salvation.

Makar Sankranti
*Commences upon the sun's entrance into Capricorn, at the
winter solstice, on or about January 14*

This Hindu three-day festival, generally falling on
January 14, is considered a day of days and marks the
beginning of an auspicious time. The beginning of
the period, when the sun travels northward, is considered highly favorable for activities. It is celebrated as
Pongal in the south, but in the north it is observed as
Makar Sankranti or Uttarayana Sankranti. On this
day Hindus bathe in the Ganges and other holy
streams. At Ganga Sagar, where the Ganges enters
the sea, a grand fair and festival is held. Devotees in
large number reach Sagar Island in boats, and bathe
there where the Ganges meets the sea. On the island,
pilgrims visit the ashram of the sage Kapil, who,
according to the Puranas, had burnt to ashes the 60
thousand sons of King Sagara of Ayodhya. These 60
thousands dead princes wereMagha Bihu subsequently
revived and ascended to heaven by the sacred waters
of the divine Ganges as it flowed over their ashes.

Makar Sankranti is a very significant day, and newly
harvested corn is cooked for the first time and offered to the Sun and other deities. The poor are fed
and given clothes and money. In the morning, people
offer libations to their dead ancestors and visit temples. Bhishma Pitamaha waited on his couch of arrows for a long period for the onset of this auspicious
season before finally dying. In Assam, this day is
called Magha Bihu or Bhogali Bihu, the festival of
feasts. Bonfires are lighted on this day, and the round
of feasts and fun continues for about a week.

In Punjab, Makar Sankranti is observed as Lohri,
marking the end of winter and the imminent advent
of summer. Bonfires are lighted, and people dance to
the tune of drums and sing folk songs around the fire.
Sweets made of sesame, ground nuts, and puffed
rice, are thrown into the fire, and then eaten by
the celebrants. Lohri is celebrated in cities, towns,
and villages alike, with great enthusiasm and
merrymaking.

See also **Pongol**.

Mardi Gras
*Between February 3 and March 9; Tuesday before Ash
Wednesday*

French for "fat Tuesday," Mardi Gras is the day
before Ash Wednesday. More commonly, Mardi Gras
refers to the pre-Lenten gala in New Orleans. The
carnival is celebrated with a myriad of parades, costume balls, and pageantry beginning right after Twelfth
Night, and concluding with the famous parade on
Shrove Tuesday. Major Mardi Gras festivals take
place in other U.S. cities as well.

Martyrdom of the Báb
July 9

In 1850, the founder of Bahá'í was executed by the
Persian government. Threatened by the Báb's teachings of religious and social reform, the traditional
political and religious powers were antagonistic toward the movement. The hostility between both powers culminated in the execution of the Báb.

Followers of Bahá'í remember this event annually on
July 9 by abstaining from commercial, agricultural,
industrial, and trade work.

Martyrdom of Joseph and Hyrum Smith
June 27

Joseph Smith, founder of the Church of Jesus Christ
of the Latter Day Saints, and his brother Hyrum were
lynched by a mob in Carthage, Illinois on June 27,
1845. It remains a date commemorated worldwide by
the Church of Jesus Christ of the Latter Day Saints
and the smaller Mormon churches.

Mary as Our Lady of Sorrows
September 15

This Roman Catholic memorial recalls the sorrows experienced by Mary in her association with Christ: the prophecy of Simeon, the flight into Egypt (Matthew 2:13-21), the three-day separation from Jesus (Luke 2:41-50). Also remembered are four incidents connected with the Passion: her meeting with Christ on the way to Calvary, the crucifixion, the removal of Christ's body from the cross, and his burial (Matthew 27:31-61; Mark 15:20-47; Luke 23:26-56; John 19:17-42). A Mass and Divine Office of the feast were celebrated by the Servites, especially, in the 17th century, and in 1817 Pope Pius VII extended the observance to the whole Church.

Mary as Our Lady of the Rosary
October 7

The Virgin Mary is commemorated on this Roman Catholic memorial day by recalling the mysteries of the Rosary which recapitulate the events of her life and the life of Christ. The feast was instituted to remember a Christian victory over invading Islamic forces at Lepanto on October 7, 1571, and was extended throughout the Church by Pope Clement XI in 1716.

Mary, The Blessed Virgin
See **Assumption of the Blessed Virgin**
See **Circumcision, Feast of the**
See **Immaculate Conception of Mary, Feast of the**
See **Immaculate Heart of Mary, Feast of the**
See **Presentation of the Blessed Virgin Mary, Feast of the**
See **Queenship of Mary**
See **Visitation of the Virgin Mary to Elizabeth**

Marymass Fair
Third, or Fourth, Monday in August

Marymass Fair is held in Irvine, Ayrshire, Scotland. It takes its name from the Feast of the Assumption on August 15, which coincides with Old Lammas Day and was celebrated locally by dances around bonfires. The fair, which dates back to at least the twelfth century, is famous for its horse races, believed to be the oldest in Europe.

Maundy Thursday
See **Easter**

Mauni Amavasya
Fifteenth day of the waning fortnight of the Hindu month of Magha (January-February)

Magha is one of the most sacred Hindu months. On Mauni Amavasya, complete silence is observed. If this day falls on Monday, then its auspiciousness increases.

Like bathing during the month of Kartika, bathing during Magha is also highly rewarding, and many aspirants live on the banks of the Ganges throughout the month and bathe daily in the sacred river. The month-long bathing and fasting ends with the observance of Mauni Amavasya, when Lord Vishnu is worshipped and the peepal tree circumambulated. In the *Gita* Lord Krishna said "Among the trees, I am Aswattha," and the Aswattha or peepal (Ficus Religiosa) is a holy tree.

Hindus believe that piety and devotion on this day at Prayag, the prince of pilgrimage centers, where the Ganges, Yamuna, and Saraswati are confluent, is highly meritorious. Aspirants come and live here for a full month and practice prescribed rituals and ceremonial sacrifices known as "Kalpa-Vas." Through the entire month, religious discourses and services are held for aspirants. Observers take one simple meal a day or ingest only fruit and milk.

Mawlid al-Nabi
Twelfth day of the month of Rabi al-Awwal

The feast of Mawlid al-Nabi, or Bara Wafat, is celebrated with enthusiasm by Muslims all over India. It commemorates the birthday of Muhammad, which in the Western calendar fell on April 12, 571 C.E. He was born at Mecca in Arabia, during a period of moral chaos and great corruption. Muhammad spent much of his time in prayer, meditation, and seclusion where he received revelations from Allah. For twenty-three years, from the time he was forty years old until his death, Muhammad succeeded in establishing a religion based on the revelations he had received, and brought a political cohesiveness to the Arab tribes that had not been previously experienced.

Around the twelfth century C.E., Muslims began celebrating his birth. On the day of Mawlid, the Prophet's teachings are repeated, the holy Qur'an is read and recited, and religious meetings are organized in the mosques. The devotees keep night vigil, spending their time in prayer and reading of the Qur'an. They invite friends and relatives to feast, and give donations to the poor.

May Day
May 1

May 1 achieved prominence as a holiday because it was the date of the Celtic festival of Beltane, which celebrated the beginning of good weather in Europe. It was a day for Maypole dances, followed by all-night outings to look for flowering branches and other prizes. Also, young women performed folk-magic rituals intended to reveal their future husbands, and gifts of flowers were given to friends and lovers. Its dedication as a festival of the Blessed Virgin Mary—marked by an annual ritual of crowning the statue of Mary in the parish church with a wreath—was intended to co-opt its ongoing importance as a folk festival, as it has never been a feast of Mary in the official Christian church calendar. As a holiday, May Day is observed the first Monday in May, observed as Labor Day throughout Great Britain and Northern Ireland.

May 9 Day
May 9

Celebrated internationally by the Church of Scientology as its Founding Day. May 9, 1950, was the date of publication of L. Ron Hubbard's *Dianetics: The Modern Science of Mental Health*, the foundation document of Scientology.

Michaelmas
September 29

This Christian feast of St. Michael the Archangel is a traditional English quarter day, whose customs included bringing the herds down from the summer high pastures, eating roast goose, going back to school, and lighting bonfires. Many of these appear to be customs also associated with the fall equinox.

The Feast of St. Michael the Archangel on September 29 is observed by the Roman Catholic, Anglican, and Lutheran churches, on the date when the first church in Italy was dedicated to him. It is a quarter day in England, and has always been associated with the opening of the Fall term at public schools and universities.

Also honored on this day are the other archangels, Raphael and Gabriel. Originally each archangel was commemorated on a separate day, but with the Roman Catholic calendar reform of 1969, the days were combined and moved to Michaelmas.

Mid-Lent Sunday
See **Mothering Sunday**

Midsummer Eve
June 22

Noted for festivities, revivals of supposedly ancient rituals, and the burning of bonfires in the British Isles; observed by the Ancient Order of Druids (founded 1781) and various other British Druid orders, some of whom stay up all night to observe the Midsummer sunrise at Stonehenge. (The National Heritage will allow Druids into Stonehenge but limits the access of other Neo-pagans and tourists.) This marks the night celebrated in Shakespeare's *A Midsummer Night's Dream*, and as many folk customs cluster about it as about May Day.

See also **Litha**.

Minakshi Float Festival
Full moon day of the Hindu month of Magha (January-February)

The Float Festival is celebrated at Madurai, which is famous for its majestic Minakshi Temple. Minakshi means the fish-eyed goddess, and it is another name of Parvati. The major part of the Minakshi temple was built during the reign of Tirumala Nayak (1623-55), whose birthday falls on Magha Purnima.

On this day, images of Minakshi and Lord Sundareshwara (Shiva) are mounted on floats and taken to Marriamman Teppakulam, Sarovar, east of Madurai. The deities are taken around the tank on richly decorated and illuminated floats, and then are drawn back and forth across the waters of the tank to the accompaniment of music and devotional songs before being returned to Madurai. The tank is fed by underground channels from the river Vaigai. In the center of the tank there stands a shrine on an island. It was built in 1641 by King Tirumala Nayak. The float festival is very popular, and thousands of pilgrims and devotees from all parts of India congregate for this occasion.

Monlam
Fourth through twenty-fifth day of the first lunar month of the Tibetan calendar; usually February

Monlam, or the Prayer Festival, is the greatest festival in Tibet following the Losar, or New Year, celebration.

Started in the fifteenth century by Tsongkhapa, the great reformist monk, the festival ensures that the new year will be successful and prosperous. In the past, celebrants thronged to Lhasa's famous Jokhang Monastery where monks created enormous butter sculptures of Buddhist heroes. A procession around the Barkor, the old city of Lhasa, carried a statue of Maitreya, the future Buddha.

Celebration of the festival ceased when the Chinese denounced religious observances in 1959, but it was revived in 1986 and has been practiced since on a smaller scale.

Most Holy Mother of God, Feast of the
See **Assumption of the Blessed Virgin**

Most Precious Blood, Feast of the
July 1

In the Roman Catholic church, July is the month of the Most Precious Blood. During the month, many Christians venerate the blood of Jesus, which, they believe, possesses life-giving power. In 1849, Pope Pius IX established the festival on the first Sunday in July. Later, Pope Pius X moved the feast to the first day of July.

Mother Seton Day
December 1

Observed by the Sisters of Charity of St. Vincent De Paul as the anniversary of their founding by St. Elizabeth Ann Bayley Seton, a Staten Island native and the first American-born saint canonized by the Roman Catholic church.

Mothering Sunday
March-April; fourth Sunday of Lent

During the seventeenth century, a custom of visiting the "Mother Church"—the church in which a person had been baptized—developed among English Christians. On the same day, many people would visit their parents with a small gift for the mother of the family. In England, the gift was often a simnel or fruit cake with an almond paste topping. In Scotland, however, a carling (a pancake made of soaked peas fried in butter) was the traditional gift. Hence, this Sunday is also known as Carling Sunday.

There are many other names for this day. It is called Laetare Sunday because the Introit of the Roman Catholic Mass begins with the word "Rejoice" which is *laetare* in Latin; Rose Sunday because of the color vestments worn by the Priests and the blessing of the Golden Rose symbol; and Mid-Lent or Refreshment Sunday because of the brief intermission it offers in the Lenten season.

Muharram
First month of Muslim calendar

Its first day is the Muslim New Year's Day, a holiday in 19 countries, and its first ten days are a New Year's celebration dedicated to the memory of Hezret Imam Hussein.

Muharram is a Muslim festival of mourning observed in the first month of the Hijri Year. The Shi'a community, in particular, celebrate it with great fervor. Muslims, in general, fast, offer prayers, and sing elegies in homage to the martyrs during the celebrations. On the final day, Tajias (symbols of tombs representing the Mausoleum of Hazrat Imam Hussein) are taken out in grand processions, accompanied by brass bands and bagpipes playing sad tunes and the beating of big drums that add to the solemnity of the occasion. The procession terminates at Karbala, where the Tajias are ceremonially buried. The alam or standard of Imam Hussein is also carried in the procession.

Alphabetical Catalogue of Religious Holidays

On the way Tajias are given offerings such as incense, as the procession makes periodic halts and different groups perform acrobatics, and battle scenes from Karbala are enacted by the people. Mourners also beat their breasts in mourning.

This sad celebration is observed with great passion at places like Lucknow, Delhi, Agra, and Jaipur, and big mourning processions are performed. Hazrat Imam Hussein was the second son of Fatima, the prophet Muhammad's daughter. Hussein was murdered along with his whole family by Yazid at Karbala in Mecca.

After the burial or immersion of the Tajias at Karbala, the devotees return home, break their fast and give food, clothes, and money to the poor, needy and sick. In other Muslim countries, Tajias are not taken out in procession; rather, Muslims observe this day of Martyrdom in peace and silence. Hindus believe that Timurlang (Tamburlaine) introduced the Tajias into India.

See also **Ashura**.

Muhammad, Birth of
See **Mawlid al-Nabi**

N

Nag Panchami
Fifth day of the waxing half of the Hindu month of Shravana (July-August)

On Nag Panchami, cobras and snakes are worshipped with milk, sweets, flowers, lamps, and sometimes sacrifices. Images of snake deities painted on walls or made from silver, stone, or wood are bathed with milk and water, then they are worshipped with the reciting of mantras.

Snakes are worshipped widely throughout India on Nag Pachami, and fairs are held in their honor at various locations. Worshippers observe a fast on this day, but the Brahmans are fed. In return for their piety, people are assured protection against snake bites in the future. One particular custom associated with Nag Pachami is that digging in the earth is prohibited, because serpents live underground, (believed to be the netherworld) and digging may hurt or annoy them. Specific rituals for snake worship are found in various Purnas of the Hindu religion.

The mythical Nagas are semi-divine beings said to have sprung from Kadru, the wife of Rishi Kashyapa. Although they live and rule Patal or the regions below the earth, the Nags roam the land wearing lustrous jewels and ornaments. The thousand-hooded Shesha Nag or Ananta is the most powerful Naga and revered even by the Gods. He bears the whole earth like a chaplet on his crown and when he nods or yawns, the earth trembles.

Nag Panchami is also observed as Bhratri Panchami, and Hindu women who have brothers worship snakes and fast to guard their beloved siblings against snakebites.

Narak Chaturdashi
Fourteenth day of the waning half of the Hindu month of Kartika (October-November)

The day after Dhan Teras is celebrated as Narak Chaturdashi. Dedicated to Yama, the god of Naraka or Hell, bathing at dawn on this day is considered of great religious merit; in fact, some texts assert that Hindus believe those who bathe on this day after sunrise have their religious merit destroyed. Therefore, the devout rise early in the morning to bathe.

After the bath, libations are offered to Yama three times to please and appease him. The hope of those who sacrifice is that he may spare them the tortures of death. A fast is observed and in the evening lamps are offered to Yama. Some Hindus believe that piety observed on this day in honor of Lord Yama liberates them from the possible tortures of hell.

Narieli Purnima
Full moon day of the Hindu month of Shravana (July-August)

Narieli Purnima is celebrated in order to appease the fury of the sea god Varuna. Marking the end of the monsoon season, it is primarily observed by sailors, fishermen, and others living in the coastal areas of south India, who offer coconuts to the sea on this occasion. If the sea happens to be far away, carry out this ritual at a nearby water source.

Narsimha Jayanti
Fourteenth day of the waxing half of the Hindu month of Vaisakha (April-May)

Vishnu incarnated himself in the Narsimha or Man-Lion form on this celebration day. Vaishnavites believe that Vishnu incarnated a Narsimha to free the world from the depredations of the demon king Hiranyakasipu, who, like his brother Hiranyaksh, had gained a boon of immunity from Brahma. Hiranyaka-sipu forbade prayer and worship to Lord Hari, and substituted worship and prayer to himself. He was very much annoyed to discover his own son Prahlad was an ardent devotee of Vishnu, and tortured Prahlad to convert him, but the child remained unmoved in his devotion to God. The king tried to kill Prahlad by trampling him under elephants, by throwing him down precipices, and by other means, but without any success.

One day Hiranyakasipu was so enraged that he rushed to kill Prahlad with his own sword, asking the child, "Where is your savior?" Instantly Vishnu stepped out of a nearby pillar in the form of Narsimha, half lion, half man, and tore Hiranyakasipu to pieces.

On this day, people fast, meditate on Narsimha, and seek his grace to have devotion like that of Prahlad. To Hindus, Narsimha symbolizes the omnipresence of God, his deep concern and love for the devotees, and the victory of good over evil.

People often demonstrate the sincerity of their devotion by giving cows, grains, gold, robes, and other goods to the poor and the Brahmans as acts charity on this day.

Nativity of the Blessed Virgin Mary, Feast of the
September 8

The birth of the Virgin Mary is one of only three births celebrated by the Christian Church. (The births of John the Baptist on June 24 and Jesus on December 25 are the other two observed.)

The date of September 8 became widely accepted for this celebration during the seventh century although there seems to be no concrete evidence that this is the actual date of Mary's birth.

Navratra
See **Durga Puja**

Naw-Ruz
March 20-21

Naw-Ruz is the Bahá'í New Year's Day which is observed from sunset to sunset on March 20 to 21.

New Church Day
June 19

Anniversary of the founding of the Church of the New Jerusalem (New Church) on June 19, 1770, by the disciples of the Swedish scientist, philosopher, and theologian, Emanuel Swedenborg.

Swedenborg taught that in 1757, a great judgment was passed in the spiritual realm, and the result was that the evil spirits were separated from the good and a new heaven was established. Jesus then called his apostles together and instructed them to preach the new doctrines to the new heaven, just as he had instructed them in the Great Commission seventeen centuries earlier. These cataclysmic events took place on June 19-20, 1757. In 1770, Swedenborg's disciples established the Church of the New Jerusalem.

In 1817, the General Convention of the New Jerusalem in the U.S.A. was founded in Philadelphia, Pennsylvania.

American members of the New Church join with members world wide in celebration of New Church Day.

New Year for Trees
Day after the winter solstice; around December 23

Observed by Neo-pagans who use Robert Graves' tree calendar which begins the day after the winter solstice.

See also **Bi-Shevat**.

Night Journey
See **Lailat al Miraj**

Nineteen-Day Feast
First day of each of the nineteen months of the Bahá'í calendar

The Bahá'í calendar is organized into 19 months of 19 days each; these 361 days, plus a four-day intercalary period, make up the Bahá'í year. A fifth day is added in leap years to keep the Bahá'í dates fixed relative to the common calendar. On the first day of each month, the Bahá'í community gathers for its Nineteen-Day Feast, which is restricted to confirmed members of the Bahá'í faith. The "Feast" actually consists of three parts: a worship service; a "town meeting" for self-governance as a community; and a social occasion with feasting and celebration.

Ninth of Av
See **Jewish Fasts**

Nirjala Ekadashi
One day in the waxing half of the Hindu month of Jyaishtha (May-June)

In all, 24 Ekadashi (eleventh-day) fasts are observed during the course of a year, but some are of relatively greater importance. Nirjala Ekadashi is one of these. Not only is a complete fast observed, but even water is not taken. In Jyaishtha it is very hot and the day is long, and so observing a fast without water is an extreme act of pious austerity. Both men and women observe a strict fast and offer puja (worship) to Vishnu to ensure happiness, prosperity, and forgiveness of transgressions and sins. On the preceding day (the tenth lunar day), sandhya is performed and only one meal is taken. In the evening Vishnu is worshipped while holding durva grass in one's hand. The night is spent in meditation and prayer.

During the Nirjala, Panchamrata is prepared by mixing together milk, ghee, curds, honey, and sugar which is then offered to the image of Vishnu or poured over the Shaligram. The deity is then adorned with rich clothes, ornaments, and jewels, and a fan is placed beside it. Then Vishnu is meditated upon as the supreme Lord of the Universe, and puja (worship) is done with flowers, lamps, water, incense, etc.

Some Hindus believe that faithful observance of the fast and other rituals on this day ensures happiness, salvation, longevity and prosperity. After the completion of the vow, clothes, grains, umbrellas, fans, and pitchers filled with water are given in charity to the Brahmans according to one's means and capacity.

Northern Navajo Fair
See **Shiprock Navajo Nation Fair**

Norway Day
See **Olsok Eve**

O

Obon Festival
July 13-15 or August 13-15

The date of the Japanese Obon Festival, or Festival of the Dead, varies from region to region, although it is always celebrated in either July or August. According to Japanese Buddhist belief, the dead revisit the earth during this time; thus Buddhist families participate in special religious services and hold family reunions to honor the dead.

The festival begins with the lighting of small bonfires outside of homes to welcome the spirits of ancestors. A traditional meal of vegetables, rice cakes, and fruit is provided for the spirits who are included in family activities as if they were physically present. On the final day of the festival, another bonfire is lit outside to guide the spirits back to the netherworld. The climax of the Obon Festival is the Bon-Odori. During this event, the town is lit with paper lanterns and people participate in folk dances which comfort the souls of the dead.

Obon is an important Japanese festival throughout the world as Japanese communities in many countries observe the traditions. In the United States, the most elaborate celebrations take place in Chicago and various locations in California.

Octave of the Birth of our Lord
See **Circumcision, Feast of**

Oimelg
See **Brigid**

Old Christmas Day
January 6

When the switch from the Julian to the Gregorian calendar was made in England, many people resisted the change because of emotional attachment to the previous system. One way in which people registered their dissatisfaction was to continue observing holidays according to the Julian calendar, placing them thirteen days later than their Gregorian counterparts. Old Christmas Day is one of these holdovers from the Julian system.

Old Christmas Eve
See **Epiphany Eve**

Olsok Eve
Norwegian festival honoring Saint and King Olaf Haraldsson, who brought Christianity to Norway; celebrated among Norwegian-Americans (as Norway Day) with bonfires, folk-dancing, food, and parties.

Omer, Counting of the
See **Counting of the Omer**

Omizutori Matsuri
March 1-14

Omizutori Matsuri, or the Water Drawing Festival, has been observed at the Buddhist Todaiji Temple in Nara (Akita Prefecture) in Japan since the twelfth century. This time of meditative rituals is characterized by the drone of devotees reciting sutras and the sound of blowing conchs echoing from the temple. The climax of the festival occurs on March 12 when young monks in the gallery of the temple shake off burning pieces from pine-branch

torches. Observers attempt to catch the sparks, believing them to have supernatural power against evil.

The Water Drawing ceremony commences at 2 a.m. on March 13. Ancient music plays as monks carry buckets to a well and the first water drawn for the year is offered to the Buddha. The monks then perform a

dramatic fire dance to the beating of drums which signals the end of the festivities.

Onam
Four days in the Malyalam month of Chingam (August-September)

Onam is the most famous festival of Kerala. It is a harvest festival characterized by four days of feasting, merrymaking, and famous 'snake' boat races. The snake boat race of Alleppey, held annually in August, is the most prominent.

A clay image of Vamana, the fifth incarnation of Vishnu, is worshipped on this day in temples and houses, and youngsters are given gifts by the elders. On the second day of the festivity, Bali is believed to visit his kingdom in Kerala. The Puranas relate that Bali, son of Virochana and grandson of Prahlad, was a virtuous demon king. He performed great magical work, defeated Indra, and extended his rule and authority over the three worlds until Vamana reclaimed them. Bali is also called Mahabali, and his capital was Mahabalipuram, near Madras.

Bali was permitted by Vamana to visit his lost kingdom and subjects once a year; this visit is regularly celebrated in Kerala, and particularly in Malabar, by his devotees on Onam. To welcome their ancient king Bali, the people of Kerala tidy up their houses and environs, decorate the houses with flowers and leaves, and arrange grand feasts and many types of amusements. The spectacular snake-boat races mark the crowning glory of these games.

P

Padva
See **Gudi Parva**

Pajjusana
An eight-day period of penance observed by Jains to commemorate the birth of their founder, Mahavira, and to honor *Kalpa Sutra*, their sacred scriptures.

Palm Sunday

Between March 15 and April 18; the Sunday preceding Easter

Palm Sunday commemorates the day on which Jesus rode into Jerusalem greeted by a cheering crowd that had heard of his miracles. The people of Jerusalem saw Jesus as a leader who could free them from Roman rule, so they honored him by waving palm branches—a traditional symbol of victory–which they then spread in the street for him to ride over. Commemoration of this day began early in the history of the Church and was adopted by Rome in the ninth century when the blessing of palm was introduced. The use of palm leaves in a procession still marks the celebration of Palm Sunday; after the leaves are used for the procession, they are dried and burned to make the ashes for the next year's Ash Wednesday.

Full liturgical observance includes the blessing of palm and a procession before the principal Mass of the day. The Passion, by Matthew, Mark, or Luke, is read during the Mass.

Parent's Day

First weekend in June

A holiday of Scientologists on which family members get together to celebrate the family unity made possible through Scientology.

Parshurama Jayanti

Third day of the waxing half of the Hindu month of

Vaisakha (April-May)

Parshurama Jayanti (Parashurama's birthday) is celebrated by worship of and prayer to Parashurama, or Rama with an Axe, who destroyed the evil Kshatriya kings and princes 21 times, including the thousand-armed King Arjuna. Hindus believe that Parashurama represents filial obedience, austerity, power, and brahmanic ideals.

Parashurama, as the sixth incarnation of Vishnu, became manifest in the world in the beginning of the Treta Yuga (the second age) primarily to terminate the tyranny of certain Kshatriya kings. His story has been told in the *Mahabharata* and the Puranas. He also appears in the *Ramayana*, as an adversary of Ramachandra, and challenges Ramachandra to a trial of strength. Finally recognizing Ramachandra's superiority, Parashurama pays him homage, and retires to the Himalayas. The Malabar region on the Western Ghat is believed to have been founded by him. On this sacred day fasting, austerities, prayer, and worship of Lord Vishnu are common.

Parsi Remembrance of the Departed

Ten days preceding the vernal equinox

This ten-day observance honoring ancestors takes place just prior to the vernal equinox during the last ten days of the year in the calendar of the Persian sect of Zoroastrianism, or Parsies. Prayers and ceremonies are offered in homes and at shrines decorated with traditional flower arrangements representing Paradise.

Partyshana Parva

Eight days during the Hindu month of Bhadrapada (August-September)

Partyshana Parva is a Jain festival, celebrated by both the Svetambar (white-clad) and the Digambar (sky-clad) sects at different times in the month of Bhadrapada (August-September). The Svetambar Jains start observing it in the waning half of the month, from the 13th day to the fifth day of the waxing half. But the Digambar (sky-clad) Jains begin to observe it from the fifth day of the waxing half of Bhadrapada and terminate it on the 13th lunar day. This festival signifies a man's emergence into a new world of spiritual and moral refinement from that of a gross and depraved world.

The ten cardinal virtues cultivated during this festival are forgiveness, charity, simplicity, contentment, truthfulness, self-restraint, fasting, detachment, humility, and continence. During the festival all of the virtues are lectured upon by the Jain saints and their cultivation stressed.

During this celebration devout Jains fast, eating only once a day; worship the Tirthankaras; and try to imbibe the qualities and virtues of the great Jain saints and preachers. This is also an occasion of self-analysis and criticism. Jains ask one another for forgiveness during this festival for offenses done knowingly or unknowingly, helping to restoring lost relations and friendships.

Passover
Begins between March 27 and April 24; Nisan 15-21 (or 22)

Passover or Pesach is the Hebrew celebration of spring and of their deliverance from slavery in Egypt and it is one of the three pilgrim festivals. The account in the book of *Exodus* relates that when Pharaoh refused to let Moses lead the Hebrews from Egypt to the Promised Land, God sent ten plagues on the Egyptians, including locusts, fire, and hailstones. Pharaoh, however, refused to yield. The tenth plague was the visitation of the Angel of Death who was sent to kill the first-born sons of the Egyptians. Hebrew families were instructed to sacrifice a lamb and place its blood on the doorposts of their homes as a signal to the Angel to "pass over" their sons. When the Egyptians discovered what had happened, they ordered the Israelites to leave the country immediately.

Passover was one of the three pilgrimage festivals established by the Deuteronomic reform in 621 B.C.E. Before the reform the combined festivals of the Passover and the Unleavened Bread had been celebrated by families in their homes. The Deuteronomic laws, however, provided that the lamb for the Passover meal could be sacrificed only at the temple in Jerusalem. This provision mandated that all Hebrew people had to come to Jerusalem for these festivals. After the destruction of the Temple by the Romans in 69 C.E., the rabbis restored the Passover to its former status as a family festival celebrated at home. Uncertainties of the ancient calendar, however, led to the custom of celebrating the Passover for eight days outside of Jerusalem during the period of the Second Temple; Orthodox and Conservative Jews living outside of Israel have retained this custom. In contrast, Reform Jews have reverted to the original seven-day dating.

The heart of the Passover celebration is the traditional liturgy known as the Seder, which indicates the order of services. The Seder is among the most universally observed elements of Judaism, even among those who do not practice most traditional Hebrew concepts. The Seder includes a customary meal which consists of symbolic foods such as a "pascal lamb," bitter herbs, and wine. Matzoh, a flat, unleavened bread, represents the hurry in which the Israelites left Egypt—they did not have time to let their bread rise.

See also **Pentecost** and **Sukkot**.

Patati
See **Jamshed Navaroz**

Pentecost
Between May 10 and June 13; Fiftieth day after the second day of Passover

This Christian festival, also called Whitsunday, is a moveable celebration held on the seventh Sunday after Easter. According to St. Luke's account in the *Acts of the Apostles*, this was the day on which the Holy Spirit descended on the Apostles, empowering Peter and the other believers there to witness to Jews in Jerusalem. Three thousand conversions were reported on that day.

Pesach
See **Passover**

Pilgrim Festivals
Seven days beginning on Nisan 15; Sivan 6; eight days beginning on Tishri 15

The Hebrew people had three festivals which required their pilgrimage to Jerusalem: Passover, Shavuot, and Sukkot. In Hebrew, the feasts are called the *shalosh regalim* or "three (foot) pilgrimages" because all adult males over the age of thirteen traditionally made a pilgrimage to Jerusalem for the celebration of those festivals. After the destruction of the Temple in Jerusalem in 70 C.E., the law requiring a central celebration of the festivals became impossible to fulfill. The holidays continued to be celebrated locally, however, with traditional merrymaking.

With the reestablishment of Israel as a nation, the pilgrimage aspect of the festivals has experienced a revival. The tenor of the pilgrimages has changed, however, and for many the journey is one of sorrow in which they join with thousands of others at the Wailing Wall to mourn the destruction of the Temple.

See also **Passover, Shavout,** and **Sukkot.**

Pioneer Day
July 24

On July 24, 1847, the first Mormon settlers arrived in the valley of the Great Salt Lake. Under the leadership of Brigham Young, they had traveled from Nauvoo, Illinois after the murder of Joseph Smith, the founder of their faith. The site of the original settlement is now Salt Lake City, Utah. Thousands of Mormon pioneers followed the original group, settling not only in Utah, but also in Idaho, Arizona, Nevada, Wyoming, and California. The anniversary of the founding of the Salt Lake City settlement is observed by Mormon churches worldwide.

Pitra Paksha
Waning half of the Hindu month of Ashvina (September-October)

Observed throughout the Hindu world, on each day of this fourteen-day ceremony oblations of water and balls of rice and meal are offered to deceased relatives by their surviving family members. These sacrifices, called Shraddha, act as a supplement to a funeral service. It is an act of reverential homage to a dead person performed by relatives, and symbolically supplies the dead with strengthening nutriment after the previous funeral ceremonies have endowed the ethereal bodies. One Hindu belief is that until Shraddha has been performed, the deceased relative is a restless, wandering ghost and has no real body. Only after the Shraddha does he attain a position among the Pitris, or Divine Fathers, in their blissful abode called Pitri-Loka. A Shraddha is most desirable and efficacious when done by a son.

The eldest son or some other elder male member of the family performs Shraddha in honor of the dead and offers oblations. Part of the food offering is given to the cows and crows. Brahmans are fed and given

Dan-dakshina, for Hindu tradition says that whatever is given to the Brahmans also reaches the departed souls. Khir, a preparation of sweet milk and rice, is specially prepared and offered to the Pitris on this occasion. On the last day of the fortnight (Amavasya, or new moon), oblations are offered to all ancestors whose day of death is unknown.

Plough Monday
January; First Monday after Epiphany

The origins of Plough Monday are thought to date back to the medieval custom of British farmers, or ploughmen, who would leave candles known as plough-lights burning in homage to the saints. Each year, the farmers would gather in town to collect money from the residents to buy the plough-lights. Although the adulation of the saints was quelled by the sixteenth-century Reformation, the festivities of the day continued.

By the nineteenth century, the day was filled with music, dancing, processions, and trick-or-treating by the local ploughmen. The trick-or-treat tradition included "The Bessy," a man dressed up as a buffoon in women's clothing, and "The Fool," a man wearing animal skins or a fur cap and tail, parading from door to door demanding money to fund their revelry. Another tradition was for the ploughmen to drag a beribboned plough from house to house, ploughing up the front yard of any homeowner who failed to financially sponsor the carousing.

These rural practices died out early in the twentieth century. The Church, however, continued to bless ploughs on Plough Sunday.

Plowing Sixth
See **Halu Shasti**

Pongal
Mid January

Pongal is a three-day solemn festival in honor of the sun, earth, and the cow. The celebration takes place in south India on Sankranti and marks the beginning of the sun's northern course. This occasion for rejoicing and merrymaking takes place when the sun passes to Capricorn from Sagittarius.

The first day is Bhogi-Pongal, the Pongal of joy. On this day, people exchange visits, sweets, and presents, and enjoy a leisurely day. The second day is dedicated to the sun. As part of the traditional celebration, people rise early in the morning, and the woman of the house puts rice to boil in milk, which makes a delightfully sweet treat. As soon as the rice begins to simmer, the family shouts together, "Pongal! Pongal!" ("It boils!") The sweet rice is then offered to the Surya, the sun god, and a portion of it is given to the cows. The family then enjoys the treat as well. On this day of the festival, people often greet one another with the phrase "Has it boiled?" to which the response is "Yes, it is boiled."

The third day, Mattu Pongal, is the Pongal of the cows. On this day cows and oxen are worshipped and proudly paraded around the village. Their horns are painted in various colors, and garlands of leaves and flowers are hung around their necks. On this day the cows are allowed to graze anywhere they like, without any restraint.

See also **Makar Sankranti**.

Pooram
During the Hindu month of Vaisakha (April-May)

The Pooram celebration is a major festival at Trichur in India. A great parade of thirty richly caparisoned elephants carrying ceremonial umbrellas is held on this occasion. They pass through the magnificent temple entrance tower and line up in the open ground. On the elephant in the center rides the temple deity Vadakkanathan (Shiva). The elephants circle around the shrine accompanied by the music of pipes and trumpets. At night, there is a spectacular display of fireworks which continues until dawn.

Presentation of Jesus
February 2

A commemoration of Jesus' presentation in the Temple, which was in accord with the prescriptions of Mosaic Law and Mary's forty-day purification follow-

ing the birth of her child. This presentation was also the occasion on which, according to the *Gospel of Luke,* Jesus was first publicly proclaimed as the Messiah by the prophets Anna and Simeon in the temple courtyard.

Also called the Feast of the Purification of the Blessed Virgin Mary, the holiday stemmed from a Jewish religious law that required a woman to abstain from sexual intercourse for forty days after the birth of a child, and undergo a ritual purification bath at the end of that time.

The date set for this holiday was February 2, forty days after the celebration of Christmas which was fixed on December 25 late in the fourth century. The feast was adopted earlier in the East than in the West and was celebrated by the Orthodox church as a feast of Jesus rather than of Mary. The Roman Catholic church, however, observed the holiday in honor of Mary until the calendar reform of 1969. At that time, the feast became known as the Presentation of Jesus in the Roman Catholic church as well as in the Orthodox church.

The secondary name for this holiday is Candlemas, which is derived from the tradition of blessing candles on this day to be used for healing and other sacred practices during the year. The blessing of candles, which became popular in the eleventh century, emerged from Simeon's proclamation of the baby Jesus as "a light for revelation to the Gentiles."

Presentation of the Blessed Virgin Mary, Feast of the
November 21

Although no one is certain of the origin of this feast, the Greek Orthodox church officially began celebrating the Presentation of the Blessed Virgin in the eight century and the Roman Catholic church followed suit later in the Middle Ages. The feast commemorates events related in the apocryphal *Book of James* of the presentation of the three-year old Mary in the Temple consecrating her to God's service.

Purification of the Blessed Virgin Mary, Feast of the
See **Presentation of Jesus**

Purim

Between February 25 and March 25; Adar 15 or We-Adar 14 in leap year

Purim is a joyful occasion to celebrate the deliverance of the Hebrews from an evil plot to exterminate them, which was put forward by an advisor to the Persian King, Ahasuerus (Xerxes I). Haman, who hated Jews but had a particular bile toward a man named Mordecai, selected the execution day by means of purim, or casting lots. Unbeknownst to King Ahasuerus or Haman, Ahasuerus's wife Queen Esther was Jewish, and Mordecai was her cousin. Esther prayed and fasted then she appealed to her husband to stop Haman's plans. (Today, Purim is preceded by Ta'anit Esther, or the Fast of Esther, which commemorates the three days of fasting observed by Esther at this time.) Ahasuerus responded to his wife's plea and had Haman executed instead.

The Book of Esther is read in the synagogue on Purim, and it is a tradition to give the children noisemakers with which they try to drown out the name of Haman whenever it is read.

From this holiday, other Purim have followed. Many Jewish communities observe their own festivals commemorating their deliverance from harrowing circumstances. For example, the Padua Purim celebrated on Sivan 11 honors the Jews' deliverance from a terrible fire in 1795. The Hitler Purim observed in Casablanca on Kislev 2 remembers the escape of the city from German domination in World War II.

Putrada Ekadashi

Eleventh day of the waxing half of the Hindu month of Shravana (July-August)

Putrada Ekadashi is observed particularly by sterile parents in order to produce a son. Fasting and piety on this day is said to ensure conception of a boy while also destroying the sins of the aspirants. Like other Ekadashis, it is also dedicated to Lord Vishnu.

A fast is observed, Vishnu is worshipped and meditated upon, and the Brahmans learned in the Vedas and sacred religious lore are fed and given robes and money on this day. At night the aspirants should sleep in the room where Vishnu had been worshipped.

Similarly, the Ekadashi falling in the waning half of the month of Shravana should be observed. This Ekadashi is known as Kamada Ekadashi, the wish-fulfilling Ekadashi.

Qing Ming Festival

Fourth or fifth day of the third moon of the Chinese calendar; usually April 5 or 6

A Confucian festival that dates back to the Han Dynasty (206 B.C.E. to 221 C.E.), Qing Ming is a day on which Chinese throughout the world honor their dead. The day is observed by the maintenance of ancestral graves; the presentation of food, wine, and flowers as offerings; and the burning of paper money at the graveside to provide the ancestors with funds in the afterworld. (Traditional Chinese belief holds that the afterlife is quite similar to this life, and that the dead live below ground in the Yellow Springs region.) In ancient China, other festivities of the day included playing Chinese football and flying kites. Today, people picnic and gather for family meals.

Quadragesima

Between February 8 and March 14; the first Sunday of Lent

This holiday is named for the Latin word "fortieth" because it falls forty days before Easter. There are three other numbered Sundays in the pre-Lent season: Quinquagesima ("fiftieth"), Sexagesima ("sixtieth"), and Septagesima ("seventieth").

These are no longer in general use; the days are now reckoned in relation to Epiphany.

Quarter Days

March/June/September/December

During the middle ages, British landowners collected quarterly rents on or near the equinoxes and solstices.

Eventually these days became known as quarter days, and they continued to be used into the early modern age.

Because of their association with the solstices and equinoxes, the quarter days have also gained religious connotations. In England, the quarter days are called: Lady Day (March 15), Midsummer Day (June 24), Michaelmas (September 29), and Christmas Day (December 25). In Scotland, the names and dates were slightly different. Candlemas fell on February 2; Whitsunday was observed on the seventh Sunday after Easter; Lammas was on August 1; and November 11 marked the celebration of Martinmas.

The observation of these days waned through the nineteenth century but has seen a resurgence in the twentieth century because of the increased popularity of the modern Neo-pagan movement. The followers of Wicca celebrate their Lesser Sabbats on these days which are most often called: Eostre (spring equinox, about March 22), Litha (summer solstice, about June 22), Mabon (fall equinox, about September 22), and Yule (winter solstice, about December 22).

Septagesima, therefore would be the first Sunday after Epiphany, and so forth until Ash Wednesday, when Lent begins.

Quasimodo Sunday
Between March 29 and May 2; Sunday after Easter

Also known as Low Sunday, Close Sunday, and Low Easterday, Quasimodo Sunday is named for the Introit of the Latin Mass recited on this day. It begins *Quasi modo geniti infantes*—"As newborn babes. . . ." Quasimodo, the famous character in Victor Hugo's *The Hunchback of Notre Dame*, was found on this day.

Queenship of Mary
August 22

This Roman Catholic observance is classed as a memorial. Commemorates Mary as Queen of heaven, angels, and mankind. Universal observance of the memorial was ordered by Pope Pius XII in the encyclical *Ad Ceali Reginam*, October 11, 1954, near the close of the Marian Year observed in connection with the centenary of the proclamation of the dogma of the Immaculate Conception, four years after the proclamation of the dogma of the Assumption. The original date of the memorial was May 31.

Race Unity Day
Second Sunday in June

Observed by Bahá'ís worldwide, Race Unity Day was established in 1957 to focus attention on the problem of racial prejudice. Participants attend discussions and meetings to promote peace and universal recognition of the connection of all humanity.

Radha Ashtami
Eighth day of the waning fortnight of the Hindu month of Bhadrapada (August-September)

The eighth and ninth days of the moon both belong to the goddess Shakti. Radha Ashtami celebrates the birth of Radha, an incarnation of Lakshmi and worshipped accordingly. Some Hindus believe that Radha, the favorite mistress and consort of Krishna during his Vrindavana days, is a symbol of the human soul drawn to the ineffable god Krishna, or the pure divine love to which the fickle love returns.

On this day, after early morning baths, the image of Radha is bathed in Panchamrita, and then richly adorned and ornamented before being offered food and worship. A fast is kept on this day and charity distributed.

Raksha Bandhan
Full-moon day of the Hindu month of Shravana (July-August)

The word "Raksha" means protection and on this auspicious day Hindu women and girls tie a thread round the right wrists of their brothers as a protection against evil during the ensuing year. The thread is called "Rakhi" and is made of a few colorful cotton or silk twisted threads. It can also be prepared from threads of gold or silver. Sisters feed their brothers with sweets, dried fruits, and other delicacies on this occasion. The brothers give their sisters gifts of money, clothes, and other valuable things in return.

Priests and Brahmans also tie this thread round the right wrists of their patrons to receive gifts. They recite a mantra or sacred formula to charge the thread with the power of protection. The empowered thread protects the wearer from possible evils.

According to Hindu scriptures, Sachi, the consort of Indra, the god of heaven, tied such a mantra-charged thread round the right wrist of her husband when he was disgraced in battle by the demon forces. Indra fought again and gained a convincing victory over the demons, and recovered his lost capitol Amaravati. The sacred amulet helped him in defeating the enemy.

In southern India, this day is celebrated as Avani Avittam. A holy thread is charged and a libation of water is offered to the ancestors and rishis on this occasion. The new thread is worshipped with saffron and turmeric paste before being worn, and the old one is discarded in the water of a pool, tank, or river. This day is specially significant for a Brahman boy who has recently been invested with a holy thread to remind him of the religious significance. Vedas are also read and recited on this day.

In Bombay coconuts are offered to the sea god Varuna on this occasion. Exchange of sweets, setting up of fairs, visiting relatives and friends, sending the rakhis by post to brothers living at far-off places, and remembering the Rishis and Gurus are other highlights of this festival.

Rama Navani

Ninth day of the waxing half of the Hindu month of Chaitra (March-April)

Rama Navani, or the birthday of Lord Rama, is a major Hindu festival celebrated all over India. It brings to a close the nine-day fast of Vasanta Navratra. Rama, the seventh incarnation of Vishnu, was born in Ayodhya. Many Hindus believe that in the Treta Yuga (the Second Age) there was one God: desireless, formless, uncreated; true being, consciousness and bliss; the supreme spirit; the all-pervading, whose shadow is the world. This being incarnates himself as Rama or Krishna and does many things out of the

love he bears for his devotees. Adi Kavi Valmiki in his celebrated *Ramayana described the advent of Rama.*

The *Ramayana* means the "Ways of Rama." It is considered sacred by Hindus who believe that it embodies the best of human ideals and contains a living sum of Indian character. Nothing surpasses India's love for the *Ramayana* as a popular religious epic and great literary work.

A fair idea of the *Ramayana*'s immense popularity can be gained from the fact that there are about 350 versions of it in Hindi alone, and the name of Rama, as "Rama! Rama!" or "Jai Ramji ki!", is a common form of salutation.

The Rama Navami festival offers an opportunity to imbibe the ideals and spirit enshrined in the ways of Rama. Vaishnavites believe that one who approaches Rama's lotus feet with love, devotion, and humility becomes noble, large-hearted, pious, peaceful, a master of the senses, and beloved of the wise. On this sacred day they fast and practice charities, visit a temple of Rama early in the morning, make a small shrine at home and install a picture of Sri Rama-Panchayatan on it, and offer prayers and puja (worship).

In Ayodhya, the birth place of Sri Rama, great celebrations are held; the temples are decorated, the *Ramayana* is read and recited, and a grand fair is held. At other places icons of Rama, along with Sita and Hanuman, are richly adorned and worshipped, and other acts of devotion and piety are observed. Chanting the holy name of Rama and lectures and discourses on Rama's life and teachings are common feature of the celebrations. People take vows to devote themselves more to their spiritual and moral evolution on this occasion. Many Hindus believe that Ram-Nam is a great magic formula (mantra) that should be repeated, recited, and meditated upon frequently.

Ramadan

Ninth month of the Islamic lunar year

Ramadan is the month during which Muslims commemorate Muhammad's reception of the divine revelations recorded in the *Qur'an*. During this month, a strict fast from sunrise to sunset is observed. This fast is one of the "Five Pillars" of the Islamic faith, and is considered a time of introspection and intensified devotion to Allah.

Each day, believers rise early and eat a light meal before dawn. They fast through the day, then after prayers they break the fast with an evening meal. In some places the end of the fast is announced by the firing of a cannon.

The first day of Ramadan occurs when the authorities in Saudi Arabia sight the new moon marking the ninth month. It is the holiest period during the Islamic year, and ends when the new moon is sighted for the next month. The Festival of Breaking Fast immediately follows the Fast of Ramadan, and is a time of rejoicing, gift-giving, and celebration.

Raphael
See **Michaelmas**

Ratha Yatra
Second day of the waxing half of the Hindu month of Ashadha (June-July)

Ratha Yatra is celebrated throughout India, and the chariot procession of Sri Jagannath (Lord of the Universe) is taken through the main markets and streets. The biggest festival is held at Puri in Orissa. The car festival of Puri is famous worldwide, and thousands of devotees participate in this spectacular religious event. The imposing twelfth-century Jagannath shrine, 60 kilometers from Bhubaneshwar, is situated on Nilachala mountain. It is one of the four great Hindu holy places, the others being Badrinath, Dwarka, and Rameshwaram.

For a devout Hindu, a pilgrimage to Jagannath Puri is a lifelong ambition. Many Hindus believe that a three-day sojourn to Puri will free a pilgrim from future births and deaths. Always crowded with pilgrims, Puri becomes a ocean of seething humanity on the occasion of Ratha Yatra. On this day Lord Jagannath is taken out in a huge procession and on an enormous chariot—45 feet high, 35 feet square, and supported by 16 wheels, seven feet in diameter. The chariot is drawn by thousands of devotees.

The event commemorates Krishna's journey to Mathura from Gokul at Kansa's invitation. The chariot procession goes along the broad avenue to Gundicha Mandir, the Lord's Summer Garden house, where it stays for seven days before returning to the temple. At the termination of the ceremony the chariot is disassembled and its materials used to manufacture religious relics.

The king of Puri, the descendant of the original temple founder King Anantavarman Chodaganga, alone has the right to carry the Lord's umbrella and other paraphernalia, and it is he who sweeps the path before the chariot. The festival is observed everywhere in India where there is a temple dedicated to Jagannath.

Ravi Das Jayanti
Ravi Das, popularly known as Raidas, like Valmiki, was a member of a disadvantaged class. He was born on Ravivar (Sunday) to a Harijan family in a village near Varanasi, and was therefore named Ravi Das. He was contemporary of another great saint, Kabir.

Ravi Das was not well educated but possessed great insight and divine powers and performed many miracles. He spent most of his time in meditation on the banks of the Ganges; the remainder he dedicated to shoe-making, his paternal profession. He also composed many beautiful hymns in praise of God.

Like Kabir, Ravi Das also contributed to social reformation through his teachings. His was a period of corruption, hypocrisy, and religious intolerance; Ravi Das did his best to educate the masses by his own example and teachings. He believed in the essential unity and equality of life and in the tenet that work is also worship.

On Ravi Das Jayanti (birthday), processions bearing his portrait are taken out to the accompaniment of music through the main bazaars and streets of the city and towns. In temples dedicated to Ravi Das, his image is worshipped. At some places, feasts are also held on this occasion. In Varanasi special celebrations are held on Ravi Das Jayanti.

Reek Sunday
Last Sunday in July

Day on which Irish pilgrims ascend Croagh Padraig, the steep mountain in County Mayo named for Ireland's patron saint.

Reformation Day
October 31

On October 31, 1517, Martin Luther posted his ninety-five theses on the Wittenberg church door. His proposals were intended to spark discussion within the Roman Catholic church about what Luther saw as doctrinal error; instead, he started one of the most influential and far-reaching movements in the history of Christianity–the Reformation. Luther's ideas spread like wildfire across Europe, inspiring many to break from Rome and begin their own churches. The Protestant churches that were a result of this event observe October 31 as the anniversary of their beginning. The Lutheran church celebrates the Sunday prior to Reformation Day as Reformation Sunday.

Refreshment Sunday
See **Mothering Sunday**

Resurrection
See **Easter**

Ridvan, Feast of
April 21-May 2

During this twelve-day feast, Bahá'ís commemorate the 1863 declaration of Baha'u'llah, the founder of the religion, as the Promised One or Mahdi. He is considered by his followers to be of the same stature as Abraham, Moses, Jesus, Muhammad, Buddha, Krishna, and Zoroaster. The first, ninth, and twelfth days of the feast are the most holy. On these days, work is suspended and believers participate in observing the celebrations of the day.

Bahá'u'lláh's declaration took place in a garden outside of Baghdad he called Ridvan or Paradise. The full revelation of Baha'u'lláh's identity was made over a twelve-day period. The first day of the process, he declared himself to his family and close friends. On the ninth day, news of his declaration spread and followers came to join him. On the ninth day, he went out into the world with his message: he was the "promised one" prophesied by the Bab nineteen years earlier and would spread Bahá'í to all the world.

The main thrust of Bahá'u'lláh's gospel was the unity of all religions and the kinship of all humanity. Throughout his life, Bahá'u'lláh wrote over one hundred works which Bahá'í regards as sacred.

Rishi Panchami
Fifth day of the waxing half of the Hindu month of Bhadra (August-September)

This day's piety and acts of devotion are dedicated to the Sapta Rishis or the seven seers, mental sons of Brahma. They are: Bhrigu, Pulastya, Kratu, Pulaha, Marichi, Atri, and Vashistha. It is primarily a women's fast and festival, but can be observed by a man for the well-being and happiness of his wife.

An earthen or copper pitcher filled with water is installed on an altar sanctified with cow dung, and an eight-petalled lotus is also made thereon. Then the seven seers are worshipped with betel leaf, flowers, camphor and lamp. Devi Arundhati, the wife of Rishi Vasishtha and a model of conjugal excellence, is also worshipped along with the seven sages. Only fruits are eaten.

Rogation Days
Between April 30 and June 3; Monday, Tuesday, and Wednesday preceding Ascension Day

These three days of prayer and fasting for the harvest have been observed in Europe since the middle ages. The tradition of praying for the crops came to the United States early and is observed by many churches on Rogation Sunday, the fifth Sunday after Easter. Since 1929, this day has also been known as Rural Life Sunday or Soil Stewardship Sunday.

In England, Rogation Days were also a time when a procession of priests, prelates, and select parishioners walked the bounds of the parish three days prior to Ascension Sunday. On these days, a tradition particular to rural England developed. The priests would drive young boys around the bounds of the parish by beating them with willow switches. The practice, known as "beating the bounds," served to both teach the boys the limits of the parish as well as purify their souls.

See also **Ascension Day**.

Rose Monday
Between February 2 and March 8; Monday before Lent

Rose Monday, or Rosenmontag, occurs before Ash Wednesday and is celebrated in Germany and German-American communities as part of the Fasching or Carnival season. The German name Rosenmontag ("Roses Monday") takes its name from a mispronunciation of Rasen Montag ("Rushing Monday") or "live-it-up Monday"—an appropriate characterization of this day of celebration.

Rose Sunday
See **Mothering Sunday**

Rosh ha-Shanah
Between September 6 and October 4; Tishri 1 and 2

This memorial day marks the beginning the Jewish New Year. The first of ten High Holy Days, Rosh ha-Shanah starts a period of introspection, abstinence, prayer, and penitence which culminates with the observance of Yom Kippur, or the Day of Atonement.

During the liturgy on Rosh ha-Shanah, the story of Abraham is read in the synagogue and the ram's horn or *shofar* is sounded to commemorate Abraham's willingness to obey God's command that he sacrifice his son Isaac. God honored Abraham's obedience by providing a ram for the sacrifice instead.

Special food is prepared for the New Year celebration, including round loaves of challah bread to symbolize the continuity of life, as well as apples dipped in honey representing sweetness and health.

Rukmani Ashtami
Eighth day of the waning half of the Hindu month of Pausha (December-January)

This fast is observed by women, both married and unmarried. Vaishnavite Hindus generally believe that Rukmani was born on this day. Rukmani was Lord Krishna's principal wife and queen. She bore him a son, Pradyumna. According to the *Harivansha Purana*, she was sought in marriage by Krishna, with whom she fell in love. But her brother Rukmin had betrothed her to Shishupala, king of Chedi. On her wedding day, as she was going to the temple, Krishna saw her, took her by the hand, and carried her away in his chariot. They were pursued by Shishupala and Rukmin, but Krishna defeated them and took her safe to Dwarka and married her.

Rukmani, Krishna, and Pradyumna are worshipped on this day. A strict fast is observed, and married women are honored. A Brahman priest is also fed and given dan-dakshina on this day. Middle-class Hindus believe that observance of this fast ensures conjugal happiness and prosperity, and also enlist the help of Rukmani in finding good husbands for unmarried girls.

Rural Life Sunday
See **Rogation Days**

S

Sabbath of Rabbi Isaac Mayer Wise
Last Sabbath in the month of March

Each year, on a date that varies in the Jewish calendar, adherents to Reformed Judaism honor both the birth and death of Rabbi Isaac Mayer Wise (1819-1900). In 1873, Rabbi Wise organized a few scattered liberal congregations into what has become the Union of American Hebrew Congregations. In 1875, he founded the Hebrew Union Seminary. And in 1879, he founded the Central Conference of American Rabbis.

Sabbats
Greater Sabbats: February 1, May 1, August 1, and November 1; Lesser Sabbats: Spring equinox, Summer solstice, Fall equinox, and Winter solstice

The eight Sabbats of the "Wheel of the Year" constitute the major holidays celebrated by members of the various Neo-pagan religions that have flourished in the United States since the mid-1960s. These Sabbats are usually supplemented holidays that are important to specific covens. The most popular ancient religious traditions observed are the Celtic, Greek, Mesopotamian, Egyptian, and Nordic. The Sabbats may sometimes be displaced from their traditional date in order to fall closer to that of a specific pagan festival. For example, the Eleusinian Mysteries in Greece were celebrated just after the full moon that fell closest to the fall equinox. Thus, if September 22 falls midweek, a coven observing the Greek traditions will often move its Sabbat to a weekend nearer the full moon.

The eight Sabbats fall into two sub-groups: the Greater Sabbats, comprising the Celtic cross-quarter days; and the Lesser Sabbats, comprising the English quarter days, i.e., the solstices and equinoxes. The most common names for the Greater Sabbats are Brigid (February 1), Beltane (May 1), Lughnasad (August 1), and Samhain (pronounced "sa-oo-en," November 1). The common names for the Lesser Sabbats are Eostre (spring equinox, about March 22), Litha (summer solstice, about June 22), Mabon (fall equinox, about September 22), and Yule (winter solstice, about December 22).

Some covens meet for an "Esbat" at each full moon during the year; each Sabbat, therefore, is observed by means of a special ritual that is inserted into the middle of the coven's ordinary ritual. Hence, there is a set of eight such special rituals in a coven's liturgical manual or *Book of Shadows*.

Since 1970, the outdoor celebration of Sabbats in the United States has increased in popularity on both the local and national level. Whereas the local gatherings may attract a few dozen to a few hundred people, there is now an annual cycle of festivals—approximately one for each Sabbat in each major region of the United States (e.g., New England, southern California, the upper Midwest, or the Southeast)—regularly attended by thousands of Neo-pagan adherents. The "Wheel of the Year" of the eight Sabbats, referring to myths about the goddess and her consort, provides the basis for the "Sabbat Ritual," which combines drama, poetry, music, costume, and dance. The working of a newly written Sabbat Ritual is usually the climax of a festival.

See also **Esbat**.

Sacred Heart of Jesus, Feast of the
Between May 22 and June 25; Friday after Corpus Christi

The Feast of the Sacred Heart of Jesus is recognized by the Roman Catholic church as a solemnity "of the greatest importance". On this day, homage is paid to Christ's all encompassing love for humanity. Devotion to the Sacred Heart was introduced into the liturgy in the 17th century through the efforts of St. John Eudes, who composed an Office and Mass for the feast. It was furthered as the result of the revelations of St. Margaret Mary Alacoque after 1675 and by the work of Claude de la Colombiere, S.J. In 1765, Pope Clement XIII approved a Mass and Office for the feast, and in 1856 Pope Pius IX extended the observance to the entire Roman Catholic church.

St. Dismas Day
See **Annunciation of the Lord, Feast of**

St. John Lateran, Dedication of
See **Dedication of St. John Lateran**

St. John's Eve
See **Midsummer Eve**

St. Michael the Archangel, Feast of
See **Michaelmas**

St. Patrick's Day
March 17

St. Patrick was born around 390 C.E. in Roman Britain. He was raised in the Christian faith but was kidnapped by pagan Irish raiders and sold into slavery when he was 16. During his time in Ireland, St. Patrick strengthened his Christian beliefs in spite of the Irish opposition, and when he gained his freedom, he returned to his home to train for the priesthood. Eventually he returned to the Irish people to share his faith with them, and he was highly successful in converting many to Christianity. The shamrock that has become a symbol of St. Patrick supposedly comes from his use of its three-part leaf to describe the Holy Trinity. St. Patrick later became the patron saint of Ireland.

The Feast of St. Patrick is celebrated by Roman Catholics, the Anglican Communion, and Lutherans on March 17. The city of Boston holds a St. Patrick's Day parade which dates back to 1737. New York City's parade is a major event for Irish-Americans and was started in 1762. Up to 125,000 participants march on the route which takes them past St. Patrick's Cathedral on Fifth Avenue in Manhattan.

See also **Sheelah's Day**.

St. Valentine's Day
February 14

The customs associated with this "Lover's Day" may have had more to do with the customs of the Roman festival of the Lupercalia than with St. Valentine. The only Valentine or Valentinus of whom there is historical record was the founder of one of the most prevalent Gnostic sects, the Valentinians. They were noted in particular for their belief in "free love" and liberal view of sexuality.

The custom of choosing a lover on February 14 seems to have come from the Lupercalian ceremony of placing girls' names in a box from which boys drew their sweetheart for the next year. During the middle ages, the church sought to Christianize the custom by substituting saints' names for those of the girls and encouraging the drawers to emulate that saint for the next year. By the sixteenth century, however, this twist had been discarded and girls were once again being selected from the box. This custom eventually gave way to the practice of sending cards to the object of one's affections.

Saints, Doctors, Missionaries, & Martyrs Day
November 8

Observed by the Anglican churches, as a counterpart to the Roman Catholic feasts of All Saints and All Souls.

Sakata Chauth
Fourth day of the waning half of the Hindu month of Magha (January-February)

On this day, a fast is observed in honor of Lord Ganesha, who is believed to have been born on this day. The fast is believed to ensure wisdom, a trouble free life, and prosperity.

The fast is observed by both men and women. After the early morning bath, a pitcher and Ganesha statue are installed and worshipped with sweets and balls made of jaggery and sesame seeds. The moon god and Rohini are also worshipped ritually and offered food. At night, with the rising of the moon, the fast is broken. The moon is worshipped and offered water (arghya).

Salvation Army Founder's Day
April 10

Salvation Army posts and chapters worldwide celebrate the birthday of their founder, William Booth, on April 10, 1829, which is celebrated as the organization's birthday as well.

Samhain
November 1

Samhain (pronounced "Sa-oo-en") is the Celtic New Year's Eve and Festival of the Dead. It is also one of the cross-quarter days, on which the Neo-pagan Greater Sabbats are celebrated.

The Celtic belief was that the boundary between this world and the netherworld of fairies, gods, spirits, and magic was at its thinnest on this night. Therefore passage between the two dimensions was easiest at this time. Visitations from the spirits of one's own departed ancestors, divine beings, or demons were believed to be possible on this evening, but not desirable. Customs of this night were directed toward understanding and propitiating these spirits by divining their desires and giving them what they wanted, thus protecting one's family from their influences. All of these motifs are summarized in the apparently simple childhood ritual of "trick-or-treat." Neighbor children appear at the door of those displaying a lit "jack-o-lantern" on the porch. The costumes worn by the children represent these undesirable spirits who demand to be bribed with a treat to keep from working a trick on the inhabitants of the house.

The Sabbats of the Neo-pagans on this night tend toward honoring the dead: calling out the names of those who have passed on, remembering what they did in life, and asking the gods to grant them a worthy rebirth.

See also **Sabbats**.

San Estevan, Feast of
September 2

This festival is the annual harvest dance and feast day in the Native American pueblo of Acoma, New Mexico. Acoma was established in the twelfth century and is the oldest continuously inhabited community in America. Home to roughly fifty year-round residents, Acoma Indians from nearby villages return annually for the feast day and celebration.

A Mass and procession begin the festivities as a statue of San Estevan, the pueblo's patron saint, is taken from the church to the plaza. There, a variety of ritual dances are performed throughout the day.

Sante Fe Fiesta
Weekend after Labor Day

This festival combines religious and secular traditions in what is said to be the oldest such event in the United States. Dating to 1712, it recalls the early history of Sante Fe, New Mexico.

The Spanish *conquistadores* were ousted from Santa Fe in 1680 by a Pueblo Indian revolt. The Spanish, led by Don Diego de Vargas, peacefully regained control in 1693. Vargas had promised to venerate *La Conquistadora*, the small statue of the Virgin Mary now enshrined in St. Francis Cathedral, if she granted them success. In fulfillment of that promise, Vargas held the first procession in her honor in 1712.

The celebration begins with an early morning Mass on the Friday following Labor Day. After this, a grand procession takes place with figures representing Vargas and the fiesta queen, *la reina*, on horseback, leading the *Caballeros de Vargas* to the Plaza. On Friday night, a forty-four-foot fabric and wood effigy of Zozobra or Old Man Gloom is burned. Thousands of spectators shout "Burn him!" as the effigy pleads for mercy. Fireworks announce the end of Gloom; the crowds then proceed to the Plaza to embark on two days of dancing, street fairs, a grand ball, and a parade with floats satirizing local politicians. The fiesta ends on the following Sunday with an evening Mass of thanksgiving and a candlelight procession to the Cross of Martyrs overlooking Sante Fe.

Saturnalia
Late December

The great festival of Saturn was celebrated by the Romans in late December, just about the same period now observed as the "Christmas season" in the United States. It was marked by "reversals": cross-dressing, Lords of Misrule, the rich serving the poor, and so on, as is still practiced to some extent in the German Fasching traditions. Many Neo-Pagans celebrate a revived Saturnalia as their Yule festival.

Seventeenth of Tammuz
See **Jewish Fasts**

Shab Barat
Fifteenth night of the Islamic lunar month of Sha'ban

Shab-Barat (or Shab-i-Barat) is the evening on which Muslims, especially Indian and Pakistani followers, entreat Allah for forgiveness of their dead. The devout often spend the night in mosques praying and reading the Qu'ran. Muslims visit graveyards to pray for the souls of their friends and ancestors. Allah's mercy is celebrated by fireworks displays, the illumination of the outside of mosques, and provision of food for the poor.

This time is also known as Laylat al-Bara'ah, or the Night of Forgiveness. It is a time of preparation for Ramadan through intense prayer. Muslim belief indicates that this is the night on which destinies of the coming year are fixed and sins absolved.

Shalako Ceremonial
Late November or Early December

The Pueblo Indians at the Zuni Pueblo in southwestern New Mexico celebrate this impressive ceremonial dance in the fall of each year. Intended to commemorate the dead and entreat the gods for good health and weather in the coming year, the ceremony involves all-night ritual dances and chants, and the blessing of houses. The dance features towering masked figures with beaks who represent the rainmaker's messengers. Moving from house to house through the Pueblo, the dancers make clacking noises to indicate the houses receiving blessings. They stop at the designated houses, remove their masks, perform chants, and share food with the inhabitants.

Others taking part in the ceremony represent rain gods, whip-carrying warriors, and the fire god.

Shankaracharya Jayanti
Fifth day (southern India) or tenth day (northern India) of the waxing half of the Hindu month of Vaisakha (April-May)

This birth anniversary celebration honors Adi Shankaracharya, one of the greatest saint-philosophers of India who symbolizes India's cultural and emotional integrity and unity. Shankaracharya's coming was a great boon and blessing to millions of Hindus, who were then groping in the darkness of ignorance and religious decay. Shankaracharya, believed to be an incarnation of Shiva, revived Brahmanism and took Vedanta philosophy to new heights. Historically believed to have lived between 788 and 820 C.E., but according to tradition flourished in 200 B.C.E., Shankaracharya was a native of Malabar in Kerala. He worked many miracles and died at age 32. He is the reputed author of many original philosophical works and commentaries on the Upanishads, Vedanta Sutras, and *Bhagavad Gita*. He has been called the "Vedanta Guru," and his philosophy is equally accessible to both the learned and the layman. He composed many popular hymns, and urged people to devote themselves to God in any of his forms and incarnations. The Hindu custom is that Shankaracharya Jayanti is a fit occasion to study his works, to fast, to meditate, and to rededicate oneself to the service of the Lord.

Sharad Purnima
Full moon of the Hindu month of Ashvina (September-October)

The Hindu moon god is also the lord of herbs, seeds, Brahmans, waters, and Nakshatras or Constellations. Some Hindus believe that on Sharad Purnima, amrit (elixir) is showered on the earth by moonbeams. On this day khir (milk thickened with rice and mixed with sugar, candy, etc.) is especially prepared in the temples and homes, and offered to Hari amidst the ringing of the bells and chanting of hymns; the next morning it is given to the devotees. The recipe is kept in the moonshine all night so that it may absorb the amrit falling from the moon and such khir is considered to possess many qualities. At night the moon god is worshipped and offered food.

Shavuot
Between May 16 and June 13; Sivan 6 in the Hebrew calendar

Shavuot, or the Feast of Weeks, occurs fifty days after Passover and is the second of the three pilgrimages festivals (see also Passover and Sukkot.) This festival, which is also called Pentecost from the Greek word for "fiftieth", marks the end of the barley harvest and the beginning of the wheat harvest.

Historically, all adult Hebrew males were required to bring their first *omer* (or sheaf) of barley to the Temple in Jerusalem on this day as an offering of thanksgiving for the harvest.

When the nation of Israel was led out of slavery in Egypt, Shavuot gained a new name, the Festival of the Giving of the Law. It is on this day that Jews celebrate Moses' descent from Mt. Sinai with the Ten Commandments given to him by God. In the homes of Orthodox and Conservative Jews, Shavuot is celebrated for two days, but Reform Jews celebrate only one.

Sheelah's Day
March 18

Observed in Ireland on March 18, with shamrocks saved from March 17 (St. Patrick's Day) to honor Sheelah, the supposed wife or mother of St. Patrick.

Shitala Ashtami
Eighth day of the waxing half of the Hindu month of Chaitra (March-April)

Shitala Ashtami is a festival honoring the Hindu goddess Shitala. She is the goddess of smallpox and her blessings are invoked for protection against the disease. Shitala is depicted as roaming the countryside riding an ass. She is identified with the devil or Durga in her role as the goddess of smallpox. On this day, which is either a Monday or Friday, Hindu women visit the Shitala shrine in the morning, and offer rice, homemade sweets, cooked food, and holy water mixed with milk. At several places colorful fairs are held on this occasion near the shrine of Shitala and there is a lot of merry-making, songs, dance, feasting and brisk buying and selling.

Shiprock Navajo Nation Fair
Usually first weekend of October

Also known as the Northern Navajo Fair, this harvest fair began in 1924 and is considered the oldest and most traditional of Navajo fairs.

The fair coincides with the end of an ancient nine-day Navajo healing ceremony called the Night Chant. The ritual involved in the Night Chant are complex and only portions are open to public attendance.

Other events of the fair include an all-Indian rodeo and inter-tribal powwow, a livestock show, a carnival, the Miss Northern Navajo Pageant, exhibits by Indian artisans, and a parade on Saturday morning.

Shivaratri
See **Mahashivaratri**

Shravani Mela
Hindu month of Shravana (July-August)

Festivities associated with this festival include a grand fair, held in Bihar at Deoghar. Throughout the month, devotees pick up water from the holy Ganges at Sultanganj, carry it on their shoulders to Deoghar, and offer it on Shiva lingam. Along the 100-kilometer route pilgrims chant "Bol Bam! Bol Bam!" Thousands of them, clad in saffron, carry the sacred water in kanwars, continuing to their destination day and night in even the most inhospitable weather conditions. In the shrine at Deoghar, pilgrims throng carrying Ganges water and shouting "Bol Bam"!

Shrimp Fleet, Blessing of the
See **Blessing of the Shrimp Fleet**

Shrove Tuesday
See **Lent**

Skanda Shashti
Tamil month of Tulam (October-November)

Skanda Shashti is celebrated in south India with great religious fervor and devotion. Skanda, the second son of Shiva, is also known as Kartikeya or Subramanya.

Shiva cast his seed into fire, and it was afterwards received by the Ganges, which "gave birth" to him. The boy was fostered by Krittika (Pleiades) and has six heads. He was born for the purpose of destroying Taraka, a demon whose austerities had made him a formidable opponent to the gods. The festivities of Skanda Shashti celebrate Taraka's defeat.

Swami Kartikeya is represented riding a peacock, holding a bow in one hand and an arrow in the other. His wife is Dev Sena or Kumari. He has many titles: Mahasena, "the warrior;" Siddha-sena, "leader of the Siddhas;" Kumara, "the boy;" Guha, "the mysterious one;" Shakti-dhara, "spear holder;" and in the south he is called Subramanya. He is also called Tarakajit, Dwadashahara (twelve-handed) and Dwadaksha (twelve-eyed).

In south India there are six places associated with his life and work, which are regarded as most holy. At these places Skanda Shashti is celebrated with great fervor, and thousands of devotees congregate at each temple to seek the lord's blessings. Hymns are sung, psalms chanted, people fed, and scenes from his life dramatized. The festivity begins six days before the Shashti. Lord Subramanya is worshipped during these days, and devotees make pilgrimages to different Subramanya shrines. A common Hindu belief is that the devotion observed on this day ensure success, prosperity, peace, and happiness.

Smith, Joseph
See **Birthday of Joseph Smith**
See **Martyrdom of Joseph and Hyrum Smith**

Snan Yatra
Full-moon day of the Hindu month of Jyaishtha (May-June)

On this occasion, a grand bathing festival is held in Orissa. Images of the Lords Jagannath, Balbhadra, Subhadra, and Sudarshan are brought in a grand procession to the bathing platform for their ceremonial baths. With the recitation of mantras from the Vedas, 108 pots of consecrated waters are poured upon the deities. Then, the deities are ceremonially attired before they retire into seclusion for fifteen days. It is an occasion of great rejoicing and merrymaking.

Soil Stewardship Sunday
See **Rogation Days**

Solemnity of Mary, Mother of God
See **Circumcision, Feast of**

Songkran
April 13

The Thai Buddhist New Year which takes place at the spring equinox. The festivities surrounding the day take place over a three-day period (April 12-14) and are religious as well as secular. In the religious ceremonies, images of the Buddha are bathed in water and, like the Hindu Holi festival from which the tradition is derived, people splash each other with water as they walk through the street. Respect is shown to older people, however, as the young honor them by sprinkling water on their hands or feet rather than splashing them indiscriminately.

Sukkot
Between September 20 and October 18; Tishri 15-21

Sukkot (also known as Sukkoth or Succoth) was the third of the three pilgrimage feasts established by the Deuteronomic reform in 621 B.C.E. and is also called the Feast of Tabernacles, Booths, or the Ingathering. Like the other pilgrimages, Sukkot was a celebration of the harvest. In later times it came to be a commemoration of the wandering of the Israelites in the wilderness, where they lived in tent-like booths.

One traditional way Jewish families observed Sukkot was to build small booths or tabernacles and live in them during the week-long festival. In more recent times, Orthodox congregations build a *sukkah* in the synagogue and Reform Jews construct centerpieces for their tables that represent the huts used by their ancestors during the years of nomadic wandering.

Four trees are used as part of the liturgy in the synagogue during the festival. Palm and willow branches, citron, and myrtle twigs are tied together and waved at special points during the service to "rejoice before the Lord."

The seventh day of Sukkot, Hoshana Rabbah, has a special significance. As an extension of the Day of Atonement, it is the last possible day for people to seek and attain forgiveness for the sins of the previous year. On this day, the ceremony in the synagogue differs from that of the other six days of the festival. The service reflects a blending of the harvest celebration with the religious significance of the day. Mankind's dependence on rain is emphasized through symbolic rituals, and a solemn liturgy for repentance from the sins of the previous year is conducted.

Summer Solstice
See **Midsummer Eve**

Surya Shashti
Sixth day of the waxing fortnight of the Hindu month of Kartika (October-November)

Observance of Surya Shashti includes a continual three-day fast for married Hindu women with children. The preceding day, only one meal is taken without salt. On Shashti, women participating in the fast abstain from taking even water, yet they worship the sun with offerings of food and water, and keep night vigil.

The next day, on Saptami, the aspirant women bathe before sunrise, worship the rising sun, and break their fast. Brahmans are also fed and given gifts on this day. Hindu women believe that the fast and piety observed on this day ensure the good health, longevity, and happiness of their progeny and husbands.

Swarupa Dwadashi
Twelfth day of the waning half of the Hindu month of Pausha (December-January)

The vow of Swarupa Dwadashi is observed by women desiring physical beauty, happiness, and healthy progeny. On the preceding day (Ekadashi), aspirant women ritually tell stories relating to Lord Vishnu. On Dwadashi they keep a strict fast, place an image of Vishnu in a vessel full of sesame, and worship it. Afterward, oblations are offered in the fire, Brahmans are fed and given charity, and the fast is broken.

T

Ta'anit Esther
See **Purim**

Tabaski
See **'Id al-Adha**

Tabernacles
See **Sukkot**

Teej
Third day of bright half of Shravana (July-August)

Teej is a Hindu festival heralding the beginning of the monsoon season. Because the monsoon symbolizes fertility, Hindu women celebrate the goddess Parvati, consort of Shiva. Teej marks the day on which Parvati (also known as Gauri) left her family home to live with Shiva. To commemorate this event, streets in every village are decorated with swings hung from trees, and women swing and sing songs in praise of Pavarotti.

Other festivities of the day include a worshipful ceremony in honor of Parvati and lively processions representing Parvati's journey to her husband's home. People bedecked in festive costumes and makeup participate in a myriad of local fairs.

Tenth of Tebet
See **Jewish Fasts**

Tet Nguyenden
First day of the first lunar month, at the new moon in Capricorn

This date, also known as Ten Nhat, marks the Vietnamese New Year.

Thanksgiving
Fourth Thursday in November

Thanksgiving Day in America traditionally commemorates the survival of the Pilgrims at the Plymouth, Massachusetts settlement. After their journey from England to North America, the settlers endured a terrible winter and an epidemic that threatened the existence of the colony. The Pilgrims were saved by native Indians who taught them how to plant crops in their new home; so, when the first bountiful harvest came in, the Pilgrims and Indians joined together to share in the goodness of the land.

Although many days of thanks have been declared and observed, the last Thursday in November was set aside by Abraham Lincoln as a day to remember the goodness of God to the United States. In 1939, Franklin D. Roosevelt changed this date to the fourth Thursday in November, although some states still observe the holiday according to Lincoln's proclamation.

Often, people attend church services on Thanksgiving morning. They may participate in a local parade, and then gather with family members for a meal usually consisting of stuffed turkey, mashed potatoes, yams, cranberry sauce, and pumpkin pie.

In Canada, Thanksgiving is normally celebrated on the second Monday in October, coinciding with Columbus Day.

Thingyan Tet
On or about April 15

The Burmese solar New Year, when the Sun enters the sign of Aries sidereally.

Third of Tishri
See **Fast of Gedaliah**
See **Jewish Fasts**

Tirupati Festival
Ten day during the Hindu month of Bhadrapada (August-September)

A grand festival, held at Tirupati, the seat of Lord Venkteshwara, a manifestation of Lord Vishnu. The festival lasts for ten days and during it devotees congregate to seek Lord Venkteshwara's blessings for material and spiritual gains. Even on ordinary days, over 20,000 pilgrims arrive to pray and worship the deity.

The shrine at Tirupati, one of the richest temples in the world, is situated on the seven Tirumala hills, which correspond to the seven hoods of the snake god Adishesha, who forms the bed of Vishnu in the cosmic ocean. Because of these seven picturesque hills, Venkteshwara is also known as the "Lord of the Seven Hills."

Tirupati is considered an essential pilgrimage center for every devout Hindu. It is tradition here that devotees, whether men or women, shave their hair off as a votive offering for a vow fulfilled. Parents bring their very young children to perform their first tonsure at the feet of the Lord.

Transfiguration of Jesus
August 6

This holiday commemorates the revelation of Jesus' divinity to Peter, James, and John on Mt. Tabor during their visit with Elijah and Moses. The feast, which is very old, was extended throughout the Church in 1457 by Pope Callistus III.

Trinity Sunday
Between May 17 and June 20; first Sunday after Pentecost in the Western Church, the Monday after Pentecost in the Orthodox tradition (called Trinity Day)

Unlike other Christian observances, Trinity Sunday is not associated with any specific saint or historical event. Instead, it honors the Christian belief in one God with a triune nature. According to Christianity, there are three manifestations of God—Father, Son, and Holy Spirit. A votive Mass of the Most Holy Trinity dates from the seventh century; an Office was composed in the 10th century; in 1334, Pope John XXII extended the feast to the entire Church.

Triumph of the Holy Cross
September 14

This Christian feast commemorates significant events relating to the cross on which Christ was crucified. These events include: the 326 C.E. discovery of fragments of the cross by St. Helena, mother of Constantine; the consecration of the basilica which was constructed in honor of the cross nearly 10 years after St. Helena's discovery; and the recovery around 628 C.E. of a major portion of the cross that had been taken from Jerusalem by the Persians. The feast originated in Jerusalem and spread through the East before being adopted in the West. General adoption followed the building at Rome of the Basilica of the Holy Cross in Jerusalem, so called because it enshrined what was believed to be a major portion of the true cross.

Trung-Thu
Full moon after the new moon in Virgo

Vietnamese autumn festival marked by street dancing and lantern-making.

Tu Bishvat
See **Bi-Shevat**

Tulsidas Jayanti
Seventh day of the waxing half of the Hindu month of Shravana (July-August)

The saintly poet Tulsidas was contemporary with Akbar the Great. He was born to Brahman parents, but was orphaned, and was thereafter raised and educated by St. Narharidas, who had been instructed to do so by God appearing to him in a dream. Tulsidas married and started living the life of a householder, but chance words of his wife awakened his ardent devotion to God, and he became a sanyasi and began to live at Varanasi. There he wrote his well-known *Ramacharitra Manas* and a dozen other books. His masterpiece *Ramayana* was written in the language of the common people for their benefit and is revered by devout Hindus. His example of sanctity and the magic of his writings have had a far-reaching impact for the spiritual uplifting of the masses—comparable to the teachings of hundreds of gurus. He and his works are so greatly revered that tradition regards him as Valmiki reborn.

Many Hindus believe that Tulsidas died on the same day that he was born; on that day, a fast is kept, and works of charity are done. The *Ramayana* is read and recited, Brahmans are fed, and Lord Rama, along with his consort Sita and devotee Hanuman, is worshipped with great religious fervor. In literary and social circles, discussions, lectures, seminars, and symposiums are organized on Tulsidas' teachings, life, and works.

Twelfth Day
See **Epiphany**

Twelfth Night
See **Epiphany Eve**

Twelve Days of Christmas
See **Christmas, Twelve Days of**

U

Ugadi Parva
First day of the Hindu month of Chaitra (March-April)

Ugadi Parva is a Hindu festival that ushers in the New Year for the inhabitants of Andhra. On this day, people visit one another, enjoy feasts, and wear new clothes. The festive day begins with ritual bath and prayers, and continues late into the night. Some Hindus believe that both Brahma's creation of the world and Lord Vishnu's first incarnation as Matsya (the fish) occurred on this day. Brahma is especially worshipped on this day.

Universal Week of Prayer
First Sunday through the second Sunday in January

This custom, begun by the World Evangelical Alliance of London, England, in 1846, has been adopted and sponsored by the National Council of Churches. It is marked by interdenominational services in many American communities; these are held in the evenings, and move from denomination to denomination during the week.

Up-Helly-Aa
Last Tuesday on January

An old Norse fire festival revived in 1889, during the first modern wave of Neo-paganism. It is observed with reconstructed pagan rituals, including the burning of a Viking ship, at Lerwick in the Shetland Islands. Also known as Antinmas, a name which may be derived from the Old Norse for "ending of the holy days".

Uttarayanna Sankranti
See **Makar Sankrati**

Vaikuntha Ekadashi
Eleventh day of both the waxing and waning fortnights in the Hindu month of Margashirsha (November-December)

Vaikuntha Ekadashi is celebrated in the south of India. Devotees observe a fast, keep vigil the whole night, and have meditation sessions. A gateway in the temple is thrown open on this day for aspirants to pass through, signifying their entrance into heaven or vaikuntha. As on any Ekadashi, rice eating is prohibited because a demon is said to dwell in rice grains on this day. A demon was born of the sweat that fell from Brahma's head, and he wanted a place to live away from Brahma. Brahma told him to go live in the rice grains eaten by people on Ekadashi and to become worms in their stomach.

Once a great demon called Mura, who had 7,000 sons, harassed the gods. The gods prayed to Vishnu for protection against Mura. Vishnu sent his Yog Maya to kill the demon and his sons, and she did it successfully. Thereupon Vishnu said that she would be known by the name of Ekadashi, and the people who observe a fast and piety on this day would be freed from all sins and get a place in heaven.

Vaisakha
See **Wesak**

Vaitarani
Eleventh day of the waning half of the Hindu month of Margashirsha (November-December)

Aspirants observe a fast and other prescribed rituals. In the evening a black cow is worshipped. She is bathed in fragrant water, sandal paste is applied on her horns, and food is offered to her. Brahmans are also given gifts of food, clothes, and a cow made of either gold and silver.

A cow is worshipped and offered food on this day because the river Vaitarani, the Hindu Styx, can only be crossed with the aid of a cow. The river, said to be filled with all kinds of filth, blood, and moral offenses must be crossed by departed souls before the infernal regions can be entered. Many Hindus believe that a cow given to Brahmans transports the dead over the river. Thus, cows are given in charity to Brahmans when there is a death in the community.

Valentine's Day
See **St. Valentine's Day**

Valmiki Jayanti
Full-moon day of the Hindu month of Ashvina (September-October)

Celebrates the birthday of the Ai Kavi (the "first Poet") Valmiki, the author of the Sanskrit *Ramayana*. A contemporary of Rama, the hero of the *Ramayana*, Valmiki himself is represented as taking part in some of the scenes he relates. He received the banished Sita into his hermitage and educated her twin sons Kusha and Lava. The invention of the "Shloka" (epic meter) is attributed to Valmiki.

Originally, Valmiki, a member of a disadvantaged class, robbed and killed people passing through the forest, but because of the influence of some sages, he repented and went to a hermitage on a hill in the district of Bonda in Bundelkhanda. There he received Sita, when banished by Rama.

He received the name "Valmiki" because when immersed in meditation he allowed himself to be overrun with ants like an anthill. Members of many disadvantaged Indian classes claim they are descended from Valmiki. On his birthday he is worshipped and prayed to, and his portraits are taken out in gay processions through the main bazaars and streets.

Vartanantz Day
Thursday preceding Ash Wednesday

Armenian commemoration of the death of their patron saint, along with 1,036 other martyrs, during the war with Persia in 451 C.E.

Vasant Panchami
Fifth day of the waxing half of the month of Magha (January-February)

This Hindu festival honors Saraswati, goddess of learning, eloquence, and the arts. During this holiday season, people wear bright yellow clothing to represent the mustard plant whose blossoms herald the coming of spring. The day of Vasant Panchami is celebrated with music, dancing, and kite-flying.

In West Bengal, Saraswati is known as the goddess of speech, learning, wisdom, fine arts, and sciences. She is credited with the invention of the Sanskrit language and the Devnagari script. Celebrations of Vasant Panchami in West Bengal include a procession in which images of her graceful figure are carried to the river for a ceremonial bath, and books and pens are placed at her shrine.

Vasanta Navratra
See **Rama Navani**

Vata Savitri
Thirteenth day of the waning fortnight of the Hindu month of Jyaishtha (May-June)

The fast of Vata Savitri is generally observed on this date, but at some places it is observed on the full moon of Jyaishtha. It is meant only for married women, who keep this vow for the sake of the longevity and well-being of their husbands.

According of the scriptures, Savitri, the daughter of King Aswapati, was the lover of Satyavan. She married him, though she was warned by a seer that Satyavan had only one year to live. One fated day Satyavan went out to cut wood, and Savitri followed him. Satyavan fell to the earth. As he lay dying, Savitri supported his body in her arms. As she did so, she observed a figure calling itself Yama and claiming the right to Satyavan's soul. Yama carried off Satyavan's soul, but Savitri followed him. Her devotion so pleased Yama, the god of death, that he restored her husband's life. Like Savitri, it is the desire of every Hindu never to die as a widow.

The Vata (banyan tree) is a sacred tree among Hindus. On the day of her husband's death, Savitri had worshipped the Vata; so on this day women get up early in the morning, and having bathed, go to worship the Vata in brightly-clad groups. They ceremonially water the tree, sprinkle red powder on it, wrap raw cotton threads around its trunk, and then circle it seven times. Returning home, they paint a Vata on the sanctified wall with turmeric powder and sandalwood, and offer it prayer and worship. After breaking their fast, they give fruits, clothes, and other articles in a bamboo basket to the Brahmans. They repeat the story of Satyavan-Savitri among themselves, and pray for the prosperity and good health of their husbands.

Vernal Equinox
See **Quarter Days**

Vesak
See **Wesak**

Vijag
Eve of Ascension Thursday

An Armenian "festival of fortune," marked by dancing, singing, and fortune-telling by means of tokens tossed into bowls of water drawn from springs believed to be especially pure on that night.

Vijay Dashami
See **Dussehra**

Vinayak
See **Ganesha Chaturthi**

Visitation of the Virgin Mary to Elizabeth
May 31 in the Roman Catholic and Protestant churches; July 2 in the Anglican church

This feast commemorates Mary's visit to her cousin Elizabeth, the mother of John the Baptist. After the Annunciation, Mary spent several months with her cousin Elizabeth in the mountains of Judea. Elizabeth reported that the baby in her womb (who would become John the Baptist, precursor of Christ) literally leapt with joy when Mary approached. According to the doctrine of the Roman Catholic church, this was the moment at which John the Baptist was cleansed from original sin and filled with heavenly grace.

The Feast of the Visitation is a feast of the Incarnation and is notable for its recall of the Magnificat, a canticle which acknowledges the unique gifts of God to Mary because of her role in the redemptive work of Christ. The canticle is recited at Vespers in the Liturgy of the Hours.

Volunteers of America Founder's Day
July 28

The Volunteers of America, an offshoot of the Salvation Army, honors the birth of their founder Ballington Booth on July 28, 1859.

W

Water Drawing Festival
See **Omizutori Matsuri**

Wesak
Full moon after the new moon in (sidereal) Taurus

Wesak is a variant on the Hindu Vaisakha, which are also spelled Vesak and Baisakhi. It is a Hindu New Year festival, but for Buddhists it celebrates the birth, enlightenment, and death of the Buddha. Wesak is generally celebrated by decorating Buddhist temples with spring flowers to honor the infant Buddha. It is one of three festivals celebrated at adjacent full moons by the followers of Alice Bailey's Arcane School and its offshoots.

See also **Baisakhi**.

Whitsunday
Pentecost

Whit (for "white") Sunday or Whitsuntide is the English name for Pentecost, possibly in reference to the white robes of converts who were baptized on that day. This is also the traditional day of Lady Godiva's ride.

See also **Pentecost**.

Williams, Roger
See **Arrival of Roger Williams in the New World**

Winter Solstice
See **Quarter days**

Wise, Rabbi Isaac Mayer
See **Sabbath of Rabbi Isaac Mayer Wise**

World Community Day
First Friday in November

A day sponsored by Church Women United to promote peace and justice.

World Day of Prayer
First Friday in March

Sponsored by Church Women United and observed in more than 170 countries.

World Invocation Day
Spring of each year at the full moon in Sagittarius

A holiday observed by the Arcane School founded by Alice A. Bailey, and by the churches and organizations descended from it. It is the third of the three Great Festivals observed in the spring of each year. The first is Easter, at the full moon in Libra; the second is Wesak, at the full moon in Scorpio; and the third is World Invocation Day, also known as the Festival of Goodwill, at the full moon in Sagittarius. The focus of its observance is a prayer written by Bailey, known as the Great Invocation, which is recited by people meeting around the world on this day. This festival is the forerunner of recent examples of "world-wide prayer meetings," such as the Harmonic Convergence in 1988.

World Peace Day
September 21 (National Spiritual Assembly of the Bahá'ís of the United States); August 24 (Church of Scientology)

The Bahá'í celebration of this day in the United States is intended to call for and support leadership in world peace.

The Church of Scientology celebrates a holiday by the same name to commemorate their first International Conference for World Peace and Social Reform, held at Anaheim, California, in 1976.

World Religion Day
Third Sunday in January

In 1950, the National Spiritual Assembly of the Bahá'ís of the United States established this day as a holiday to focus world attention on the harmony of all religions. The Bahá'í maintain that all religion is intended to create unity, ease suffering, and bring about peace; everyone should, therefore, work together to accomplish these goals. People gather in homes, or hold public meetings and panel discussions to observe the day.

Wuwuchim
Eve of the new moon in November

Wuwuchim is the new year for Hopi Indians and is observed in Hopiland in northeastern Arizona. As the most significant of Hopi rituals, it establishes the rhythms for the year to come.

Over a four-day period, priests offer prayers, songs, and dances for a prosperous and safe new year. Other traditions include dances performed by men of the tribe costumed in embroidered kilts. Their dance is accompanied by the creation-myth chants of priests from the Bear Clan.

Y

Yom Ha-Shoah
Nisan 27

This solemn occasion is observed by Jews as the "Day of the Holocaust." It commemorates the mass killing of six million Jews by the Nazis during World War II. People of many faiths also mourn on this day in remembrance of Jewish victims as well as the other six million people who were exterminated in Nazi death camps during the same period.

Observance of Yom Ha-Shoah focuses on the impact of this catastrophe that shocked and impoverished all mankind. It is dedicated to the hope that human beings will never forget the horror of the Holocaust and assure that it never happens again.

Yom Kippur
Tishri 10

The Jewish "Day of Atonement"; the holiest day of the Jewish year. Also known as Yom Tov, the "Day of

Goodness," it is observed by strict fasting and ceremonial repentance.

The synagogue services on the eve of Yom Kippur are traditionally called the *Kol Nidre* services, after the prayer which begins with the Hebrew words for "all vows." In the prayer, the people renounce all thoughtless vows they may have made during the preceding year, and forgive all debts owed to them and all wrongs done to them during the year; only then, it is believed, will God forgive them for their violations of his laws during the year. In the Middle Ages, it was understood that the *Kol Nidre* prayer was a renunciation of any vows a Jew had been forced to make under threats of violence or death. This prayer, therefore, allowed Jews to renounce forced conversions to Christianity (which were common in Spain, for example) and to continue to be accepted as Jews by the Jewish community.

Young, Brigham
See **Birthday of Brigham Young**

Yule
Winter solstice; around December 22

Yule is still used as an alternative name for Christmas, but it was originally the Saxon name for their winter-solstice festival. Neo-pagans hold one of their four Lesser Sabbats on the winter solstice and have adopted this term as its name.

The Yule Sabbat ritual usually focuses on the themes of the return of light, of the birth of the new king, and of the giving of presents, which was a pagan custom long before Christianity.

See also **Sabbats**.

Bibliography

Adler, Margot. *Drawing Down the Moon: Witches, Pagans, Druids, and Other Goddess-Worshippers in America Today.* 2d ed. NY: Viking Press, 1979. Boston: Beacon Press, 1987.

Allen, Richard. *The Life Experience and Gospel Labors of the Rt. Rev. Richard Allen.* Nashville: Abingdon Press, 1960.

Arcana Workshops. *The Full Moon Story.* Beverly Hills, CA: Arcana Workshops, 1967.

Asimov, Isaac. *The Clock We Live On.* Revised ed. New York: Abelard-Schumann, 1965.

Attwater, Donald. *The Penguin Dictionary of Saints.* New York: Penguin, 1965.

Bahá'í Meetings: The Nineteen Day Feast; Extracts from the Writings of Bahá'u'lláh, 'Abdu'l-Bahá, and Shoghi Effendi. Wilmette, IL: Bahá'í Publishing Trust, 1976.

Bamberger, Bernard J. *The Bible: A Modern Jewish Approach.* New York: B'nai B'rith Hillel Foundations, 1955.

Barashango, Ishakamusa. *Afrikan People and European Holidays: A Mental Genocide, Book I.* Washington, D.C.: IV Dynasty Publishing, 1980.

Barrett, Michael. *Footprints of the Ancient Scottish Church.* N.p., 1914.

Bede. *A History of the English Church and People.* Translated by Leo Sherley-Price. Baltimore, MD: Penguin, 1955.

Bloch, Abraham P. *The Biblical and Historical Background of the Jewish Holy Days.* New York: Ktav, 1978.

Brand, John, and Henry Ellis. *Observations on the Popular Antiquities of Great Britain.* 3 vols. London: Bohn, 1853.

Buckland, Raymond. *The Tree: The Complete Book of Saxon Witchcraft.* York Beach, ME: Samuel Weiser, 1974.

Burkert, Walter. *Homo Necans.* Berkeley: University of California Press, 1983.

Burland, C. A. *Echoes of Magic: A Study of Seasonal Festivals Through the Ages.* London: Peter Davies, 1972.

Butler, Alban. *The Lives of the Fathers, Martyrs, and Other Principal Saints.* 12 vols. 1846. Reprint (12 vols. in 4). New York: Sadlier, 1857.

Campbell, Joseph. *The Masks of God, Vol. 3: Occidental Mythology.* New York: Viking, 1964.

Campbell, Joseph, ed. *The Mysteries: Papers from the Eranos Yearbooks.* Translated by Ralph Manheim & R. F. C. Hull. Princeton, NJ: Princeton University Press, 1955.

Clinton, Kevin. "The Sacred Officials of the Eleusinian Mysteries." *Transactions,* n.s. Vol. 63, pt. 3. Philadelphia, 1974.

Cole, W. Owen, and Piara Singh Sambhi. *The Sikhs: Their Religious Beliefs and Practices.* London: Routledge & Kegan Paul, 1978.

Colson, F.H. *The Week.* Cambridge, Eng.: Cambridge University Press, 1926.

Cook, Arthur Bernard. *Zeus: A Study of Ancient Religion.* 3 vols. Cambridge, Eng.: Cambridge University Press, 1914-1940.

Cowie, L. W., and John S. Gummer. *The Christian Calendar: A Complete Guide to the Seasons of the Christian Year.* Springfield, MA: Merriam-Webster, 1974.

Crowley, Aleister. *Magick in Theory and Practice.* NY: Dover Publications, 1976.

De Bles, Arthur. *How to Distinguish the Saints in Art by Their Costumes, Symbols, and Attributes.* New York: Art Culture Publications, 1925.

Deems, Edward Mark. *Holy-days and Holidays.* 1902. Reprint. Detroit, MI: Gale Research Co. , 1968.

Delehaye, Hippolyte. *The Legends of the Saints.* Translated by D. Attwater. New York: Fordham University Press, 1962.

Delaney, John J. *Dictionary of Saints.* New York: Doubleday, 1980.

Drake, Maurice, and Wilfred Drake. *Saints and Their Emblems.* 1916. Reprint. Detroit: Gale Research, 1971.

Eisenberg, Azriel Louis. *The Story of the Jewish Calendar.* London and New York: Abelard-Schuman, 1958.

Ellwood, Robert S., Jr. *Religious and Spiritual Groups in Modern America.* Engleweed Cliffs, N.J.: Prentice-Hall, Inc., 1973.

Engelbert, Omer. *The Lives of the Saints.* Translated by Christopher Fremantle and Anne Fremantle. David McKay, 1951.

Farnell, Lewis R. *The Cults of the Greek States.* 5 vols. London: Oxford University Press, 1896-1909.

Farrar, Stewart, and Janet Farrar. *Eight Sabbats for Witches.* London: Robert Hale, 1981.

Farrar, Stewart, and Janet Farrar. *The Witches' Way: Principles, Rituals, amd Beliefs of Modern Witchcraft.* London: Robert Hale, 1984.

Fasts and Festivals of India. New Delhi: Diamond, n.d.

Ferguson, John. *The Religions of the Roman Empire.* Ithaca, N.Y.: Cornell University Press, 1970.

Fitch, Ed, and Janine Renee. *Magical Rites from the Crystal Well.* St. Paul, MN: Llewellyn, 1984.

Fontenrose, Joseph. *Python: A Study of Delphic Myth and Its Origin.* Berkeley: University of California Press, 1959.

Fowler, W. Warde. *The Roman Festivals of the Period of the Republic: An Introduction to the Study of the Religion of the Romans.* London: Macmillan, 1899.

Frazer, Sir James G. *The Golden Bough.* 3d ed. 13 vols. London: Macmillan, 1912.

Gardner, Gerald B. *Witchcraft Today.* London: Jarrolds, 1954.

Gaster, Theodore H. *Festivals of the Jewish Year: A Modern Interpretation and Guide.* New York: William Sloane, 1953.

Gaster, Theodore H. *Thespis: Ritual, Myth, and Drama in the Ancient Near East.* 2d ed. New York: Doubleday, 1961.

Gaver, Jessyca Russell. *The Bahá'í Faith.* New York: Award Books, 1967.

Goodman, Philip. *The Rosh Hashanah Anthology.* Philadelphia: The Jewish Publication Society of America, 1973.

Graves, Robert. *The Greek Myths.* 2 vols. New York: Penguin, 1955.

Graves, Robert. *The White Goddess: A Historical Grammar of Poetic Myth.* 3d ed. London: Faber & Faber, 1948.

Green, Marian. *A Harvest of Festivals.* London: Longman, 1980.

Gregory, Ruth W. *Anniversaries and Holidays.* 4th ed. Chicago: American Library Assn, 1983.

Hammond, N. G. L., and H. H. Scullard. *The Oxford Classical Dictionary.* 2d ed. Oxford, Eng.: The Clarendon Press, 1970.

Harper, Howard V. *Days and Customs of All Faiths.* New York: Fleet Publishing, 1957.

Harrison, Jane Ellen. *Prolegomena to the Study of Greek Religion.* 1903. Reprint. Princeton: Princeton Univer. Press, 1991.

Hawkins, Gerald S. *Stonehenge Decoded.* NY: Doubleday, 1965.

Hoyle, Sir Fred. *Stonehenge.* San Francisco: W. H. Freeman, 1976.

Hubbard, L. Ron. *What Is Scientology?* Los Angeles, CA: Church of Scientology of California, 1978.

Hutchison, Ruth, and Ruth Adams. *Every Day's a Holiday.* New York: Harper & Row, 1951.

Ickis, Marguerite. *The Book of Festivals and Holidays the World Over.* New York: Dodd, Mead, 1970.

Jumsai, M. L. Manich. *Understanding Thai Buddhism.* 2d ed. Bangkok, Thailand: Chalermnit Press, 1973.

Jung, Carl G., and C. Kerényi. *Essays on a Science of Mythology: The Myth of the Divine Child and the Mysteries of Eleusis.* Translated by R. F. C. Hull, 1949. 2d ed. Reprint. Princeton, NJ: Princeton University Press, 1963.

Kenneth, Br., C.G.A. *A Pocket Calendar of Saints and People to Remember.* Oxford, Eng.: A. R. Mowbray, 1981.

Kerényi, C. *Eleusis: Archetypal Image of Mother and Daughter.* Trans. by Ralph Manheim. 1960. Reprint. New York: Pantheon, Bollingen Series 65:4, 1967.

Kightly, Charles. *The Customs and Ceremonies of Britain: An Encyclopaedia of Living Traditions.* London: Thames & Hudson, 1986.

Mathers, S. L. MacGregor, ed. and trans. *The Greater Key of Solomon.* Chicago: De Laurence, Scott, 1914.

Melton, Gordon J. *The Encyclopedia of American Religions.* 3d ed. Detroit, MI: Gale Research Inc., 1989.

Mossman, Jennifer, ed. *Holidays and Anniversaries of the World.* Detroit, MI: Gale Research, 1985.

Murray, Margaret A. *The God of the Witches.* London: Oxford University Press, 1931.

Murray, Margaret A. *The Witch-Cult in Western Europe.* London: Oxford University Press, 1962.

Mylonas, George E. *Eleusis and the Eleusinian Mysteries.* Princeton, NJ: Princeton University Press, 1961.

National Conference of Catholic Bishops. *Holy Days in the United States: History, Theology, Celebration.* Washington, D.C.: United States Catholic Conference, 1984.

National Spiritual Assembly of the Bahá'ís of the United States. *The Bahá'í World: A Biennial International Record* XII (1950-1954) Wilmette, IL: Bahá'í Publishing Trust, 1956.

Neugebauer, Otto, and H. B. van Hoesen. *Greek Horoscopes.* Philadelphia: American Philosophical Society, 1959.

Nilsson, Martin P. *Greek Folk Religion.* New York: Columbia University Press, 1940.

Nilsson, Martin P. *Primitive Time-Reckoning: A Study in the Origins and First Development of the Art of Counting Time Among the Primitive and Early Culture Peoples.* Lund, Norway: Gleerup, 1920.

O'Flaherty, Wendy Doniger. *Hindu Myths.* Middlesex, England: Penguin Books, 1975.

Ogilvie, R. M. *The Romans and Their Gods in the Age of Augustus.* New York: W.W. Norton & Company, Inc., 1969.

O'Neil, W. M. *Time and the Calendars.* Sydney, Australia: Sydney University Press, 1975.

Oxbridge Omnibus of Holiday Observances Around the World. New York: Oxbridge Communications, 1976.

Parise, Frank, ed. *The Book of Calendars.* New York: Facts on File, 1982.

Perkins, Mary, and Philip Hainsworth. *The Bahá'í Faith.* London: Ward Lock Educational, 1980.

Pfeiffer, Robert H. *Introduction to the Old Testament.* 2d ed. New York: Harper, 1948.

Pollard, John. *Seers, Shrines, and Sirens: The Greek Religious Revolution in the Sixth Century B.C.* New York: A. S. Barnes, 1965.

Price, Nancy. *Pagan's Progress: High Days and Holy Days.* London: Museum Press, 1954.

Rees, Aylwin, and Brinsley Rees. *Celtic Heritage: Ancient Tradition in Ireland and Wales.* London: Thames & Hudson, 1961.

Regardie, Israel. *The Golden Dawn: An Account of the Teachings, Rites, and Ceremonies of the Order of the Golden Dawn.* 2d ed. Minneapolis, MN: Hazel Hills, 1969.

Renfrew, Colin. "Carbon-14 and the Prehistory of Europe." *Scientific American,* Oct. 1971:63-72.

Renfrew, Colin. "The Origins of Indo-European Languages." *Scientific American,* Oct. 1989:106-114.

Roeder, Helen. *Saints and Their Attributes, with a Guide to Localities and Patronage.* London: Longmans, Green, 1955.

Rose, H. J. *A Handbook of Greek Mythology.* 6th ed. London, England: Methuen & Co. Ltd., 1958.

Rose, H. J. *Religion in Greece.* New York: Harper, 1946.

Rose, H. J. *Religion in Greece and Rome.* New York: Harper, 1948.

Rosenau, William. *Jewish Ceremonial Institutions and Customs.* 4th ed. New York: Bloch, 1929.

Ross, Anne. *Pagan Celtic Britain: Studies in Iconography and Tradition.* New York: Columbia University Press, 1967.

Ryan, Charles J. *H. P. Blavatsky and the Theosophical Movement.* Pasadena, CA: Theosophical University Press, 1974.

Shemanski, Frances. *A Guide to World Fairs and Festivals.* Westport, Conn.: Greenwood Press, 1985.

Smart, Ninian. *The Religious Experience of Mankind.* New York: Charles Scribner's Sons, 1969.

Spangler, David. *Festivals in the New Age.* Moray, Scotland: Findhorn Foundation, 1975.

Spicer, Dorothy, Gladys. *The Book of Festivals.* Detroit, MI: Gale Research, 1969.

Stapleton, Michael. *The Illustrated Dictionary of Greek and Roman Mythology.* London: The Hamlyn Publishing Group Ltd., 1978.

Starhawk. *The Spiral Dance: A Rebirth of the Ancient Religion of the Great Goddess.* 2d ed. San Francisco, CA: Harper & Row, 1989.

Stutley, Margaret. *Hinduism.* Wellingborough, Northamptonshire: The Aquarian Press, 1985.

Thomson, George. *Studies in Ancient Greek Society.* Vol. I. 3d ed. London: Lawrence & Wishart, 1961. Vol. II, London: Lawrence & Wishart, 1955.

The Three Festivals of Spring. Ojai, CA: MGNA Publications, 1971.

Tillem, Ivan L. *The Jewish Directory and Almanac.* Vol. I. New York: Pacific Press, 1984.

Tolkien, J.R.R. *The Silmarillion.* New York: Houghton, Mifflin, 1977.

Trepp, Leo. *The Complete Book of Jewish Observance.* New York: Behrman House and Summit Books, 1980.

Valiente, Doreen. *The Rebirth of Witchcraft.* London: Robert Hale, 1989.

Waddell, L. A. *The Buddhism of Tibet or Lamaism.* 2d ed. Cambridge, Eng.: Heffer, 1939.

Wasserman, Paul, Esther Herman, and Elizabeth Root, eds. *Festivals Sourcebook.* Detroit, MI: Gale Research, 1977.

Weiser, Francis X. *Handbook of Christian Feasts and Customs: The Year of the Lord in Liturgy and Folklore.* New York: Harcourt, Brace, 1952.

Weiser, Francis X. *The Holyday Book.* New York: Harcourt, Brace, 1956.

Wilson, P. W. *The Romance of the Calendar.* New York: Norton, 1937.

Wolverton, Robert E. *An Outline of Classical Mythology.* Totowa, N. J.: Littlefield, Adams & Co., 1975.

Wright, Lawrence. *Clockwork Man: The Story of Time, Its Origins, Its Uses, Its Tyranny.* New York: Horizon, 1968.

Zen Lotus Society. *Handbook of the Zen Lotus Society.* Toronto: Zen Lotus Society, 1986.

Zerubavel, Eviatar. *The Seven-Day Circle: The History and Meaning of the Week.* New York: Macmillan Free Press, 1985.

Monthly Index
of
Holidays

January

Baptism of the Lord, The Feast of the	First Sunday following Epiphany
Bhishma Ashtami	Eighth lunar day of Magha Shulka
Birthday of Martin Luther King, Jr.	Third Monday in January
Blessing of Animals	Sunday nearest to January 17
Carnival	Begins with Epiphany, ends with Shrove Tuesday
Circumcision, Feast of the	January 1
Death of George Fox	January 13
Epiphany	January 6; Sunday between January 2 and January 8 in the Roman Catholic Church in the United States
Epiphany Eve	January 5; Saturday between January 1 and January 7 in the Roman Catholic Church in the United States
Esbats	Full or new moon evening of each month
Ganjitsu	January 1
Magha Purnima	Full moon day of the Hindu month of Magha
Makar Sankranti	Commences upon the sun's entrance into Capricorn, at the winter solstice, on or about January 14
Mauni Amavasya	Fifteenth day of the waning fortnight of the Hindu month of Magha
Minakshi Float Festival	Full moon day of the Hindu month of Magha
Old Christmas Day	January 6
Plough Monday	First Monday after Epiphany
Pongal	Mid-January
Sakata Chauth	Fourth day of the waning half of the Hindu month of Magha
Universal Week of Prayer	First Sunday through the second Sunday in January
Up-Helly-Aa	Last Tuesday in January
Vasant Panchami	Fifth day of the waxing half of the Hindu month of Magha
World Religion Day	Third Sunday in January

February

Amalaka Ekadashi	Eleventh day of the waxing half of the Hindu month of Phalguna (February-March)
Arrival of Roger Williams in New World . . .	February 5

Ash Wednesday	Moveable: six and one-half weeks before Easter (between February 4 and March 10)
Ayyam-i-Ha	February 25-March 1
Birthday of Richard Allen	February 11
Brigid	February 1
Candlemas	February 2
Collop Monday	Between February 2 and March 8; the Monday preceding Shrove Tuesday
Cross-Quarter Days	February 1
Esbats	Full or new moon evening of each month
Fasching	Between February 2 and March 8; the three days preceding Ash Wednesday
Holi	Fourteenth day of the waxing half of the Hindu month of Phalguna
Homstrom	First Sunday of February
Leap Year Day	February 29
Lent	Between Febraury 2 and March 8; forty days before Easter (West), seven weeks before Easter (East)
Losar	Movable date
Mahashivaratri	Fourteenth day of the waning half of the Hindu month of Phalguna
Mardi Gras	Between February 3 and March 9; Tuesday before Ash Wednesday
Monlam	Fourteenth to the twenty-fifth day of the first lunar month of the Tibetan calendar; usually February
Presentation of Jesus	February 2
Purification of Mary	February 2
Purim	Between February 25 and March 25; Adar 15 or We-Adar 14 in leap year
Quadragesima	Between February 8 and March 14, the first Sunday of Lent
Rose Monday	Between February 2 and March 8; Monday before Lent
Shrove Tuesday	Between February 3 and March 9; Tuesday before Ash Wednesday
St. Valentine's Day	February 14

March

Annunciation of the Lord, Feast of	March 25
Ashokashtami	Eighth day of the waxing half of the Hindu month of Chaitra
Birthday of L. Ron Hubbard	March 13
Chaitra Parb	Full-moon day of the Hindu month of Chaitra
Chaitra Purnima	Ten days in the Hindu month of Chaitra
Easter Sunday	Between March 22 and April 25 (West); between April 4 and May 8 (East)
Eostre	On or near March 22
Esbats	Full or new moon evening of each month
Gangaur	Two weeks after *Holi*
Good Friday	Friday before Easter

Gudi Parva	First day of the Hindu month of Chaitra
Hanuman Jayanti	Full-moon day of the Hindu month of Chaitra
Jamshed Navaroz	Month of March
Mahavir Jayanti	Thirteenth day of the waxing half of the Hindu month of Chaitra
Mothering Sunday	Fourth Sunday before Lent
Naw-Ruz	March 20-21
Omizutori Matsuri	March 1-14
Palm Sunday	Between March 14 and April 18; the Sunday preceding Easter
Passover	Begins between March 27 and April 24; Nisan 15-21/22
Quasimodo Sunday	Between March 29 and May 2; Sunday after Easter
Rama Navani	Ninth day of the waxing half of the Hindu month of Chaitra
Sabbath of Rabbi Isaac Mayer Wise	Last Sabbath in the month of March
Sheelah's Day	March 18
Shitala Ashtami	Eighth day of the waxing half of the Hindu month of Chaitra
St. Patrick's Day	March 17
Ugada Parva	First day of the Hindu month of chaitra
World Day of Prayer	First Friday in March

April

Akshya Tritiya	Third day of the waxing half of the Hindu month of Vaisakha
Ascension Day	Between April 30 and June 3; forty days after Easter, held on a Thursday
Baisakhi	April 13
Birthday of Joseph Smith	April 24
Buddha Purnima	Full-moon day of the month of Vaisakha. Also called "Full Moon of the Buddha"
Chandan Yatra	Twenty days beginning on the third day of the waxing half of the Hindu month of Vaisakha
Founding of the Church of Jesus Christ of Latter-Day Saints	April 6
Esbats	Full or new moon evening of each month
Janaki Navami	Ninth day of the waxing half of the Hindu month of Vaisakha
Narsimha Jayanti	Fourteenth day of the waxing half of the Hindu month of Vaisakha
Parshurama Jayanti	Third day of the waxing half of the Hindu month of Vaisakha
Pooram	During the Hindu month of Vaisakha
Qing Ming Festival	Fourth of fifth day of the third moon of the Chinese calendar; usually April 5 or 6
Ridvan, Feast of	April 21 through May 2
Rogation Days	Between April 30 and June 3; Monday, Tuesday and Wednesday preceding Ascension Day
Salvation Army Founder's Day	April 10
Shankaracharya Jayanti	Fifth day (southern India) or tenth day (northern India) of the waxing half of the Hindu month of Vaisakha
Songkran	April 13
Thingyan Tet	April 15

May

Abbotsbury Garland Day	May 13
Aldersgate Experience	Sunday nearest to May 24
Ascension of Baha'u'llah	May 29
Beltane	May 1
Birth of 'Abdu'l-Bahá	May 23
Corpus Christi	Between May 21 and June 24; Thursday after Trinity Sunday
Cross-Quarter Days	May 1
Death of Helena Petrovna Blavatsky	May 8
Declaration of the Báb	May 23
Esbats	Full or new noon evening of each month
Family Week	Begins the first Sunday in May
Ganga Dussehra	Tenth day of the waxing half of the Hindu month of Jyaistha
Jyaistha Ashtami	Eighth day of the waxing half of the Hindu month of Jyaistha
May Day	May 1
May 9 Day	May 9
Nirjala Ekadashi	One day in the waxing half of the Hindu month of Jyaishtha
Pentecost	Between May 10 and June 13; fiftieth day after the second day of Passover
Sacred Heart of Jesus	Between May 22 and June 25; Friday after Corpus Christi
Shavuot	Between May 16 and June 13; Sivan 6 in the Hebrew calendar
Snan Yatra	Full-moon day of the Hindu month of Jyaishtha
Trinity Sunday	Between May 17 and June 20; first Sunday after Pentecost in the Western Church, the Monday after Pentecost in the Orthodox tradition
Vata Savitri	Thirteenth day of the waning fortnight of the Hindu month of Jyaishtha
Visitation of the Virgin Mary to Elizabeth	May 31 in the Roman Catholic and Protestant churches; July 2 in the Anglican church

June

Birthday of Brigham Young	June 1
Blessing of the Shrimp Fleet	Last weekend in June
Childrens' Day	Second Sunday in June
Esbats	Full or new moon evening of each month
Footwashing Day	Sunday in early summer
Guru Purnima	Full-moon day of the Hindu month of Ashadha
Hemis Festival	Three days in June or July
Litha	Summer soltice; on or about June 22
Magna Carta Day	June 15
Martyrdom of Joseph and Hyrum Smith	June 27
New Church Day	June 19
Parent's Day	First weekend in June
Race Unity Day	Second Sunday in June
Ratha Yatra	Second day of the waxing half of the Hindu month of Ashadha

July

Birthday of Mary Baker Eddy	July 16

Esbats . . . . Full or new moon evening of each month
Hariyali Teej . . . . Third day of the waxing half of the Hindu month of Shravana
Hill Cumorah Pageant . . . . Nine days in late July
Jhulan Latra . . . . Full moon of the Hindu month of Shravana
Kamada Ekadashi . . . . Waning half of the Hindu month of Shravana
Lughnasad . . . . July 31
Martyrdom of the Báb . . . . July 9
Most Precious Blood, Feast of the . . . . July 1
Nag Panchami . . . . Fifth day of the waxing half of the Hindu month of Shravana
Narieli Purnima . . . . Full-moon day of the Hindu month of Shravana
Obon Festival . . . . July 13-15 or August 13-15
Pioneer Day . . . . July 24
Putrada Ekadashi . . . . Eleventh day of the waxing half of the Hindu month of Shravana
Raksha Bandhan . . . . Full-moon day of the Hindu month of Shravana
Reek Sunday . . . . Last Sunday in July
Teej . . . . Third day of the bright half of the Hindu month of Shravana
Tulsidas Jayanti . . . . Seventh day of the waxing half of the Hindu month of Shravana
Volunteers of America Founder's Day . . . . . . July 28

August

Abbey Fair . . . . Moveable date in early August
African Methodist Quarterly Meeting Day . . . Last Saturday in August
Anant Chaturdashi . . . . Fourteenth day of the waxing half of the Hindu month of
      Bhadrapada
Assumption of the Blessed Virgin . . . . August 15
Carnea . . . . Month-long celebration
Christ the King, Feast of . . . . Last Sunday in August
Cross-quarter days . . . . August 1
Esbats . . . . Full or new moon evening of each month
Floating Lantern Ceremony . . . . August 15
Ganesha Chaturthi . . . . Fourth day of the waxing half of the Hindu month of
      Bhadrapada
Hala Shashti . . . . Sixth day of the waxing half of the Hindu month of Bhadrapada
Janamashtami . . . . Eight day of the waning half of the Hindu month of Bhadrapada
Lammas . . . . August 1
Marymass Fair . . . . Third or fourth Monday in August
Onam . . . . Four days in the Malyalam month of Chingam
Partyshana Parva . . . . Eight days during the Hindu month of Bhadrapada
Queenship of Mary . . . . August 22
Radha Ashtami . . . . Eighth day of the waning fortnight of the Hindu month of
      Bhadrapada
Rishi Panchami . . . . Fifth day of the waxing half of the Hindu month of Bhadrapada
Tirupati Festival . . . . Ten days during the Hindu month of Bhadrapada
Transfiguration of Jesus . . . . August 6
World Peace Day . . . . August 24 (Church of Scientology); September 21 (National
      Spiritual Assembly of the Bahá'ís of the U.S.)

September

Auditors' Day	Second Sunday in September
Dasain	Waxing half of the Hindu month of Asvina
Dussehra	Tenth day of the waxing half of the Asvina
Esbats	Full or new moon evening of each month
Festa de Serreta	September 8 through 15
Kojagara	Full moon in the Hindu month of Asvina
Mabon	Autumnal equinox, on or about September 22
Mary as Our Lady of Sorrows	September 15
Michaelmas	September 29
Nativity of the Blessed Virgin Mary, Feast of	September 8
Pitra Padsha	Waning half of the Hindu month of Ashvina
Rosh ha-Shanah	Between September 6 and October 4; Tishri 1 and 2
San Estevan, Feast of	September 2
Santa Fe Fiesta	Weekend after Labor Day
Sharad Purnima	Full moon of the Hindu month of Ashvina
Sukkot	Between September 20 and October 18; Tishri 15-21
Triumph of the Holy Cross	September 14
Valmiki Jayanati	Full-moon day of the Hindu month of Ashvina
World Peace Day	September 21 (National Spiritual Assembly of the Bahá'ís of the U.S.); August 24 (Church of Scientology)
Yom Kippur	Between September 15 and October 13; Tishri 10

October

Bhaiya Duj	Second day of the waxing fortnight of the Hindu month of Kartika; the day following the Govardhan Puja
Birth of the Báb	October 20
Christ the King, Feast of	Last Sunday in October
Dewali	Fifteenth day of the waning half of Kartika
Devathani Ekadashi	Eleventh day of the waxing half of the Hindu month of Kartika
Dhan Teras	Thirteenth day of the waning half of the Hindu month of Kartika
Esbats	Full of new moon evening of each month
Govardhan Puja and Annakut	First day of the waxing fortnight of the Hindu month of Kartika
Guardian Angels	October 2
Guru Parab	Full-moon day of the Hindu month of Kartika
Hallowe'en	October 31
Hari-Shayani Ekadashi	Eleventh day of the waxing fortnight of the Hindu month of Kartika
Kartika Purnima	Full moon in the Hindu month of Kartika
Kartika Snan	Hindu month of Kartika–October/November
Karwa Chauth	Fourth day of the waning half of the hindu month of Kartika
Mary as Our Lady of the Rosary	October 7
Narak Chaturdashi	Fourteenth day of the waning half of the Hindu month of Kartika
Reformation Day	October 31
Shiprock Navajo Nation Fair	Usually first weekend of October

Skanda Shashti	Tamil month of Tulam
Surya Shashti	Sixth day of the waxing fortnight of the Hindu month of Kartika

November

Advent	Movable: Sunday closest to November 30, through December 24 (Western Church), November 15 through December 24 (Eastern Church)
All Saints' Day	November 1
All Souls' Day	November 2 (West), three Saturdays prior to Lent and the the day before Pentecost (East)
Ascension of 'Abdu'l-Bahá	November 28
Bhairava Ashtami	Eighth lunar day of the waning half of the Hindu month of Margashirsha
Bible Sunday	Last Sunday in November
Birth of Bahá'u'lláh	November 12
Birthday of Martin Luther	November 10
Cross-Quarter Days	November 1
Dattatreya Jayanti	Full-moon day of the Hindu month of Margashirsha
Day of the Covenant	November 26
Dedication of St. John Lateran	November 9
Esbats	Full or new moon evening of each month
Gita Jayanti	Eleventh day of the waxing half of the Hindu month of Margashirsha
Presentation of the Blessed Virgin Mary, Feast of the	November 21
Saints, Doctors, Missionaries, and Martyrs Day	November 8
Samhain	November 1
Shalako Ceremonial	Late November or early December
Thanksgiving	Fourth Thursday in November
Vaikuntha Ekadashi	Eleventh day of both the waxing and waning fortnights in the Hindu month of Margashirsha
Vaitarani	Eleventh day of the waning half of the Hindu month of Margashirsha
World Community Day	First Friday in November
Wuwuchim	Eve of the new moon in November

December

Christmas Day	December 25
Christmas Eve	December 24
Christmas, Twelve Days of	December 25
Esbats	Full or new moon evening of each month
Freedom Day	December 30
Hanukkah	Eight days, beginning Kislev 25
Holy Innocents' Day	December 28
Immaculate Conception of Mary, Feast of . . .	December 8
Kwanza	December 26 through January 2

Las Posadas	December 16 through 25
Lucia Day	December 13
Mother Seton Day	December 1
New Year for Trees	Day after the winter solstice; around December 23
Rukmani Ashtami	Eighth day of the waning half of the Hindu month of Pausha
Saturnalia	Late December
Swarupa Dwadashi	Twelfth day of the waning half of the Hindu month of Pausha
Yule	Winter solstice; around December 22

Religions Index

Bahá'í

Ascension of 'Abdu'l-Bahá . . . . November 28
Ascension of Bahá'u'lláh . . . . May 29
Ayyam-i-Ha . . . . February 25 through March 1
Birth of 'Abdu'l-Bahá . . . . May 23
Birth of the Báb . . . . October 20
Birth of Bahá'u'lláh . . . . November 12
Day of the Covenant . . . . November 26
Declaration of the Báb . . . . May 23
Martyrdom of the Báb . . . . July 9
Naw-Ruz . . . . March 20-21
Nineteen-Day Feast . . . . First day of each month in the Bahá'í calendar
Race Unity Day . . . . Second Sunday in June
Ridvan, Feast of . . . . April 21-May 2
World Peace Day . . . . September 21
World Religion Day . . . . Third Sunday in January

Buddhism

Buddha Purnima . . . . April-May
Floating Lantern Ceremony . . . . August 15
Hemis Festival . . . . Three days in June or July
Losar . . . . Usually in February
Monlam . . . . Fourth throught the twenty-fifth day of the first lunar month of
  the Tibetan calendar; usually February
Obon Festival . . . . July 13-14, or August 13-15
Songkran . . . . April 13

Christian Science

Birthday of Mary Baker Eddy . . . . July 16

Christianity

Abbey Fair . . . . August

Advent	November-December
Aldersgate Experience	Sunday nearest to May 24
All Saints' Day	November 1
All Souls' Day	November 2 (West), three Saturdays prior to Lent and the day before Pentecost (East)
Annunciation of the Lord, Feast of the	March 25
Arrival of Roger Williams in the New World	February 5
Ascension Day	Between April 30 and June 3; forty days after Easter
Ash Wednesday	Movable, six and one-half weeks before Easter (between February 4 and March 10)
Assumption of the Blessed Virgin	August 15
Baptism of the Lord, The Feast of the	First Sunday following Epiphany
Bible Sunday	Last Sunday in November
Birthday of Martin Luther	November 10
Birthday of Richard Allen	February 11
Carnival	Begins with Epiphany, ends with Shrove Tuesday
Children's Day	Second Sunday in June
Christ the King, Feast of	Last Sunday in October (Roman Catholic); last Sunday in August (Protestant)
Christmas Day	December 25
Christmas Eve	December 24
Christmas, Twelve Days of	December 25 through January 5
Circumcision, Feast of the	January 1
Collop Monday	February-March
Corpus Christi	Between May 21 and June 24
Death of George Fox	January 13
Dedication of St. John Lateran	November 9
Easter	Between March 22 and April 25 (West); between April 4 and May 8 (East)
Epiphany	January 6; Sunday between January 2 and January 8 in the U.S. Roman Catholic Church
Epiphany Eve	January 5; Saturday between January 1 and January 7 in the Roman Catholic Church in the U.S.
Family Week	Begins first Sunday in May
Fasching	Austria and Germany Between February 2 and March 8; the three days preceding Ash Wednesday
Footwashing Day	Sunday in early summer
Good Friday	Friday before Easter
Guardian Angels	October 2
Holy Family, Feast of the	Sunday after Epiphany
Immaculate Conception of Mary, Feast of the	December 8
Immaculate Heart of Mary, Feast of the	Saturday following the second Sunday after Pentecost
Las Posadas	December 16 through 25
Lent	Between February 2 and March 8; forty days before Easter (West), seven weeks before Easter (East)
Mary as Our Lady of the Rosary	October 7

Mary as Our Lady of Sorrows . . . . September 15

Michaelmas . . . . September 29

Most Precious Blood, Feast of the . . . . July 1

Mother Seton Day . . . . December 1

Mothering Sunday . . . . March-April; fourth Sunday before Lent

Nativity of the Blessed Virgin Mary,

    Feast of . . . . September 8

Old Christmas Day . . . . January 6

Palm Sunday . . . . Between March 15 and April 18; the Sunday preceding Easter

Pentecost . . . . Between May 10 and June 13; fiftieth day after the second day of
                                 Passover

Plough Monday . . . . January; first Monday after Epiphany

Presentation of Jesus . . . . February 2

Presentation of the Blessed Virgin Mary,

    Feast of the . . . . November 21

Quadragesima . . . . Between February 8 and March 14; the first Sunday of Lent

Quasimodo Sunday . . . . Between March 29 and May 2; Sunday after Easter

Queenship of Mary . . . . August 22

Reformation Day . . . . October 31

Rose Monday . . . . Between February 2 and March 8; Monday before Lent

Sacred Heart of Jesus . . . . Between May 22 and June 25; Friday after Corpus Christi

St. Patrick's Day . . . . March 17

Saints, Doctors, Missionaries, and

    Martyrs Day . . . . November 8

Salvation Army Founder's Day . . . . April 10

Shrove Tuesday . . . . Between February 3 and March 9; Tuesday before Ash
                                 Wednesday

Transfiguration of Jesus . . . . August 6

Trinity Sunday . . . . Between May 17 and June 20; first Sunday after Pentecost in the
                                 Western Church, the Monday after Pentecost in the Orthodox
                                 tradition

Triumph of the Holy Cross . . . . September 14

Universal Week of Prayer . . . . First Sunday through the second Sunday in January

Visitation of the Virgin Mary to Elizabeth . . . May 31 in the Roman Catholic and Protestant churches; July 2 in
                                 the Anglican church

Whitsunday . . . . Pentecost

Church of Jesus Christ of Latter-Day Saints

Birthday of Brigham Young . . . . June 1

Birthday of Joseph Smith . . . . April 24

Founding of the Church of Latter Day

    Saints . . . . April 6

Hill Cumorah Pageant . . . . July

Martyrdom of Joseph and Hyrum Smith . . . . . June 27

Pioneer Day . . . . July 24

Church of the New Jerusalem

New Church Day . . . . June 19

Church of Scientology

Auditors' Day	Second Sunday in September
Birthday of L. Ron Hubbard	March 13
Freedom Day	December 30
May 9 Day	May 9
Parent's Day	First weekend in June
World Peace Day	August 24

Hinduism

Akshya Tritiya	April-May
Amalaka Ekadashi	February-March
Anant Chaturdashi	August-September
Ashokashtami	March-April
Baisakhi	April 13
Bhairava Ashtami	November-December
Bhaiya Duj	October-November
Bhishma Ashtami	January-February
Chaitra Parb	March-April
Chaitra Purnima	March-April
Chandan Yatra	April-May
Dasain	September-October
Dattatreya Jayanti	November-December
Dewali	October-November
Devathani Ekadashi	October-November
Dhan Teras	October-November
Dol Purnima	Full moon day of Hindu month of Dol
Durga Puja	March-April and September-October
Dussehra	September-October
Ganesha Chaturthi	August-September
Ganga Dussehra	May-June
Gangaur	March-April
Gita Jayanti	November-December
Govardhan Puja and Annakut	October-November
Gudi Parva	March-April
Guru Parab	October-November
Guru Purnima	June-July
Hala Shashti	August-September
Hanuman Jayanti	March-April
Hari-Shayani Ekadashi	October-November
Haritalika Teej	August-September
Hariyali Teej	July-August
Holi	February-March
Janaki Navami	April-May
Janamashtami	August-September
Jhulan Latra	July-August
Jyaistha Ashtami	May-June

Kalpa Vruksha	Hindu New Year
Kamada Ekadashi	July-August
Kartika Purnima	October-November
Kartika Snan	October-November
Karwa Chauth	October-November
Kojara	September-October
Magha Purnima	January-February
Mahashivaratri	February-March
Mahavir Jayanti	March-April
Makar Sankranti	Commences upon the sun's entrance into Capricorn, at the winter solstice, or about January 14
Mauni Amavasya	January-February
Minakshi Float Festival	January-February
Nag Panchami	July-August
Narak Chaturdashi	October-November
Narieli Purnima	July-August
Narsimha Jayanti	April-May
Nirjala Ekadashi	May-June
Parshurama Jayanti	April-May
Partyshana Parva	August-September
Pitra Paksha	September-October
Pooram	April-May
Putrada Ekadashi	July-August
Radha Ashtami	August-September
Raksha Bandhan	July-August
Rama Navani	March-April
Ratha Yatra	June-July
Rishi Panchami	August-September
Rukmani Ashtami	December-January
Sakata Chauth	January-February
Shankaracharya Jayanti	April-May
Sharad Purnima	September-October
Shitala Ashtami	March-April
Shravani Mela	July-August
Skanda Shashti	October-November
Snan Yatra	May-June
Surya Shashti	October-November
Swarupa Dwadashi	December-January
Teej	July-August
Tirupati Festival	August-September
Tulsidas Jayanti	July-August
Ugadi Parva	March-April
Vaikuntha Ekadashi	November-December
Vaitarani	November-December
Valmiki Jayanti	September-October
Vasant Panchami	January-February
Vata Savitri	May-June

Islam

Al-'id al-Kabir	Tenth day of Dhu al-Hijjah
Ashura	Tenth day of Muharram
Awwal Muharram	First day of the lunar month of Muharram
Death of Imam 'Ali	Holiday for Shi'ite Muslims
Hajj	First day of Shawwal through the tenth day of Dhu al-Hijjah
'Id al-Adha	Days 10-12 of Dhu al-Hijjah, the twelfth Islamic month
'Id al-Fitr	First day of Shawwal
Lailat at Miraj	Twenty-seventh day of Rajab
Mawlid al-Nabi	Twelfth day of the month of Rabi al-Awwal
Muharram	First month of the Muslim calendar
Ramadan	Ninth month of Islamic lunar calendar
Shab Barat	Fifteenth night of Sha'ban

Jainism

Pajjusana	Eight-day penance

Judaism

Bi-Shevat	Fifteenth day of Shevat
Counting of the Omer	Between Passover and Shavuot
Fast of the First-born	Nisan 14
Hanukkah	Eight days, beginning on Kislev 25
Jewish Fasts	Four different days associated with destruction of Jerusalem
Passover	Begins between March 27 and April 24; Nisan 15-21/22
Pilgrim Festivals	Begins on Nisan 15, Sivan 16, and Tishri 15
Purim	Between February 25 and March 25; Adar 15 or We-Adar 14 in leap year
Rosh ha-Shanah	Between September 6 and October 4; Tishri 1 and 2
Sabbath of Rabbi Isaac Mayer Wise	Last Sabbath in the month of March
Shavuot	Between May 16 and June 13; Sivan 6 in the Hebrew calendar
Sukkot	Between September 20 and October 18; Tishri 15-21
Yom Ha-Shoah	Nisan 27
Yom Kippur	Tishri 10

Neo-Pagan

Beltane	May 1
Brigid	February 1
Carnea	August
Cross-Quarter Days	February 1, May 1, August 1, November 1
Eostre	On or about March 22
Esbats	Full or new moon evening of each month
Hallowe'en	October 31
Homstrom	First Sunday in February
Lammas	August 1
Litha	Summer Solstice; on or about June 22

Lughnasad . . . . July 31
Mabon . . . . Autumnal equinox, or or about September 22
Marymass Fair . . . . Third or fourth Monday in August
May Day . . . . May 1
Midsummer Eve . . . . June 22
New Year for Trees . . . . Day after the winter solstice; around December 23
Samhain . . . . November 1
Saturnalia . . . . Late December
St. Valentine's Day . . . . February 14
Up-Helly-Aa . . . . Last Tuesday in January
Yule . . . . Winter solstice; around December 22

Theosophical Society
Death of Helena Petrovna Blavatsky . . . . May 8

Volunteers of America
Founder's Day . . . . July 28

Zoroastrianism
Jamshed Navaroz . . . . March
Parsi Remembrance of the Dead . . . . Ten days preceding the vernal equinox

Master Index

Abbas Effendi 62
Abbey Fair 55
Abbey of Regina Laudis 55
Abbotsbury Garland Day 55
Abbotsbury, Dorset, England 55
Abdu'l-Bahá 55, 58, 62
Abraham 30, 37, 84, 109, 110, 117
Acoma Indians 113
Acropolis 28
Acts of the Apostles 58, 102
Adar 11, 12, 23, 105
Adi Kavi Valmiki 107
Adi Shankaracharya 39
Advent 25, 55, 68, 72, 83, 87, 93, 107
Advent calendar 55
Advent wreath 55
Adventist churches 68
African Methodist Episcopal Church 63
African Methodist Quarterly Meeting Day 56
African Union Methodist Protestant
    Church 56
Afterlitha 19
Afteryule 19
Agrionia 28
Ahasuerus 105
Ahmad 30
Ahmad, Shaykh 30
Ai Kavi 120
Akshya Tritiya 39, 56
Al Jumah 30
Al-'id al-Kabir 37, 81
Alá 38
Alaska 49

Albania 49
Alder 21
Aldersgate Experience 56
Alexander the Great 11, 33, 45
Ali, Imam 70
Ali, Mirza Husayn 58, 62
Ali-Muhammad 30, 62, 71
Ali-Muhammad, Mirza 62
Ali-Muhammad, Siyyid 30
Alkmene 27
All Hallows Eve 19
All Hallows' Day 56
All Saints' Day 56, 81
All Souls' Day 57
All Souls' Eve 57
Allah 29, 62, 63, 84, 89, 94, 108, 113
Allen, Richard 57, 63
Amalaha Ekadashi 41
Amavasya 33, 41, 94, 103
Amitabha 34, 42
Anant Chaturdashi 40, 57
Ananta 57, 97
Anarhusis 25
Ancient Order of Druids 95
Angel of Death 76, 102
Anglican Communion 55-57, 67, 75, 95,
    111, 112, 121
Anna 104
Annakut 40, 80
Annunciation of the Blessed Virgin Mary 57
Annunciation of the Lord, Feast of 57, 89,
    111
Anodos 25

Anthesteria 27
Anthesterion 12, 14, 26
Antinmas 57, 119
Apaturia 25
Aphrodite 24-28
Apollo 14, 24-28, 65
April 17-19, 21, 31, 38, 51, 56-60, 62-66, 72, 73, 77-80, 82, 86, 88, 92, 94, 96, 98, 101, 102, 104, 105, 107, 109, 112, 114, 116, 117, 119
April Fool's Day 21
Aprilis 45
Aquarius 33, 35
Arcane School 121, 122
Arjuna 62, 79, 86, 101
Armenian Church 66, 120, 121
Arrhephoria 28
Artemis 24-28
Ascension Day 18, 58, 64, 109
Ascension of 'Abdu'l-Bahá 55, 58
Ascension of Bahá'u'lláh 38, 58, 60, 71
Ascension Sunday 58, 109
Ascension Thursday 58, 121
Ascention of the Prophet 89
Ash Wednesday 18, 58, 59, 65, 76, 90, 93, 101, 106, 110, 120
Ashadha 39, 59, 71, 81, 108
Ashadha Purnima 59, 81
Ashadha Shukla 39
Ashokashtami 59
Ashtami 33, 39-41, 61, 87, 106, 110, 114
Ashura 37, 59, 84, 97
Ashvina 40, 72, 73, 88, 103, 114, 120
Ashvina Krishna 40
Ashvina Shukla 40
Asmá 38
Aspen 21
Assumption Day 59
Assumption of the Blessed Virgin 59, 94, 96
Assyrian 8
Asvina 69
Aswapati 120
Aswattha 94
Athena 24, 25, 28
Athenian 12-14, 24, 26
Athens 14, 24-28
Atri 70, 109
Auditors' Day 59

August 19, 21, 38, 45, 49, 51, 55-57, 59, 61, 64-66, 69, 77, 80-83, 86, 87, 89, 94, 97, 99-101, 105, 106, 109-111, 115, 117, 118, 122
Augustine of Canterbury 16, 20
Augustus 45, 47
Autumnal 19, 36, 50, 59, 91
Av 23, 86, 99
Avadhuta Gita 70
Avani Avittam 40, 107
Aviv 10
Awwal Muharram 59
Ayyám-i-Há 38
Azamat 38

B

Báb 30, 31, 38, 60, 62, 71, 93
Bábis 30, 71
Babi 62
Babylonian 6, 8-11, 76
Bahá 30, 31, 38, 55, 58, 60, 62, 70, 71, 93, 98, 99, 106, 109, 122
Bahá'í 30, 31, 58, 60, 62, 71, 93, 98, 99, 109, 122
Bahá'u'lláh 31, 38, 58, 60, 62, 70, 71, 109
Bailey, Alice 121
Baisakhi 60, 121
Bakrid 60, 84
Balarama 81
Balarama Shasti 81
Balbhadra 115
Bali 100
Baptist 30, 58, 71, 75, 98, 121
Bara Wafat 60, 63, 94
Basilinna 27
Bastille 50
Bear Clan 122
Belgium 48
Beltane 21, 22, 60, 61, 64, 69, 95, 111
Bendis 28
Bengal 41, 72, 73, 120
Bessy 103
Bhadra 40, 81, 109
Bhadra Krishna 40
Bhadra Shukla 40
Bhadrapada 57, 77, 82, 86, 101, 106, 117
Bhagavad Gita 41, 79, 86, 114

Bhairava   41, 42, 61
Bhairava Ashtami   41, 42, 61
Bhaiya Duj   40, 61
Bhishma Ashtami   41, 61
Bhishma Pitamaha   61, 93
Bhogali Bihu   93
Bhogi-Pongal   104
Bhrigu   109
Bible   62, 90
Bible Sunday   62
Big Dipper   35
Birch   21
Birth of 'Abdu'l-Bahá   38, 62
Birth of Bahá'u'lláh   38, 62
Birth of the Báb   38, 62
Birthday of Brigham Young   62
Birthday of Joseph Smith   62
Birthday of L. Ron Hubbard   63
Birthday of Martin Luther   63
Birthday of Martin Luther King, Jr.   63
Birthday of Mary Baker Eddy   63
Birthday of Muhammad   63
Birthday of Richard Allen   63
Blake, William   21
Blavatsky, Helena Petrovna   63, 70
Blessing of Animals 64
Blessing of Animals   27, 57, 64, 69, 73, 75,
     89, 96, 101, 104, 113-115
Blessing of the Shrimp Fleet   64
Bloodmonth   19
Bodhi Day   43
Boedromia   24
Boedromion   12, 14, 15, 24
Boeotia   28
Bon-Odori   99
Bonfire nights   64
Book of Shadows   111
Booth, Ballington   121
Booth, William   112
Boukolion   27
Bounds Thursday   58, 64
Brahma   32, 33, 61, 70, 74, 92, 98, 109, 119
Brahmans   56, 57, 60, 78, 80, 83, 91, 97-99,
     103, 105, 107, 114, 116, 118-121
Brauron   27
Brauronia   27
Brigid   22, 61, 64, 69, 84, 85, 100, 111
Britain   18, 19, 22, 48, 49, 64, 89, 95, 111

British Isles   19-21, 95
Britons   19
Brumaire   51
Buddha   32-34, 39, 42, 43, 64, 77, 92, 96,
     100, 109, 116, 121
Buddha Purnima   39, 64, 77
Buddhism   33, 34, 83, 90
Buddhist   33, 34, 42, 43, 64, 77, 79, 83, 96,
     99, 100, 116, 121
Bul   10
Bulgaria   49
Buphonia   28
Byzantium   28

C

Cairo   30
Callippic   13, 14
Callippus of Cyzicus   13
Canaanite   9
Candlemas   19, 21, 65, 104, 106
Capitoline Hill   46
Capricorn   33, 93, 104, 117
Carling Sunday   65, 96
Carnea   65
Carneus   65
Carnival   42, 43, 65, 90, 93, 110, 115
Celestial Equator   14
Celtic   19, 20, 22, 49, 61, 64, 69, 75, 81, 84,
     95, 110-112
Ch'ing ming   42
Ch'ung Yang   43
Chaitanya Mahaprabhu   41, 72
Chaitra   31, 39, 59, 65, 66, 72, 80, 82, 92,
     107, 114, 119
Chaitra Parb   65
Chaitra Purnima   39, 65
Chaitra Shukla   39
Chalisa   82
Chalkeia   25
Chandan Yatra   39, 66
Chandrashekhra   92
Charilla   25
Chaturdashi   33, 40, 41, 57, 92, 97
Chaturmas   82
Chaturthi   33, 40, 77, 78, 121
Chau   35

Cheesefare Sunday   66, 90
Chi hsi   42
Childermas   66, 84
Children's Day   66
China   33, 34, 49, 89, 105
Chinese   33-35, 42, 43, 89, 91, 96, 105
Chingam   100
Chitra Gupta   39, 66
Choes   27
Chou   35
Christ   8, 15, 16, 18, 20, 58, 62, 66-69, 73-75, 77, 79, 80, 85, 86, 89, 93, 94, 111, 118, 121
Christ the King, Feast of   66, 86
Christian   4, 13, 15, 16, 18, 20-22, 47, 48, 55-58, 60, 62, 63, 66-68, 73-77, 89, 94, 95, 98, 102, 111, 118
Christian Science   63
Christianity   15-18, 20, 21, 33, 57, 68, 75, 100, 109, 111, 118, 123
Christians   15-17, 21, 57, 58, 66-68, 73, 74, 79, 82, 90, 96
Christmas   4, 18, 21, 55, 56, 66-68, 75, 82, 86, 100, 104, 106, 113, 119, 123
Christmas carol   68
Christmas Day   55, 66-68, 75, 100, 106
Christmas decorations   67
Christmas Eve   4, 55, 67, 68, 75, 100
Christmas lights   67
Christmas presents   67
Christmas tree   67
Christmas, Twelve Days of   68, 119
Chung yüan   43
Church Fathers   17, 18
Church of Jesus Christ of the Latter Day Saints   77, 93
Church of Scientology   59, 63, 77, 95, 122
Church of the New Jerusalem   98
Church Women United   122
Chytroi   27
Circumcision of Jesus   68
Circumcision, Feast of the   68, 94
Clavius   47, 48
Cleostratus of Tenedos   13
Clepsydra   5
Clockwork Man   8
Close Sunday   68, 106
Collop Monday   69

Colombiere, Claude de la   111
Columbus Day   117
Communism   34
Confucianism   34
Constantine   15, 16, 71, 118
Copernicus   7
Corpus Christi   18, 69, 111
Council of Nicaea   16-18, 47
Council of Trent   47
Council of Whitby   20
Counting of the Omer   4, 18, 35, 47, 69, 100
Croagh Padraig   108
Cross-Quarter days   19, 21, 22, 64, 69, 75, 111, 112
Crucifixion   16, 18, 73, 94
Curia Calabra   46
Cycle   4, 6, 7, 9-14, 17-20, 24, 27, 29, 32, 35, 44-48, 75, 111
Cycles   6-10, 12-14, 35, 44, 48, 50

D

d'Eglantine, Fabre   50
Dairy Sunday   69
Dali Lama   33, 42
Dan-dakshina   91, 103, 110
Danda-pani   61
Dasain   69
Dasara   69
Dashami   33, 73, 121
Dattatreya   41, 70
Dattatreya Jayanti   41, 70
Day of Atonement   23, 70, 110, 116, 122
Day of the Covenant   38, 69, 70
Day of the Holocaust   122
Day of the Three Wise Men   75
Death of George Fox   70
Death of Helena Petrovna Blavatsky   70
Death of Imam 'Ali   70
December   16, 18, 19, 38, 45, 47, 48, 51, 55, 61, 66-68, 70, 74-77, 79, 80, 82, 84, 85, 89-91, 96, 98, 104-106, 110, 111, 113, 116, 119, 123
Decemvirate   45
Declaration of the Báb   38, 60, 62, 71
Dedication of St. John Lateran   111

Deepvali 71
Definition 16, 32, 35
Deities 24, 25, 57, 65, 66, 71, 93, 95, 97, 115
Delian League 12
Delphi 24-26
Demeter 14, 25, 26, 28
Demon of Bad Luck 42, 71
Demosthenes 25
Denmark 48
Dev Sena 115
Devas 33
Devathani 40, 71, 74
Devathani Ekadashi 40, 71, 74
Devi 39, 72, 82, 109
Devi Arundhati 109
Dewali 71, 72, 77, 80
Dhamma Day 42
Dhan Teras 41, 72, 97
Dhanvantri 41, 72
Dhanvantri Trayodashi 41, 72
Dharma 33, 79, 80
Dhu al-Hijjah 37, 56, 81, 84
Dhu al-Qa'da 37
Dianetics: The Modern Science of Mental
    Health 95
Diasia 27
Diaspora 11
Digambar 40, 101
Diipolia 28
Diisoteria 28
Diocletian 15, 20
Dionysian period 18
Dionysius Exiguus 18, 20
Dionysus 14, 26-28
Divine Fathers 103
Diwali 41
Dol Purnima 41, 72
Dominical Letters 17
Dragon Boat Festival 42
Druids 18, 19, 67, 95
Dumuzi 22
Durga 39, 40, 69, 72, 73, 78, 98, 114
Durga Puja 40, 69, 72, 73, 98
Dussehra 39, 40, 69, 72, 73, 78, 121
Dvadashi 33
Dvitiya 33, 40, 61
Dwadaksha 115
Dwadashahara 115

E

Easter 13, 16-18, 20, 21, 47-49, 56-58, 73,
    74, 76, 79, 84, 86, 90, 94, 101, 102, 105,
    106, 109, 122
Easter Monday 76
Easter Rabbit 20
Eastern 4, 5, 16, 17, 20, 29, 48, 55, 66, 68,
    75, 90
Eastern Orthodox Church 48, 55, 68
Ecclesiastical History of the English People 18,
    20
Ecliptic 14, 32
Ecumenical Council 16
Eddy, Mary Baker 63, 74
Eed ed Keeber 30
Eed es Sagheer 30
Effendi, Abbas 58, 62
Egypt 29, 44-46, 49, 64, 76, 94, 102, 114
Egyptian 16, 18, 44-46, 110
Eirene 24
Eiresione 28
Elaphebolia 27
Elaphebolion 12, 27
Elder 21, 81, 103
Eleusinian Mysteries 14, 16, 22, 24, 111
Eleusis 14, 25, 27
Elijah 58, 90, 118
Elul 23
Elwood, Robert S. 34
Ember Days 74
Emperor Jamshed 86
Empire 4, 14-16, 20, 29
England 17, 19-21, 55, 57, 58, 67, 75, 92,
    95, 96, 100, 106, 109, 111, 117, 119
English 9, 18, 20, 35, 51, 55, 74, 75, 90, 95,
    96, 111, 121
Enuma elish 9
Eostre 20, 22, 74, 75, 90, 106, 111
Eostremonth 19
Epiphany 16, 60, 65-68, 75, 84, 100, 103,
    105, 106, 118, 119
Equinox 9, 12, 17, 19-22, 36, 47, 50, 59, 73,
    75, 76, 90, 91, 95, 101, 106, 110, 111, 116,
    121
Equirria 46
Era 4, 12, 17, 18, 20, 29-31, 60, 72

Esbats 75
Essenes 15
Esther 11, 23, 105, 117
Estonia 49
Etanim 10
Eucharist 69, 77
Euctemon 13
Eudoxus of Cnidus 13

F

Fall equinox 20, 21, 75, 76, 90, 91, 95, 106, 110, 111
Family Day 76
Family Week 76
Fasching 65, 76, 110, 113
Fast of Esther 23, 105
Fast of Gedaliah 23, 76, 79, 87, 117
Fast of Tammuz 23
Fast of the First-born 76
Fasti 47
Fat Tuesday 76, 93
Father Christmas 67
Fatima 97
Feast Days 15, 30, 56
Feasts 10, 11, 15, 18, 21, 24, 30, 32, 47, 60, 74, 75, 87, 91, 93, 100, 102, 108, 112, 116, 119
Februarius 45
February 17, 19, 35, 38, 42, 45-47, 49, 51, 57, 58, 60, 61, 63, 64, 69, 76, 83, 84, 86, 88, 90-96, 104-106, 110-112, 120
Federation Day 24
Festa de Serreta 76
Festivals 4, 10, 11, 14, 16, 19-22, 25, 32, 34, 37, 46, 47, 50, 69, 72, 73, 77, 79, 83, 89-93, 102, 105, 111, 114, 121, 122
Flavius 45
Floating Lantern Ceremony 77
Floréal 51
Fool 21, 103
Footwashing Day 77
Forelitha 19
Foreyule 19
Founding of the Church of the Latter Day Saints 45, 77, 89, 95, 96, 98, 103
Fox, George 70, 77

France 48, 50, 51, 69
Franciade 50
Frazer, Sir James 11
Freedom Day 77
French 50, 51, 93
French Republican 50, 51
Friday 11, 18, 20, 30, 73, 74, 79, 90, 111, 113, 114, 122
Frimaire 51
Fructidor 51
Furze 21

G

Gabriel 18, 57, 77, 95
Galileo 5, 7
Gamelia 26
Gamelion 12, 26
Games of Hera at Olympus 88, 91
Gandhi 33, 63
Ganesh Chaturthi 40
Ganesha 33, 40, 41, 72, 77, 78, 112, 121
Ganesha Chaturthi 77, 78, 121
Ganga Dussehra 39, 78
Gangaur 39, 78
Ganges 39, 56, 60, 61, 78, 87, 88, 91-94, 108, 115
Ganjitsu 79
Gardnerian Witches 61, 91
Gauri 39, 78, 117
Gedaliah 23, 76, 79, 87, 117
Genesia 24
George Washington 49
Germans 48, 67
Germinal 51
Gezer 9
Gezer Calendar 9
Girisha 92
Gita Jayanti 41, 79
Glastonbury Thorn 75
Gnostics 15
God 9, 10, 15, 16, 24-31, 37, 39-41, 43, 44, 57, 59, 62, 65, 68, 70, 72, 77-80, 82, 84, 87, 92, 96-98, 102, 104, 106-108, 110, 112, 114, 116-118, 120, 121, 123
God-Fearers 15
Golden Bough 11

Golden numbers   17, 48
Good Friday   18, 20, 73, 79, 90
Gospel of John   16, 77, 79
Gospel of Luke   20, 104
Gospel of Matthew   20, 66
Gospels   16, 30
Govardhan Puja   40, 57, 80
Graves, Robert   22
Great Festival of Theseus   25
Great Lent   56, 90
Great Night of Shiva   92
Great Paschal period   18
Great Pitier   42
Great Renunciation   42
Greece   14, 16, 49, 91, 111
Greek   6, 9, 12-15, 18, 24, 32, 33, 48, 65,
   104, 110, 111, 114
Gregorian   14, 29, 31, 34, 47-51, 55, 91, 100
Gregorian reform   47, 48, 55, 91
Gregory the Great   58, 90
Grisma   31
Groundhog Day   21, 69
Guardian Angels   80
Gudi Padva   39
Gudi Parva   80, 100
Guh-ldan monastery   43
Guha   115
Gule of August   80, 89
Guru Nanak   40, 80, 87
Guru Nanak's Day   80
Guru Padmasambhava   83
Guru Parab   40, 80, 87, 88
Guru Purnima   59, 81
Guru Vyas Purnima   81
Guy Fawkes' Day   21
Guyakala   43

H

Hai   35
Hajj   37, 56, 81
Hala Shashti   40, 60, 81
Halai   27
Halloween   4, 21, 69, 81
Haloa   26
Haman   105

Han Dynasty   105
Hanukkah   23, 82
Hanuman   39, 82, 107, 118
Hanuman Jayanti   39, 82
Hari   39, 41, 72, 74, 82, 83, 98, 114
Hari Tritiya   82, 83
Hari-Shayani Ekadashi   39, 74, 82
Haritalika Teej   40, 82
Harivansha Purana   110
Hariyali Teej   39, 82, 83
Harmonic Convergence   122
Harvest Festival   21, 43, 49, 59, 88, 89, 100
Harvestmonth   19, 20
Hawthorn   21
Hazel   21
Heather   21
Hebrew   4, 7, 9-15, 17, 20, 30, 59, 63, 68,
   69, 76, 87, 102, 110, 114, 123
Hecatombaion   12
Hejira   29, 59
Hekate   24-28
Hekatombaia   24
Hekatombaion   24
Hell   97
Hemanta   31
Hemis Festival   83
Hemis Gompa   83
Hephaestia   25
Hephaestus   25
Hera   24-26
Herakles   24-28
Hermes   24-28, 67
Herois   25
Heshvan   10
Hierokeryx   14
Hierophant   14
High Priest   5, 10, 11, 14
High Priestess   9
Hilkiah   10
Hill Cumorah Pageant   83
Hillel II   11, 12
Hindu   6, 31-34, 56, 57, 59-61, 65, 66, 69-
   74, 77-83, 86-88, 91-95, 97-99, 101, 103-
   110, 112, 114-121
Hindu Trimurti   70
Hinduism   32, 33, 80
Hipparchus   13, 14
Hiranyakasipu   83, 98

Hitler Purim   105
Hlyda   20
Hlydamonth   19
Holi   41, 57, 72, 78, 83, 84, 116
Holidays   3, 10, 11, 14, 17, 19-22, 31-34, 42, 44-46, 49, 53, 60, 61, 64, 66, 68, 69, 81, 90, 91, 100, 102, 110
Holika   83, 84
Holly   21, 67
Holy Family   18, 68, 84
Holy Family, Feast of the   84
Holy Innocents' Day   66, 84, 85
Holy Saturday   64, 73, 84
Holy Spirit   15, 102, 118
Holy Thursday   84
Holy Trinity   111, 118
Holy Week   20, 57, 73, 74, 79
Holymonth   19, 20
Homer   25
Homstrom   84
Hopi Indians   122
Horus   44
Hoshana Rabbah   116
Hsu   35
Hsun   35
Hubbard, L. Ron   63, 84, 95
Hungary   48
Husain, Mulla   30
Hussein Day   84
Hussein, Hezret Imam   59, 96
Huygens, Christiaan   5
Hyakinthia   24
Hymn To Demeter   14

I

I-chaw   35
Id al-Adha   37, 60, 84, 117
Id al-Fitr   85
Ides   45, 46
Ilm   38
Imbolg   85
Immaculate Conception   18, 85, 94, 106
Immaculate Conception of Mary, Feast of the   85, 94
Immaculate Heart of Mary, Feast of the   85, 94

Inanna   22
Independence Day   33
India   31-33, 39, 43, 63, 65, 66, 70-73, 77, 78, 80-86, 88, 91, 92, 94, 96, 97, 103, 104, 107, 108, 114, 115, 119
Indian   32, 33, 43, 60, 72, 83, 86, 107, 113, 115, 120
Indra   33, 65, 73, 80, 93, 100, 107
Ingathering, Feast of the   85
Intercalation   6, 8, 12, 17, 32, 35, 44-46
International Conference for World Peace and Social Reform   122
International Fixed Calendar   50, 51
Iran   29, 59
Iranian   30
Ireland   20, 21, 49, 57, 85, 95, 108, 111, 114
Irish   20, 60, 64, 67, 108, 111
Isaac   30, 84, 110, 121
Ishmael   37, 84
Ishtar   11, 22
Isis   16, 44
Islam   29, 30, 32, 59, 62, 80, 81
Islamic   7, 29-31, 56, 59, 81, 84, 94, 107, 108, 113
Israel   10, 63, 102, 114
Israelites   10, 90, 102, 116
Isthmian Games   27
Italy   48, 67, 95
Iti dirig   8
Ivy   21, 67
Iyar   10, 23
Izzat   38

J

Jagannath   39, 59, 66, 87, 108, 115
Jain   72, 92, 101
Jainism   39, 92
Jains   32, 40, 41, 72, 92, 93, 100-102
Jamshed Navaroz   85, 102
Janaki Navami   39, 86
Janamashtami   40, 86, 89
Januarius   45
January   17-19, 38, 47, 48, 51, 60, 61, 63, 64, 66, 68, 70, 75, 79, 80, 88, 89, 91, 93-95, 100, 103, 110, 112, 116, 119, 120, 122
Japan   33, 49, 100

Japanese   34, 79, 99
Jehovah's Witnesses   68
Jerusalem   10, 11, 15, 37, 58, 59, 73, 76, 82,
    86, 87, 98, 101, 102, 114, 118
Jesus   15, 18, 20, 30, 32, 57-60, 62, 65-68,
    71, 73, 75, 77, 80, 84-86, 89, 90, 93, 94, 96,
    98, 101, 104, 109, 111, 118
Jewish   9-12, 15, 16, 18, 63, 68, 69, 76, 82,
    86, 99, 104, 105, 110, 113, 116, 117, 122,
    123
Jewish Fasts   76, 86, 99, 113, 117
Jews   10, 11, 15, 87, 102, 105, 114, 116, 122,
    123
Jhulan Latra   39, 87
Jin   35
Jivanmukta Gita   70
John the Baptist   30, 71, 75, 98, 121
John Wesley   56
Jordan   29
Joseph of Arimathea   75
Josiah   10
Judaic Law   11
Judaism   10, 15-17, 33, 76, 102, 110
Judea   10, 121
Judeans   10
Julian   14, 29, 45-48, 66, 68, 100
Julian calendar   45, 47, 48, 66, 68, 100
Julius Caesar   46, 47, 90
July   19, 21, 29, 31, 38, 50, 51, 63, 71, 81, 83,
    87, 91, 93, 96, 97, 99, 103, 105, 106, 108,
    115, 117, 118, 121
Jumada al-Aula   37
Jumada al-Ukhra   37
June   19, 21, 22, 38, 51, 58, 62, 64, 66, 69,
    71, 75, 78, 81, 83, 87, 90, 92, 93, 95, 98, 99,
    101, 102, 105, 106, 108, 109, 111, 114, 115,
    118, 120
Junis   45
Jupiter   9
Jyaishtha   39, 78, 87, 99, 115, 120
Jyaishtha Shukla   39
Jyaistha Ashtami   39, 87

K

Kabir   37, 56, 81, 108
Kadru   97

Kah-chih   35
Kah-gyur   43
Kai-tsu   35
Kalachakra Revelation   42
Kali   31, 32, 41, 72
Kali Yuga   31, 32
Kalimát   38
Kalligeneia   25
Kallynteria   28
Kalpa Sutra   100
Kalpa Vruksha   87
Kamada Ekadashi   40, 74, 87, 105
Kamadeva   41
Kang   35
Kapil   93
Kartika   40, 41, 61, 71, 72, 80, 82, 87, 88, 91,
    94, 97, 116
Kartika Amavasya   41
Kartika Krishna   41
Kartika Purnima   40, 80, 87, 91
Kartika Shukla   40
Kartika Snan   40, 88
Kartikeya   33, 88, 115
Karwa Chauth   41, 88
Kazim, Siyyid   30
Keats, John   21
Kerala   40, 100, 114
Khir   39, 87, 103, 114
Khir Bhawani   39, 87
Ki   35, 107
Kiah   35
King Anantavarman Chodaganga   108
King Henry II   75
King Herod   84
King Janaka   86
King John   92
King Olaf Haraldsson   100
King Sagara   93
King Tirumala Nayak   96
King, Martin Luther, Jr.   63, 88
Kislev   11, 12, 23, 82, 105
Knecht Rupprecht   67
Kojagara   40, 88
Kol Nidre   123
Kore   14, 25, 26
Kos   28
Koureotis   25
Kourotrophos   27

Kratu   109
Kris Kringle   67
Krishna   32, 39-41, 57, 71, 72, 79-81, 84, 86,
   89, 94, 106-108, 110
Krishna Dwaipayna   81
Krittika   115
Kronos   24
Kumara   115
Kumari   115
Kusha   120
Kwanza   89
Kwei   35

L

Lady Day   57, 89, 106
Laetare Sunday   89, 96
Lag ba'Omer   23
Lagrange, Joseph-Louis   50
Lailat al Miraj   37, 58, 89, 98
Lakshmi   39-41, 56, 57, 70-72, 86, 88, 89,
   106
Lamaism   90
Lammas   19, 21, 22, 64, 80, 89, 94, 106
Lantern Festival   89
Las Posadas   89
Last Supper   15, 18, 73, 77
Latvia   49
Laurel wreaths   67
Lava   120
Law   10, 11, 15, 23, 30, 77, 83, 88, 102, 104,
   114
Law of Moses   10
Laylat al-Bara'ah   113
Leap Year Day   90
Lenaia   26
Lent   14, 43, 55-59, 65, 66, 69, 73-76, 90,
   95, 96, 105, 106, 110, 115
Leto   24
Lilius   48
Limnae   27
Lincoln, Abraham   117
Litha   19, 22, 75, 90, 95, 106, 111
Lithuania   49
Little Lent   55
Lohri   93
Loi Krathong   90

Lord Badri   56
Lord Ganesha   41, 77, 78, 112
Lord Jagannath   39, 59, 66, 87, 108
Lord Lingaraja   59
Lord Sundareswara   65
Lord Vardhamana Mahavira   92
Lords of Misrule   43, 113
Losar   90, 91, 96
Low Easterday   106
Low Sunday   91, 106
Lucia Day   91
Lughnasad   21, 22, 49, 61, 64, 69, 91, 111
Lunar   7, 8, 10-13, 19, 29, 32-35, 42, 44-46,
   48, 59, 61, 72, 84, 89, 90, 96, 99, 101, 107,
   113, 117
Lunisolar   7, 11, 19, 34, 35, 44
Luther, Martin   56, 63, 91, 109
Lutheran Church   57, 63, 67, 75, 95, 109
Luxembourg   48

M

Mabon   22, 75, 76, 90, 91, 106, 111
Macedonian   11
Macrobius   46
Magha   41, 42, 61, 88, 91-95, 112, 120
Magha Bihu   93
Magha Krishna   41
Magha Mela   92
Magha Puja   42
Magha Purnima   41, 91, 95
Magha Shukla   41
Magi   67, 68, 75
Magna Carta Day   92
Magnificat   121
Mahabali   100
Mahabharata   62, 78, 79, 81, 101
Mahadeva   92
Mahakala   92
Mahasena   115
Mahashivaratri   92, 115
Mahavir Jayanti   39, 92
Mahavira   39, 41, 72, 92, 93, 100
Mahayana   33, 34, 42, 43
Mahayogi   92
Mahdi   30, 31, 109
Maia   27

Maimactrerion 12
Maimakteria 25
Maimakterion 25
Maius 45
Makar Sankranti 93, 104
Manger scene 68
Mao 35
March 17-20, 29, 30, 38, 45-47, 51, 57-60,
    63, 65, 66, 72, 73, 75, 76, 78-80, 82, 83, 85,
    86, 90, 92, 93, 96, 98, 100-102, 105-107,
    110-112, 114, 119, 122
Mardi Gras 65, 76, 90, 93
Marduk 11
Margashirsha 41, 61, 70, 79, 119
Margashirsha Krishna 41
Margashirsha Shukla 41
Marheshvan 11, 12, 23
Marichi 109
Mars 9
Marseshvan 23
Martin Luther 56, 63, 88, 91, 109
Martinmas 106
Martius 45
Martyrdom of Joseph and Hyrum Smith 93,
    115
Martyrdom of the Báb 38, 60, 71, 93
Mary 18, 57, 59, 61-63, 68, 74, 84, 85, 89,
    94, 95, 98, 104, 106, 111, 113, 116, 121
Mary as Our Lady of Sorrows 94
Mary as Our Lady of the Rosary 94
Marymass Fair 94
Masá'il 38
Mashíyyat 38
Mass of the Most Holy Trinity 118
Maternity of Mary 68
Matsya 40, 80, 87, 119
Matsya Avatar 80, 87
Mattu Pongal 104
Maundy Thursday 18, 74, 77, 94
Mauni Amavasya 41, 94
Mawlid al-Nabi 37, 63, 94, 97
May 4, 6, 8, 9, 12, 14, 18, 19, 21, 22, 30, 31,
    35, 38, 43, 45, 51, 55-58, 60-62, 64-67, 69-
    76, 78, 80, 86-91, 95, 97-99, 101, 102, 104,
    106, 109-112, 114, 115, 117-121, 123
May 9 Day 95
May Day 21, 55, 61, 69, 95
May Eve 21, 64

May Queen 61
Meadmonth 19
Mecca 29, 37, 59, 63, 81, 94, 97
Medicine Buddha 34, 42, 72
Medina 29, 30, 59
Mercury 9
Messiah 15, 18, 62, 71, 104
Messidor 51
Metageitnia 24
Metageitnion 12, 24
Methodist Church 56, 66
Meton 13, 14
Metonic 12-14, 17, 18, 48
Mi-'krugs-pa 43
Michaelmas 21, 58, 77, 80, 95, 106, 108, 111
Midsummer Eve 64, 95, 111, 116
Minakshi 65, 95
Minakshi-kalyanam 65
Minyas 28
Mistletoe 67
Mithras 16
Monday 21, 59, 63, 69, 76, 83, 90, 94, 95,
    103, 109, 110, 114, 117, 118
Monge, Gaspart 50
Monlam 96
Moon 5-13, 16-18, 20, 24, 27-30, 32, 33,
    35, 39, 40, 43, 44, 46, 48, 64-66, 70, 72-75,
    77, 78, 80-82, 86-92, 95, 97, 103, 105, 106,
    108, 111, 112, 114, 115, 117, 118, 120-122
Mordecai 11, 105
Mormon 62, 77, 83, 93, 103
Morocco 29
Moses 10, 58, 90, 102, 109, 114, 118
Most Precious Blood, Feast of the 86, 96
Mother Seton Day 96
Mother's Day 76
Mothering Sunday 65, 89, 95, 96, 109, 110
Mounichion 27
Mufti 30
Muhammad 29, 30, 32, 59, 60, 62, 63, 70,
    71, 89, 94, 97, 107, 109
Muharram 29, 30, 37, 59, 96
Mulk 38
Munychia 27
Mura 119
Muslim 29, 30, 34, 81, 84, 85, 89, 96, 97,
    113
Myhayana 33

Mysteries of Isis   16

N

Nag   39, 62, 82, 97
Nag Panchami   39, 62, 97
Nagas   97
Narak Chaturdashi   41, 97
Naraka   97
Narieli Purnima   39, 97
Narsimha   39, 98
National Council of Churches   10, 22, 50, 56, 66, 76, 95, 111, 119, 122
Nativity of the Blessed Virgin Mary, Feast of   62, 66, 98
Navajo   99, 115
Navami   33, 39, 72, 86, 107
Navrata   40, 72
Naw-Ruz   38, 98
Nebuchadnezzar   76, 86, 87
Nekusia   24
Nemean Games   24
Nemesia   24
Neo-pagan   14, 21, 22, 60, 64, 75, 89, 91, 106, 110-112
Nephthys   44
Nesteia   25
Netherlands   48
New Church Day   98
New Covenant   15
New Year   4, 9-12, 20, 23, 29, 33, 35-39, 42, 43, 47, 48, 50, 59, 60, 63, 68, 71, 79-81, 85-87, 89, 91, 96, 98, 110, 112, 116, 117, 119, 121, 122
New Year's Day   20, 33, 39, 68, 79, 96, 98
New Year's Eve   4, 79, 112
Nicaea   16-18, 47
Nicaean Council   16
Night Chant   115
Night Journey   89, 98
Night of Forgiveness   20, 31, 41, 83, 92, 113
Nile   44
Nine Gods of Immortality   43
Nineteen-Day Feast   31, 99
Ninth of Av   99

Nirjala Ekadashi   39, 74, 99
Nirvana   42
Nisan   10, 12, 16, 23, 76, 102, 122
Nisanu   9, 10
Nivôse   51
Noah   37, 59
Nones   45, 46
Northern Navajo Fair   4, 10, 19, 32, 60, 61, 67, 68, 73, 78, 80, 81, 83, 89, 95, 99, 103, 114, 115
Norway Day   99, 100
Nossa Senhora dos Milagres (Our Lady of Miracles)   76
November   18, 19, 31, 38, 45, 47, 51, 55-58, 61-64, 69-72, 79, 80, 82, 87, 88, 90, 97, 104, 106, 110-113, 115-117, 119, 122
Numa   45
Nur   38

O

Oak   21
Obon Festival   77, 99
Octaëteris   13
Octave of the Birth of Our Lord   68, 99
October   19, 38, 45, 47, 50, 51, 61, 62, 66, 68, 69, 71-73, 80-82, 87, 88, 94, 97, 103, 106, 109, 110, 114-117, 120
Oimbelg   21
Old Christmas   66, 75, 100
Old Christmas Day   75, 100
Old Christmas Eve   75, 100
Old Man Winter   84
Old May Day   55
Old Testament   9
Olsok Eve   99, 100
Olympic Games   24
Omizutori Matsuri   100, 121
Onam   40, 100
Origen   15
Orissa   39, 65, 66, 87, 108, 115
Orthodox   15, 32, 48, 55, 57, 59, 60, 66, 68, 75, 102, 104, 114, 116, 118
Oschophoria   25
Osiris   16, 44

Ovid   47

P

Padma-sambhava   42
Padua Purim   105
Painted Porch in Athens   14
Pajjusana   100
Pakshas   32
Palm Sunday   18, 73, 74, 101
Panchami   33, 39-41, 62, 97, 109, 120
Panchamrita   106
Pandia   27
Parashurama   101
Parent's Day   61, 101
Parinirvana   42
Parshurama   39, 101
Parshurama Jayanti   39, 101
Parsi   85, 86, 101
Parsi Remembrance of the Departed   101
Partyshana Parva   40, 101
Parvati   39-41, 70, 78, 82, 88, 95, 117
Pasch   20
Paschal   17, 18, 74
Pashupati   92
Passover   10-12, 15-18, 20, 23, 68, 69, 76,
   102, 103, 114
Patati   85, 102
Pausha   41, 80, 110, 116
Pausha Krishna   41
Peitho   24
Pentecost   10, 15, 18, 23, 56, 57, 73, 85, 102,
   114, 118, 121
Persephone   14
Persian   16, 29, 30, 62, 93, 101, 105
Pesach   23, 102
Phalguna   41, 57, 83, 86, 92
Pharisees   15
Pharmakoi   28
Picture Feast   42
Pilgrim festivals   102
Ping   35
Pioneer Day   103
Pithoigia   27
Pitra Paksha   40, 103

Pitri-Loka   103
Pitris   103
Plough Monday   103
Plough Sunday   103
Plowing Sixth   40, 103
Plutarch   8
Pluviôse   51
Plynteria   28
Poinsettia   67
Pongal   33, 93, 103, 104
Pontifex maximus   46
Pooram   104
Pope Benedict XIII   71
Pope Benedict XV   84
Pope Calixtus I   74
Pope Callistus III   118
Pope Clement X   80
Pope Clement XI   94
Pope Clement XIII   111
Pope Gregory I   56
Pope Gregory IV   56
Pope Gregory XIII   47
Pope Hilarius   18
Pope Innocent X   71
Pope John XXII   118
Pope Leo XIII   71
Pope Paul III   47
Pope Paul V   80
Pope Pius IX   85, 96, 111
Pope Pius VII   94
Pope Pius X   96
Pope Pius XI   66
Pope Pius XII   59, 85, 106
Pope Sylvester   71
Pope Urban IV   69
Portugal   48
Poseidea   26
Posideon   26
Pradyumna   110
Prahlad   83, 84, 98, 100
Prairial   51
Prayer Festival   96
Pre-Julian   45
Presentation of Jesus   65, 86, 104
Presentation of the Blessed Virgin Mary, Feast
   of the   104
Priests   11, 18, 19, 22, 45, 55, 69, 79, 90, 96,
   107, 109, 122

Priyakarini   93
Procession of the Mysteries   14
Proclamation of the Mysteries   15
Proetus   28
Protestant   48, 49, 56, 57, 62, 66, 67, 77, 79,
   109, 121
Ptolemy   6, 45
Pueblo Indians   113
Pulaha   109
Pulastya   109
Punjab   32, 60, 93
Pure Land   34
Purification of the Blessed Virgin Mary, Feast
   of the   104
Purim   11, 23, 105, 117
Purnima   33, 39-41, 59, 64, 65, 72, 77, 80,
   81, 87, 91, 95, 97, 114
Putrada Ekadashi   39, 74, 87, 105
Pyanopsia   25
Pyanopsion   12, 25
Pythian Way   25
Python   25

Q

Qawl   38
Qing Ming Festival   105
Quadragesima   105
Quarter days   19, 21, 22, 59, 64, 69, 75, 90,
   105, 106, 111, 112, 121
Quartodecimans   16, 17
Quasimodo Sunday   68, 91, 106
Qudi   30
Qudrat   38
Queenship of Mary   94, 106
Quinctilis   45, 47
Quinquagesima   105
Quintodecimans   16
Qur'an   29, 30, 37, 62, 63, 71, 95, 107

R

Rabbis   15, 102, 110
Rabi al-Awwal   63, 94
Rabi I   30

Rabi II   30
Rabi'al-Akhir   37
Rabi'al-Awal   37
Race Unity Day   106
Radha   40, 72, 106
Radha Ashtami   40, 106
Rahmat   38
Raidas   108
Rajab   37, 89
Raksha Bandhan   39, 106
Ram-Nam   107
Rama   32, 39-41, 71-73, 78, 82, 101, 107,
   118, 120
Rama Navami   39, 72, 107
Rama Navani   107, 120
Ramachandra   101
Ramacharitra Manas   118
Ramadan   30, 37, 85, 107, 108, 113
Ramayana   69, 73, 82, 101, 107, 118, 120
Ramcharitra Manas   78
Rape of Kore   14
Rasen Montag   110
Ratha Yatra   39, 59, 108
Ravi Das Jayanti   108
Ravidas   41
Ravidas Jayanti   41
Red Road   34
Reed   21
Reek Sunday   108
Rees, Aylwin and Brinsley   19
Reformation   48, 67, 103, 108, 109
Reformation Day   109
Refreshment Sunday   96, 109
Regifugium   46
Rejab   30
Religious and Spiritual Groups in Modern
   America   34
Renaissance   14, 21
Republic Day   33, 50
Restoration   67
Resurrection of Christ   15, 16, 73
Reza Shah Pahlavi   29
Rhodes   13, 28
Ridvan, Feast of   109
Rishi Kashyapa   97
Rishi Panchami   40, 109
Rishi Vasishtha   109
Rishi Vyasa   81

Rites of Atonement   9
Rogation Days   58, 60, 109, 110, 116
Roman   5, 14-20, 45-48, 55-57, 60, 61, 63, 64, 66-69, 71, 74-76, 79, 80, 84, 85, 90, 94-96, 101, 104, 106, 109, 111, 112, 121
Roman Catholic Church   18, 55, 60, 64, 66, 68, 69, 75, 84, 96, 104, 109, 111, 121
Romania   49
Romanticists   21
Rome   4, 16, 20, 44-46, 48, 56, 59, 66, 75, 101, 109, 118
Romme, Charles-Gilbert   50
Romulus   45
Roosevelt, Franklin D.   117
Rosary   94
Rose Monday   76, 110
Rose Sunday   96, 110
Rosenmontag   110
Rosh ha-Shanah   11, 23, 76, 110
Rowan   21
Rudra   33
Rukmani   41, 110
Rukmani Ashtami   41, 110
Rukmin   110
Rural Life Sunday   109, 110
Russia   49

S

Sabbat   22, 64, 75, 91, 111, 123
Sabbath   9, 15, 110, 121
Sabbath of Rabbi Isaac Mayer Wise   121
Sabbats   22, 60, 61, 64, 69, 75, 90, 91, 106, 110-112, 123
Sachi   107
Sacred Heart of Jesus, Feast of the   111
Sacrificial Lamb   16
Sadducees   15
Safar   37
Saints, Doctors, Missionaries, & Martyrs Day   112
Sakata Chauth   41, 112
Salamis   24, 27
Salvation Army   112, 121
Salvation Army Founder's Day   112
Sambhara   42

Samhain   19, 21, 22, 56, 61, 64, 69, 81, 111, 112
San Estevan, Feast of   113
Santa Claus   67, 68
Sante Fe Fiesta   113
Sapta Rishis   109
Saptimi   33
Sarad   31
Saraswati   41, 70, 72, 94, 120
Saturday   9, 51, 56, 64, 73-75, 84, 85, 115
Saturn   9, 113
Saturnalia   66, 113
Satya-Yuga   56
Satyavan   120, 121
Saudi Arabia   29, 108
Savitri   39, 120, 121
Scirophorion   12
Second Vatican Council   69
Seder   68, 102
Selene   14, 24-28
Septagesima   105, 106
September   18, 19, 38, 45, 47, 49-51, 55, 57, 59, 69, 72-77, 81, 82, 86, 88, 90, 91, 94, 95, 98, 100, 101, 103, 105, 106, 109-111, 113, 114, 116-118, 120, 122
Seventeenth of Tammuz   113
Sexagesima   105
Sextilis   45, 47
Sha'ban   30, 37
Shab Barat   113
Shaikiya   62
Shakti   33, 106, 115
Shakti-dhara   115
Shakyamuni Buddha   42
Shakyamuni's Descent from Heaven   43
Shalako Ceremonial   113
Shalosh regalim   102
Shankara   82, 87, 92
Shankaracharya Jayanti   39, 114
Shankhasura   71
Sharad   40, 114
Sharad Purnima   40, 114
Sharaf   38
Shashti   33, 40, 60, 81, 115, 116
Shavuot   69, 77, 102, 114
Shawwal   30, 37, 81, 85
Shearmonth   19
Shebat   23

Sheelah's Day   112, 114
Shelley, Percy Bysse   21
Shesha   57, 73, 82, 97
Shevat   63, 81
Shimchas Toirah   23
Shin   35
Shintoism   34
Shiprock Navajo Nation Fair   99, 115
Shiráz   30
Shishupala   110
Shitala   39, 114
Shitala Ashtami   39, 114
Shiva   32, 33, 39-41, 61, 70, 72, 73, 78, 82,
    87, 88, 92, 95, 104, 114, 115, 117
Shiva Chaturdashi   92
Shivan   23
Shivaratri   41, 115
Shoghi Effendi   31
Shraddha   103
Shravana   39, 40, 83, 87, 97, 105, 106, 115,
    117, 118
Shravani Mela   40, 115
Shrove Monday   90
Shrove Tuesday   18, 65, 76, 90, 93, 115
Shrovetide   76
Siddha-sena   115
Siddhartha Gautama   33, 64
Sidereal   6, 31, 33, 121
Sikh   80
Sikh Dharma   80
Sikhism   40, 80, 87
Sikhs   32, 80, 87
Silver Fir   21
Simeon   94, 104
Sin   35, 59, 76, 85, 121
Sirius   44, 45
Sisira   31
Sisters of Charity of St. Vincent De Paul   96
Sita   39, 40, 78, 86, 107, 118, 120
Siuh   35
Sivan   102, 105, 114
Skanda   40, 115
Skanda Shashti   40, 115
Skira   25, 28
Skirophoria   28
Skirophorion   28
Smith, Joseph   62, 77, 83, 115
Snan Yatra   39, 115

Soil Stewardship Sunday   109, 116
Solar   6-13, 18, 19, 29, 31, 32, 34, 35, 44, 46-
    48, 117
Solemnity of Christ the King   18
Solemnity of Mary, the Mother of God   68
Solmonth   19
Solstice   19, 21, 24, 36, 66, 75, 90, 91, 93, 98,
    106, 110, 111, 116, 121, 123
Songkran   116
Sosigenes   47
Sothic   44, 45
Sothis   44
Soviet Union   51
Spain   48, 80, 123
Sparta   28
Spencer, Peter   56
Spring   9, 12, 21, 22, 31, 36, 47, 63, 74, 75,
    83, 87, 89, 90, 102, 106, 110, 111, 116, 120-
    122
Sproutkale   19
Sri Krishna   57, 72
Sri Rama   107
Sri Rama-Panchayatan   107
St. Andrew's Day   55
St. Anthony of Egypt   64
St. Dismas   18, 57, 111
St. Dismas Day   57, 111
St. Francis of Assisi   64, 68
St. Helena   118
St. John Eudes   21, 71, 85, 111
St. John's Eve   21, 111
St. Joseph   84, 89
St. Margaret Mary Alacoque   111
St. Narharidas   118
St. Odilo of Cluny   57
St. Patrick   111, 112, 114
St. Patrick's Day   111, 114
St. Valentine's Day   112, 120
Stepterion   25
Sthenia   25
Stonehenge   18, 95
Subhadra   115
Subramanya   40, 115
Succoth   116
Sudarshan   115
Sukkot   10, 23, 64, 85, 102, 103, 114, 116,
    117
Sultán   38

Sumerian 8
Summer 4, 19, 21, 24, 31, 36, 43, 61, 66, 75, 77, 90, 93, 95, 106, 108, 110, 111, 116
Summer solstice 19, 21, 24, 36, 75, 90, 106, 110, 111, 116
Sun 4-7, 9, 11, 13, 14, 16, 32-35, 61, 62, 66, 83, 93, 103, 104, 116, 117
Sunday 9, 11, 15-18, 49, 51, 55, 56, 58-60, 62-69, 73-77, 83-85, 89-91, 95, 96, 101-103, 105, 106, 108-110, 113, 116, 118, 119, 121, 122
Surya 40, 73, 104, 116
Surya Shashti 40, 116
Svathira 43
Svetambras 93
Swarupa Dwadashi 41, 116
Swaswa 61
Sweden 49
Swedenborg, Emanuel 98
Switzerland 48
Synodic 13
Synodical 5, 6
Synoekia 25
Syria 29

T

Ta'anit Esther 105, 117
Tabaski 37, 117
Tabulae Rudolphinae 48
Tajias 96, 97
Tammuz 22, 23, 86, 87, 113
Tantric Buddhism 83
Taoism 34
Taraka 115
Tarakajit 115
Tatric 33
Tauropolia 27
Taurus 33, 121
Tebet 23, 86, 117
Teej 39, 40, 82, 83, 117
Telesterion 14
Tempe 25
Ten Commandments 114
Ten Nhat 117
Teng Chieh 42
Tenth of Tebet 117

Tet Nguyenden 117
Thanksgiving 89, 113, 114, 117
Thargelia 28
Thargelion 12, 27
Theravada 33, 34, 42
Thermidor 51
Theseus 24-28
Thesmophoria 14, 25
Thesmophorion 25
Thingyan Tet 117
Third of Tishri 116, 117, 122
Thor 67
Thoth 44, 45
Three Kings' Day 75
Threelitha 19
Threemilks 19
Thursday 18, 58, 64, 69, 74, 77, 84, 94, 117, 120, 121
Tibet 33, 83, 91, 96
Timurlang 97
Ting 35
Tirthankaras 101
Tirupati Festival 117, 118
Tisha b'Av 23
Tishri 10, 23, 87, 102, 110, 116, 117, 122
Tor-gyak 43
Toro Nagashi 77
Transfiguration of Jesus 86, 118
Trayodashi 33, 41, 72
Tree 21, 22, 51, 57, 63, 67, 75, 81, 87, 93, 94, 98, 120
Treta Yuga 101, 107
Trinity Sunday 69, 118
Tripurari 40, 87
Tripurasura 87
Trisala 92
Tritiya 33, 39, 56, 82, 83
Triumph of the Holy Cross 86, 118
Tropical 13, 14, 31, 47
Trung-Thu 118
Tsao chün 43
Tse 35
Tsongkhapa 96
Tsou K'apa 43
Tu-K'or 42
Tuan yang chieh 42
Tuesday 18, 65, 76, 90, 93, 109, 115, 119
Tulam 115

Tulsi   40, 56, 78, 88
Tulsi Vivahotsava   40
Tulsidas   39, 118
Turkey   29, 49, 59, 67, 117
Turkish   29
Twelfth Day   30, 63, 75, 94, 116, 118
Twelfth Night   64, 68, 75, 119
Twelfthtide   75
Twelve Days of Christmas   68, 119
Tzu   35

U

Ugadi Parva   119
Ullambana Day   43
Umar I   29
Union of American Hebrew
  Congregations   110
Universal Week of Prayer   119
Universalist Church   66
Up-Helly-Aa   57, 119
Uttarayana Sankranti   93

V

Vadakkanathan   104
Vaikuntha Ekadashi   41, 74, 119
Vaisakha   39, 56, 60, 64, 66, 86, 88, 98, 101,
  104, 114, 119, 121
Vaisakhi   33, 60
Vaishali Mahotsava   92
Vaitarani   41, 119
Vaitarani Vrata   41
Valmiki   40, 107, 108, 118, 120
Valmiki Jayanti   40
Vamana   100
Vardhama   93
Varro   46
Varsa   31
Vartanantz Day   120
Varuna   39, 73, 97, 107
Vasant Panchami   41, 120
Vasanta   31, 107, 120
Vasanta Navratra   107, 120
Vashistha   109
Vasus   33

Vata Savitri   39, 120
Vendémiaire   51
Venkteshwara   117, 118
Ventôse   51
Venus   9
Vernal equinox   17, 36, 73, 75, 101, 121
Vesak   121
Victorian   18, 20
Victorian Period   18
Victorius of Aquitaine   18
Vidhatr   33
Vighnesha   78
Vijag   121
Vijay Dashami   73, 121
Vijay Dussehra   40
Vinayak   77, 121
Vine   21
Virgin   16, 57, 59, 61, 62, 84, 94-96, 98, 104,
  113, 121
Vishnu   32, 33, 39-41, 56, 57, 61, 70-73, 81,
  82, 86, 88, 92, 94, 98-101, 105, 107, 116-
  119
Vishnupriya   88
Vishwanath   92
Visitation of the Virgin Mary to
  Elizabeth   94, 121
Volunteers of America   121
Volunteers of America Founder's Day   121
Vyasa   39, 78, 81

W

Wailing Wall   103
Washington, George   49
Water Drawing Festival   100, 121
Water-clock   5
We-Adar   11, 12, 23, 105
Wednesday   11, 18, 58, 59, 65, 74, 76, 90, 93,
  101, 106, 109, 110, 120
Weedmonth   19, 20
Wesak   33, 64, 119, 121, 122
Wesley, John   56
Western   3-6, 8, 9, 16, 17, 19-21, 29-35, 38,
  42, 44, 47, 49-51, 55, 58, 63, 70, 75, 94,
  101, 118
Wheel of the Year   22, 60, 64, 69, 75, 90, 91,
  110, 111

White Goddess 22
White Road 35
White Tara 42
Whitsunday 18, 74, 102, 106, 121
Whitsuntide 21, 121
Wi 35
Wicca 106
Williams, Roger 58, 121
Willow 21, 58, 109, 116
Winter 4, 19, 21, 26, 31, 36, 56, 66, 67, 75, 83, 84, 90, 91, 93, 98, 106, 110, 111, 117, 121, 123
Winter Solstice 19, 21, 36, 66, 75, 90, 91, 93, 98, 106, 110, 111, 121, 123
Winterfull 19, 20
Wise, Isaac Mayer 110
Wittenberg 109
Wolfmonth 19
World Community Day 122
World Day of Prayer 122
World Evangelical Alliance 119
World Invocation Day 77, 122
World Peace Day 122
World Religion Day 122
Wotan 67
Wright, Lawrence 8
Wu 35
Wuwuchim 122

X

Xerxes 105

Y

Yama 33, 40, 41, 61, 66, 97, 120
Yama Dvitiya 40, 61
Yellow Road 35
Yemen 29
Yew 21
Yih 35
Yin 35
Yog Maya 119
Yom Ha-Shoah 84, 122
Yom Kippur 23, 59, 70, 110, 122, 123
Yom Tov 122
Young, Brigham 62, 123
Yu 35, 42, 43
Yüan tan 42
Yugoslavia 49
Yule 19, 22, 75, 90, 106, 111, 113, 123

Z

Zealots 15
Zen 34
Zen Buddhism 34
Zeus 14, 24, 25, 27, 28
Ziv 10
Zodiac 6, 9, 31, 35
Zoroastrian 85

DATE DUE
